'This is book is a must have for any therapist working with severely traumatized children and young people. It's written with such clear explanations and a step-by-step guide on how to apply the method within practice. I found it to be enriched by the case studies. Arianne, yet again captures the importance of sensitivity when working with traumatized children. This is underpinned by the care and attention of introducing the "sleeping dogs" model, which offers a structured way of working, creating the appropriate therapeutic environment.'

Simon Carpenter, *Chief Executive of CLEAR UK , Accredited MBACP, Accredited EMDR Children / Young Persons Practitioner*

'Arianne Struik has developed a brilliant theory based on her many years of experience working with traumatized children and young people. For the past three years, Arianne Struik has been working on major new projects, in which she shows her ability to develop and refine both the theory and practice of working with traumatized children. She is an excellent teacher and her ability to convey complex knowledge relating to traumatized children to other professionals is both nuanced and precise.

This book charts the way in which we, in The Copenhagen Community Social Services, have been able to work together with Arianne Struik over the past three years. It has been an amazing journey for us in which we have been able to develop and deepen our understanding of the best ways to work with traumatized children. I strongly recommend all professionals read the new edition of *Sleeping Dogs* – and be inspired.'

Claus Gosvig, *Former Center Manager, Copenhagen Community, Social Security*

'Struik incorporated vast experience with theoretical concepts in neuroscience in order to provide a significant challenge to all therapists treating traumatized children. Despite the multitude of information available about treatment of traumatized children, the vast majority of therapists are still too afraid to "disturb" the trauma. By this inaction, many children continue to suffer complex behaviours. By implementing the Sleeping Dogs method, even therapists new to the world of treating traumatized children, will be able to systematically follow a safe and effective protocol in the preparation and treatment of traumatized children. This book is a "must read" for child therapists.'

Dr Renée Potgieter Marks, *Consultant Therapist, UK*

Treating Chronically Traumatized Children

When children refuse or seem unable to talk about their traumatic memories, it might be tempting to 'let sleeping dogs lie'. However, if left untreated, the memories of childhood abuse and neglect can have a devastating effect on the development of children and young people. How can these children be motivated and engage in trauma-focused therapy? *Treating Chronically Traumatized Children: The Sleeping Dogs Method* describes a structured method to overcome resistance and enable children to wake these sleeping dogs safely, so these children heal from their trauma.

The 'Sleeping Dogs method' is a comprehensive approach to treating chronically traumatized children, first preparing the child to such an extent that he or she can engage in therapy to process traumatic memories, then by the trauma processing and integration phase. Collaboration with the child's network, the child's biological family including the abuser-parent and child protection services, are key elements of the Sleeping Dogs method. The underlying theory about the consequences of traumatization, such as disturbed attachment and dissociation, is described in a comprehensive, easy-to-read manner illustrated with case studies, and is accompanied by downloadable worksheets. This new edition has been updated to include the clinical experience in working with this method and the most recent literature and research, as well as entirely new chapters that apply the 'Sleeping Dogs method' to the experiences of children in foster care and residential care, and those with an intellectual disability.

Treating Chronically Traumatized Children will have a wide appeal, including psychologists, psychiatrists, psychotherapists, counsellors, family therapists, social workers, child protection, frontline, foster care and youth workers, inpatient and residential staff, and (foster or adoptive) parents.

Arianne Struik is a clinical psychologist, family therapist and EMDR consultant, director of the Institute for Chronically Traumatized Children (ICTC) in Australia. She provides specialized trauma treatment and teaches internationally on the treatment of trauma and dissociation in children. She is a member of the European Society for Trauma and Dissociation.

Treating Chronically Traumatized Children

The Sleeping Dogs Method
2nd Edition

Arianne Struik

Routledge
Taylor & Francis Group

LONDON AND NEW YORK

Second edition published 2019
by Routledge
2 Park Square, Milton Park, Abingdon, Oxon, OX14 4RN

and by Routledge
52 Vanderbilt Avenue, New York, NY 10017

Routledge is an imprint of the Taylor & Francis Group, an informa business

© 2019 Arianne Struik

Illustrations: R.P.K. Struik's Gravenhage: the Netherlands.

First edition published by Routledge 2014

British Library Cataloguing-in-Publication Data
A catalogue record for this book is available from the British Library

Library of Congress Cataloging-in-Publication Data
A catalog record for this book has been requested

ISBN: 978-0-367-07614-6 (hbk)
ISBN: 978-0-367-07615-3 (pbk)
ISBN: 978-0-429-02161-9 (ebk)

Typeset in Times New Roman
by Wearset Ltd, Boldon, Tyne and Wear

Visit the eResource: http://www.routledge.com/9780367076153

For Brett my partner, you light up my life

Contents

Preface

There are many traumatized children who do not receive (adequate) treatment. In a lot of cases traumatization is not recognized. Most children with a dissociative disorder are not even diagnosed, because many still believe that children cannot suffer from this disorder. On the other hand it is difficult to find the right treatment for this group of children and, even then, these treatments often do not work. The symptoms do not disappear after treatment, or only partly. 'The child isn't ready', is the conclusion, and the caregivers are given the advice to return when he is ready. But this seldom happens spontaneously, and then what? The trauma fades to the background: 'He never mentions it anymore, so I assume he got over it. He forgot, it is such a long time ago.' The advice generally is to let sleeping dogs lie, and not to stir up the past.

This can cause children to suffer serious symptoms for years, often unnecessarily. These children can be anxious, depressed, violent, use drugs and alcohol, display sexualized behaviours, self-harm or be suicidal. Some try and commit suicide and some unfortunately succeed. They can be diagnosed with suspected attention deficit hyperactivity disorder (ADHD) or autism spectrum disorder, bipolar disorder or behavioural problems. Many of them are in out of home care and move from one foster family to another, because of their difficult behaviour. Sometimes children are even placed in a residential facility for prolonged periods of time. It is said that they are unable to form attachment relationships and some children even receive this 'life sentence' when they are only four years old.

It is for these children that this method has been developed, so that more children may receive trauma-focused treatment. With the Sleeping Dogs method an analysis is made of reasons why the child may not be able to engage in trauma-focused treatment. These barriers are addressed with interventions so the child is prepared for trauma processing. Motivation and psychoeducation take a prominent place. After the trauma-processing phase, interventions support integration and make the child resilient to new traumatization.

The Sleeping Dogs method is based on a method for adults with chronic childhood trauma: the Three Tests (Spierings, 2012). Joany Spierings works with adults who did not receive adequate trauma treatment when they were children.

They were the children whose trauma had supposedly 'faded to the background'. Their sleeping dogs were not woken up and they still suffer the consequences. Joany inspired me to adapt her method for children. By waking up sleeping dogs for children and helping them to heal from their trauma they hopefully can become healthy adults, breaking the cycle of intergeneration abuse for their children. The Sleeping Dogs method is a structured method with a clear theoretical framework and a practical section with exercises, similar to the Three Tests. I share Joany's opinion that the theoretical framework and the structure of the method are much more important than the interventions. The interventions can only be applied correctly if the underlying theory and the reasons for using these are fully understood. I have made an effort to simplify the theory on trauma and to limit it to what is strictly needed for the application of the method – which was not an easy task.

Waking up sleeping dogs in children should be done consciously and carefully as it makes children, their parents and caregivers vulnerable. When interventions are done incorrectly or in the wrong order they can damage children and parents. When this method is not taught correctly in training or supervision, or when the tools are not correctly translated, that can have serious consequences. Therefore I have decided in 2018 to register Sleeping Dogs as a trademark. With this trademark Sleeping Dogs® trainers, training materials and tools can easily be identified.

In this second edition I have made many changes and improvements to the structure. In the last eight years, more than 3500 clinicians from all over the world have been trained in the use of this method. Organizations have implemented this method or adaptions of this method into their organizations and translated the tools into different languages. The Sleeping Dogs method has been used to structure and improve collaboration between therapists, child protection and youth care workers, residential and foster care organizations. I have moved from the Netherlands to Australia and used the Sleeping Dogs method with Indigenous children and families. The Sleeping Dogs method combined with eye movement desensitization and reprocessing (EMDR) therapy is delivered as a fly-in–fly-out model in remote areas of Australia and New Zealand. My team of trainers and I have received feedback from experienced clinicians through training and supervision. Several research projects on the Sleeping Dogs method have been carried out or have commenced. New research and methods on chronic traumatization in children have been published. This information, feedback, clinical experience and experiences with implementation have led to this second edition of the Sleeping Dogs method. I hope that this method may serve to answer some of the many questions that there still are. At the same time the method also raises new questions, which have not yet been answered. The Sleeping Dogs method remains a work in progress. In the future, my team and I may be able to make further choices and improve this method based on new experiences and research.

I have tried to keep this book simple and manageable, offering practical advice to psychologists, psychiatrists, psychotherapists, family therapists, child protection, frontline, foster care and youth workers, social workers, and inpatient and residential staff and (foster or adoptive) parents. In my work with these chronically traumatized children I have learnt that it is easier to apply theory in practice when it can be pictured. That is why I have added many examples and descriptions of children to illustrate the theory. In the second edition the Barriers Form has replaced the Six Tests, and the Action Plan has replaced the Planning Forms and I added a new form, the Case Conceptualization Form, which all together are called the Sleeping Dogs tools.

This method is accompanied by worksheets, which can be found on the accompanying e-resource for this title, http://www.routledge.com/9780367076153 and on www.ariannestruik.com, making it easy to print them out. Copying is permitted.

The Sleeping Dogs method is used all over the world. Clinicians find it easier to use the tools in their own language and the forms have been translated in some. Anyone who is interested in translating the Sleeping Dogs tools into their language can contact me.

Acknowledgements

I would like to thank Joany Spierings for continuing to inspire me, for the use of her material and for her input in the development of this method. Also, I would like to thank professionals from Altra, de Combinatie Widdonck, Jeugdformaat, Juzt, Rubicon, Sterk Huis in the Netherlands, the Department for Child Protection in Western and South Australia, Oranga Tamariki in New Zealand, Barbara van Blanken, Linda Coolen, Fransien Jans, Jim Knipe, Rikke Ludvigsen, Sonja Parker, Paul van Rooij, Joss Schrijver, Reitse-Pieter Struik, Susan van der Woude, Brigitte Ubachs, the facilitators team from Københavns Kommune Denmark, Brett, Coco, Ans and Bea for sharing their experiences and contributions to the second edition of this book. To Claus Gosvig, who believed in this method and his project team Lisa Maria Bahn Rasmussen, Zandra Olesen, Cecilie Bille-Brahe Raahauge and Kristian Bo Jørgensen, thank you for the inspiring journey of adapting the Sleeping Dogs method into a collaboration model for the Københavns Kommune, Denmark. To Brechtje, my loyal assistant, thank you for your support, you are always there for me. Special thanks to my trainers team Danny de Bakker, Caroline Dierkx and Mirjam Pijpers, for their feedback on the manuscript. I hope this book will contribute to a better treatment for traumatized children. And those sleeping dogs...? Wake them up!

Arianne Struik

January 2019, summer in Australia, winter in Europe

Introduction

Target group

Children, ages zero to eighteen who were severely and chronically traumatized in early childhood, for whom 'standard' trauma treatment is not possible. Chronic traumatization in early childhood refers to events that occurred before the child was eight years old. It is assumed – though this has not been researched sufficiently – that chronic traumatization at an early age has more serious consequences than traumatization that starts at a later age.

Goal

The goal of this method is to help children who were chronically traumatized in early childhood overcome their barriers, so they can participate in trauma processing and integrate their trauma. Trauma processing relieves their symptoms instead of only stabilizing them by teaching them how to manage their symptoms. This is in line with the international guidelines on the treatment of PTSD in children, which state:

> Trauma-focused psychotherapies should be considered first-line treatments for children and adolescents with PTSD. Among psychotherapies there is convincing evidence that trauma-focused therapies, that is, those that specifically address the child's traumatic experiences, are superior to nonspecific or nondirective therapies in resolving PTSD symptoms.
>
> (Cohen et al., 2010, p. 421)

The target group for this method is children for whom this is difficult or seems impossible. They say they have forgotten what happened or don't want to talk about their traumatic memories. The advice of caregivers, child protection workers or therapists is to 'let sleeping dogs lie' and not to focus treatment on the trauma, strangely contrary to the international guidelines:

> Timing and pacing of trauma-focused therapies are guided in part by children's responses that therapists and parents monitor during the course of

treatment. Clinical worsening may suggest the need to strengthen mastery of previous treatment components through a variety of interventions, rather than abandoning a trauma-focused approach.

(Cohen et al., 2010, pp. 421–422)

I think it is unwise to leave such traumas untreated. The 'sleeping dogs' (traumatic memories) are more dangerous than they appear. These children are chronically stressed and alert, they trust no one and are attached to no one. They are lonely, afraid to seek comfort and yet unable to soothe themselves. The apparently sleeping dogs 'bite' them from the inside and these internal injuries have a disastrous effect on their development. These children are in fact much in need of treatment, instead of having their avoidance confirmed. But how can this be done? I strongly believe that we should 'wake those sleeping dogs' and this book describes a trauma-focused treatment method to accomplish that.

The Sleeping Dogs® method

The Sleeping Dogs method consists of tools to analyse the child's circumstances and possible barriers to treatment. The customized treatment plan consists of practical interventions to overcome the identified barriers, support trauma processing and integration. The Sleeping Dogs method can be combined with other methods and is *always* combined with a therapy to process traumatic memories, such as trauma-focused cognitive behavioural therapy (TF-CBT) or eye movement desensitization and reprocessing (EMDR) therapy. In everyday practice I find EMDR therapy the most suitable method of trauma processing for these children. It is a protocol-based method, suitable for children of all ages, as opposed to other methods that have a minimum age for the application of the method. Besides, the method does not make large demands on verbal abilities, which are often underdeveloped in these children. If a different method is preferred, the word EMDR, found in some of the examples, can be replaced by 'trauma processing'. Sleeping Dogs treatment consists of work with the child's biological family, if applicable caregivers, residential staff, foster care workers and the child protection worker. Sessions with the child are reduced to the minimum.

Stabilization

Recently the use of the phased model has been challenged, because there is not enough evidence that supports the necessity of the use of this model. De Jongh et al. (2016) argue that evidence-based treatments, such as EMDR therapy or TF-CBT, should be used without stabilization, however De Jongh et al. fail to provide any evidence for this viewpoint as well. Chronically traumatized children should participate in evidence-based treatments, such as EMDR therapy or TF-CBT as soon as possible (Cohen et al., 2010). Unnecessary stabilization is potentially damaging as it prolongs the time these children have to suffer from the consequences of trauma preventing their healthy development. However, even without evidence, it is obvious that children who refuse to discuss their memories or claim amnesia, either need stabilization to prepare them or they do not process their memories at all. The Sleeping Dogs method is for those children and should therefore only be used when it is impossible to start with processing the child's traumatic memories. When the child *does* talk about his or her memories and has awake dogs, evidence-based treatments to process traumatic memories are preferred.

Research

This target group is to hard study because the Sleeping Dogs method is used only for chronically traumatized children who are unable to engage in trauma processing. Research needs to be conducted in a multi-centred set-up, over a long period of time and requires a high level of flexibility in treatment procedures. Contextual factors can make it hard to recruit a large number of participants. Participants are suddenly transferred to another location, major life events such as divorce, a suicide or incarceration of a biological parent, and child protection issues with for example acquiring consent for participation complicate inclusion.

Examples of the use of the Sleeping Dogs method are described in several case studies. These case studies describe a variety of children living at home, in foster care and residential care, in an urban setting or living in remote Indigenous communities (Struik, 2015, 2017b, 2017c, 2018).

A pilot study (Struik, Lindauer, & Ensink, 2017) explored whether chronically traumatized children, who presented as unable or unwilling to engage in trauma processing, could be prepared with the Sleeping Dogs method to complete EMDR therapy, and whether there was sufficient reduction in posttraumatic stress symptoms to enable positive placement decisions. Participants were fourteen children, age three to nine, refusing to participate in EMDR therapy. All were living in residential care or with foster families and were considered stuck cases because of their severe problems. With the treatment package of 'Sleeping Dogs' plus EMDR therapy all children completed EMDR therapy in an average of 7.57 sessions with the child, leading to the resolution of all identified traumatic memories. Two-thirds of the children who were in residential care at study onset were placed in foster families within two months after the last session, some even during treatment. This is the first study on the Sleeping Dogs method. The findings suggest important directions for future study and currently some research projects are being undertaken and set up.

Who can use the Sleeping Dogs method?

The Sleeping Dogs method can be used by individual clinicians, by multidisciplinary teams, by foster care or residential teams, and by child protection, frontline and youth workers. Trauma processing is preferably done by the same therapist who did the stabilization work, but can be done by another therapist as well.

What can the Sleeping Dogs method be used for?

The Sleeping Dogs method can be used to plan trauma-focused treatment for the child and support the parents and caregivers. The Sleeping Dogs method can be used to guide decision-making by child protection services around disclosures, safety, contact arrangements with biological parents, contact between foster parents and biological parents, and reunification. The Sleeping Dogs method can also be used by child protection or youth care workers or to assess the child's development, health and wellbeing and plan interventions to improve that.

Set up of this book

In Chapter 1 the impact of traumatization is explained. Chapter 2 outlines why children become avoidant and resistant. Chapter 3 describes what is needed to overcome resistance and Chapter 4 describes how the Sleeping Dogs method can be used for that. Chapter 5 consists of practical examples to provide psychoeducation to motivate children. Chapter 6–10 contain interventions to overcome the barriers described per item. Chapter 11 consists of the Motivation and Nutshell Checks, after which trauma processing and integration are described in Chapter 12. Chapter 13 describes specific aspects of children in out of home care. Chapter 14 outlines specific aspects of the use of the Sleeping Dogs method with children with a dissociative disorder and conversion, adaptations for people with an intellectual disability and cultural aspects. In the last chapter the execution and planning of the method are discussed. The book ends with the tools in the appendices and the worksheets.

Practical matters

To be able to draw up a treatment plan and to provide psychoeducation, it is important to understand something about the way the brain and the body functions. The theory in this book is limited to what is needed to be able to that. The reality is simplified and the descriptions may not be completely correct in every detail to make the theory understandable for children and parents. Sentences are used like: 'your brain then automatically does…', or 'your body now thinks…'. Strictly speaking this is incorrect, since the brain and the body are not a person. But such descriptions make it much easier for the children to understand. The out of home care systems differ greatly between countries. This can call for an adaptation of the interventions described in this book to the system in the country that it is used in.

Some of the theoretical background information is organized into text boxes for easy reference. These text boxes provide definitions or summaries, or they consist of sentences taken from the main text, which are important to remember and consider more closely. For the sake of convenience this book uses the term 'children' throughout, to refer to children who were chronically traumatized in early childhood. This book often refers to parents. Parents play an important role in the life of a child when it comes to attachment and caretaking. Some children will have foster or adoptive parents or residential staff that take on (part of) the caretaking and parental role, apart from their biological parents. In order to avoid confusion the terms 'biological parent' is used for the child's parents and the term caregiver for either the child's parent, foster parent, residential staff or other caregivers. When interventions focus on the biological parent's responsibility for the abuse, the terms abuser-parent and non-protecting parent are used for clarity purposes. Obviously every parent is more than just an abuser-parent or non-protecting parent.

The pronoun 'he' can also be read as 'she'. Where it says 'he', 'she' can also be read. Where it says 'child', 'adolescent' can also be read. Where it says residential staff or unit, inpatient staff or inpatient facility can also be used. Where it says 'therapist' the term counsellor, practitioner or psychotherapist can be read. The term child protection worker is used for the person responsible for the child's safety, such as a caseworker or case manager. This person can also be the child's legal guardian. The whole set of interventions I refer to as the (trauma-focused) treatment. The sessions with the child and the parents themselves I call the therapy. Trauma-focused treatment means treatment focused on processing traumatic experiences. Treatment for traumatized children can also focus on their symptoms only, without addressing the trauma underlying these symptoms, which is not trauma-focused treatment. For the sake of convenience, the term 'treatment' is used in the rest of the book to indicate trauma-focused treatment.

Basically, the exercises are suitable for all age groups, but they focus mainly on younger children. When working with adolescents it may be necessary to adapt the language. Separate exercises for adolescents have not been included as adaptation is quite simple.

All interventions described in this book are presented in a shaded box; all case histories are presented in a clear square box and summaries are in a clear curved box.

Acknowledgement

This book contains a large number of techniques. I have tried to find the original exercises and refer to the original author where possible. But I have been using many of these exercises for years and it is impossible to trace the origin of some of them because they come from an oral history of psychotherapy traditions. I apologize if I have unintentionally failed to cite sources and would welcome any suggestions for the next edition.

Chapter 1

What is the impact of traumatization in children?

Chronically traumatized children can have huge problems in daily life, moving from placement to placement. Their parents, foster caregivers or residential staff are struggling to manage their behaviours, but they say that they feel fine, or deny that anything has happened. They do not need any therapy and they are not traumatized. Some refuse to see a therapist, or have walked out of sessions and refuse to come back. They are afraid to talk about their traumas, afraid of becoming angry, of things getting stirred up again and causing them nightmares. It is too pain ful to talk about and they rather avoid. Some do not even realize that their symptoms are caused by their experiences in the past. Chronically traumatized children can have severe problems in daily life as a consequence of their trauma. If they would participate in trauma treatment, those problems could be resolved, but what to do if that is not possible?

Other children actually manage quite well. They are seemingly stable and never talk about the past. Sometimes the therapist may be unaware of what they have been through, because they never talk about it. They suspect some trauma, based on their symptoms, but do not know how to address it. Parents, caregivers or therapist can believe it is better to focus on the child's behaviour, rather than their trauma. 'He does not talk about the sexual abuse, so he probably forgot. Let's not "wake up sleeping dogs" by talking about the abuse because it might make him upset again. We should focus on medication for his ADHD.' They are afraid to upset the child and make things worse.

This was the case with Sandra.

Sandra (1)

Sandra is seven years old and has been living with her foster family, the Smiths, for three years. She is referred for assessment of her learning difficulties. She has been subjected to serious abuse, neglect and sexual violence. She never talks about it anymore and denies her past. 'My last name is Smith', she says. When her foster family talk about her biological family, she yells: 'Shut up, stop it!' She is doing fairly well. Sometimes she gets very angry but it is manageable. The only thing that is out of the ordinary is that her foster parents have the feeling of being exchangeable. Sandra does not seem to have formed an attachment relationship with them. When they hug her, Sandra freezes. When she hurts herself, she laughs and does not seek comfort. The foster parents worked very hard and Sandra's behaviour has improved a lot. They do not want trauma treatment for Sandra because they are afraid it will stir up old memories again and her violent behaviour will get worse. They just want to enjoy the stability they have reached.

Because it is so obvious that Sandra does not want to talk about what happened to her, it might be tempting to avoid disturbing the relative balance. Sandra has managed to survive by herself, and she has suppressed her memories –it seems unwise to stir things up. However it is unwise to leave such traumas untreated.

Children like Sandra are chronically stressed and alert, they trust no one and are attached to no one. They are lonely, are afraid to seek comfort and yet are unable to soothe themselves. These children do need help, but it is not clear where to start or how to find an opening. They do not want to talk about their memories or the child and/or caregivers or professionals believe the child will decompensate or destabilize or dissociate when the traumatic memories would be addressed. This chapter describes the impact of chronic traumatization on children, to demonstrate why it is needed to address the trauma.

1.1 Traumatizing events

Most of these children have been exposed to traumatizing events at an early age (before the age of eight), such as psychological, physical and sexual abuse, emotional and physical neglect (e.g. by parents with psychiatric problems or drug and alcohol abuse), domestic violence, threats and/or conflicts between parents witnessed by the child, war circumstances, discontinuity in the attachment process caused for instance by the death of a parent, adoption or a prolonged hospitalization, or an emotionally unavailable parent or painful medical procedures or diseases. The traumatization has happened within their families. Their parents or another caregiver such as grandparents or a stepparent, who are supposed to provide safety and protect them, have abused them. Child protection services have been involved and many are or have been removed from their biological parents.

1.2 Symptoms

As a result of traumatizing events, children may develop diverse trauma-related symptoms affecting most areas of development, such as:

- Affective and physiological dysregulation. For instance, children may be impulsive and become very angry or anxious without being able to control themselves. Or conversely, they may seem detached and without emotion. They can have diminished awareness and dissociation of sensations and emotions.

- Attentional and behavioural dysregulation. The children may have trouble learning or concentrating at school. Or they may be hyper-alert and easily distracted. They can be preoccupied with danger, have too much or too little self-protection, or they may self-harm.
- Self and relational dysregulation. They can have a disturbed self-image and distorted ideas about others and the world (guilt, blame, distrust). The children may fight a lot and have few friends and are often unable to sustain long-term relationships. They may keep their attachment figures at a distance, or conversely cling to them.
- Posttraumatic spectrum symptoms such as flashbacks, nightmares, avoidance (Van der Kolk et al., 2009).

David is such a child.

David (1)

Ten-year-old David has witnessed domestic violence since birth and his father was physically violent towards his mother and the children on a regular basis. His father was a sadistic man who enjoyed humiliating and tormenting David. At the age of seven, David called the police when his father assaulted his mother once again. His father became so angry that he almost strangled David. After that, his mother divorced his father and started a relationship with a new boyfriend. David does not see his father anymore.

David's teacher thinks that he has ADHD. He has trouble concentrating and learning. He has fallen behind considerably in arithmetic and reading comprehension, and his integrative and deductive capacities seem limited. David cannot sit still for a second. He is always on the move and is unable to relax. He is quickly irritated, shouts out in class and has fits of rage in which he attacks other children and throws chairs. He often feels no one loves him and complains. He requires a lot of attention, but this never seems to be enough. When the teacher is helping another child, David will misbehave up to the point where the teacher has to intervene and send him out of the classroom.

David is suspicious and distrustful. David is reckless and sometimes deliberately hurts himself. He does not show pain and does not ask to be comforted. He seems unhappy, but never talks about his feelings. The teacher has never seen him enjoy himself. David is dominant and when he plays with other children, it invariably leads to fighting. David then behaves aggressively, and his eyes turn 'mean'. He says things like: 'I'll stab you to death, I'll rip you open and tear your guts out.' At home,

David attacks his younger brother, and sometimes his stepfather has to intervene because David loses control completely, kicking, screaming and biting, seemingly in a trance and out of reach. 'Stop it, don't hit me,' he screams.

David is not popular at school. He bullies other children and they are afraid of him. He tries to trip them, punches them 'by accident' and then innocently says: 'Oh, sorry.' Frequently things go missing or are broken in school with David being the suspected culprit, but he denies any involvement and cannot explain why he behaves in this way. David does not seem to realize the consequences of his actions and he does not learn from his experiences.

He prefers playing games involving violence, his drawings are full of violence and death. His mother has found notes written by David which read: 'I am going to kill myself, that is better for you. I hate myself.' When she confronts him, David denies having written them.

David has trouble falling asleep and his mother frequently hears him screaming in his sleep: 'Stop it, let me go!' He says he does not have nightmares, but his mother suspects that he does. When they are having a good time, David tends to ruin the occasion by picking a fight. A pleasant evening always ends negative.

Chronic traumatization can also lead to different symptoms. Children may be confused and disoriented, have fragmented perception, be forgetful and chaotic, dreamy and absent, they may dissociate or have flashbacks and nightmares. They may literally be out of touch with their body and their feelings, like five-year-old Demi below.

Demi (1)

Five-year-old Demi was sexually abused by her grandfather between the ages of two and four years. A year ago the abuse stopped when Demi told her mother. Mother had suspected for quite some time that something was wrong. Demi had inexplicable stomach-aches and headaches, twice had a sexually transmitted disease and complained about an itch around her genitals.

Demi sometimes wets herself during daytime and night-time. She has nightmares and sleeps with her mother because she is afraid to sleep alone. Demi is afraid to sleep over, to go to the bathroom alone or to go upstairs alone. She does not play outside and she does not ask other children to come and play. When she is invited, she usually refuses the invitation. Demi sometimes talks in an infantile way and acts like a baby. Demi is often tired and hangs on the couch. She hardly ever plays. Most days she doesn't want to go to school and clings to her mother. Demi is dreamy at school and has trouble concentrating. She has few friends because she makes weird, inappropriate remarks and does not know how to interact with other children.

Demi has a negative self-image and thinks she is stupid. She is insecure and has a fear of failure. She thinks that other children laugh at her or think she is stupid without any reason. She cannot stand up for herself and does not seem to have an opinion of her own. She copies other children and has a hard time making her own choices. She can be manipulated into bullying another child, for which she then takes the blame. She then feels very bad and guilty.

Demi masturbates every day and also touches her genitals with other people around. Sometimes she inserts objects into her vagina. Mother caught her one time while she was pushing a pencil into the anus of her three-year-old cousin, who of course was crying loudly. A few times she sat on a man's lap, rubbed against him and tried to kiss them on the mouth. She seems to flirt with men. She may suddenly take off all her clothes in public. She somehow attracts 'dirty old men'. Her aunt has twice caught her in the hot tub of the swimming pool, sitting next to a man whom her aunt did not trust. Demi does not seem to sense any danger. Her mother, who was sexually abused herself, does not sense it either. She allowed Demi to stay in the hot tub beside those men. This surprises the aunt, because Demi's mother should know better.

Demi does not want to talk about the abuse because she is ashamed. But she does often play sexual and violent games with her Barbie dolls.

Adolescents may be ashamed of their vulnerability and suppress their emotions. Some tend to blame themselves and have more internalizing problems such as depression, fear and feelings of guilt, learning difficulties, self-harming, suicidal thoughts or attempts, and substance abuse. Tracy is such a girl.

Tracy is sixteen years old. Together with her brother Roger, she grew up in an environment of emotional neglect. Their father is an introverted man who is always working. Their mother displays traits of borderline personality disorder and is emotionally unstable. She can become very angry and then humiliate her children and abuse them psychologically. From quite an early age Tracy has often had to comfort her mother. Roger was a child with behavioural problems, in need of a lot of attention. There were many conflicts, and Tracy always kept quiet so as not to cause any problems.

> Tracy is depressed and has negative thoughts about herself. She smokes cannabis daily, saying that it helps her to sleep. She has trouble concentrating at school and her grades are getting worse. She is mistrustful of her boyfriend and jealous. When she feels bad, she shuts him out. She then cuts herself and picks fights with him. She shouts at him, telling him she does not need him and that she hates him, until he leaves. Then she feels guilty and bad about herself, and sometimes drinks a lot of alcohol. The following day she then apologizes and is pleasing and extra-sweet to him.

Some children cover up their negative feelings with externalizing behavioural problems, trying to put the blame outside themselves. They misbehave at school, have conflicts, abuse alcohol and drugs, and are violent. Some re-enact the traumatizing events in their behaviour. Such is the case with Roger, Tracy's brother, who re-enacts the rejection by his biological parents.

> Roger is seventeen years old and was adopted from Colombia at the age of two. In the children's home where he was since birth he was physically and emotionally neglected. After the adoption he hardly responded to contact, which only improved after a year. In the following years his behavioural problems became worse. Roger was expelled from two schools and was sentenced to community service for stealing. He keeps promising to do better, but he never succeeds. Roger feels really bad about doing this to his parents, but he never manages to keep his promises. He steals money from his mother, stays out all night and frequently uses drugs. Roger has friends who have a bad influence on him and sometimes manipulate him into doing things he does not want to do. He is afraid of saying no to them because he worries that they will think he is a loser. His mother says that Roger is insensitive and not social. He has trouble anticipating other people's behaviour and often has no clue what others might think or feel. His parents wonder whether he is autistic. Roger thinks this is nonsense.

Roger is probably right; his symptoms seem autistic, but they may very well be caused by traumatization. Traumatization of children or adolescents may present in different ways, sometimes covered up with behavioural problems or not visible at all. During or after traumatic experiences there may be a period in which the child seems not to have symptoms. Trying to survive, he cannot afford to stand out and show any strong reaction. Nonetheless, his development is seriously threatened, making treatment necessary.

1.3 The impact of traumatization on the body and brain

1.3.1 The three parts of the brain

In their book *Trauma and the Body*, Ogden, Minton and Pain (2006) describe a theory about the brain and the body and the way it functions, which is useful to explain traumatic stress reactions to children and their parents so they can understand themselves and each other better. A simplified version of this theory is summarized in the following paragraphs.

There are three levels of brain architecture (MacLean, 1985): the sensorimotor level of information processing, the emotional level of processing (Cozolino, 2002) and the cognitive level of processing. In ordinary circumstances these 'three brains' function as a well-coordinated and integrated whole (Fisher, Murray, & Bundy, 1991). The most primitive part, the reptilian brain, is responsible for the automatic functions in the body, such as breathing and heartbeat. In this part of the brain, information is processed on a sensorimotor level. The mammalian brain, where information is processed on an emotional level, is also called the limbic system or the emotional brain. The cognitive level is the neocortex, which is responsible for talking, planning, abstract thinking and reasoning.

The reptilian brain dominates the activities of very young children, as the other parts of the brain are not yet sufficiently developed (bottom-up). Young children react well to sensorimotor stimuli, such as rocking, touching or a soft voice, which are processed in the reptilian brain. This stimulation forms the basis for the further development of the mammalian and the human brain (the higher parts of the brain). By stimulating the reptilian brain with sensorimotor stimuli, the tissue structures grow and the mammalian and human brain develop (Perry & Dobson, 2013). When the higher parts of the brains have further developed and matured, activities are coordinated more and more by the mammalian and the human brain (Ogden, Minton, & Pain, 2006).

When the brain is fully developed, the human brain (the cognitive level) functions as a control centre for the three parts (Schore, 1994), and the human brain coordinates activities (top-down). For instance, when a child is travelling in a car and feels hungry, he can use his human brain to realize that it is almost dinnertime and that he must wait until he gets home. The child then suppresses the physical sensation of 'hunger' from his reptilian brain with his human brain. The same applies to the mammalian brain. A child who is told he can't have something in a shop can throw a tantrum in the shop or wait until later and discuss the matter in the car. Young children are unable to do this. As children grow older, they learn to delay or suppress gratification of their needs. The three brains already function reasonably well in children of primary school age, but they develop further into adult age.

1.3.2 Action systems

Another theory, very useful for understanding the way chronically traumatized children react, is the theory of action systems described by Van der Hart, Nijenhuis and Steele (2006). A simplified version of this theory is summarized in the following paragraphs.

Animals have action systems to secure their survival and the survival of their kind. The same applies to human beings. Action systems are the basic elements of the personality. They are psychobiological systems that regulate mental actions and motives, behaviour and emotions. They are complex systems consisting of subsystems with separate elements. The action system of energy management, for instance, consists of subsystems such as eating and sleeping. And the subsystem of eating in turn consists of different mental actions and behaviour. Action systems secure a human being's survival by helping to distinguish between threatening and beneficial experiences and adapting maximally to the circumstances. Action systems determine to a large degree what we find attractive or aversive, and then generate tendencies to approach or avoid accordingly (Timberlake, 1994).

Van der Hart et al. (2006) describe action systems for reproduction/sexuality, attachment, caretaking, energy management (sleeping and eating), exploration and play, achievement of personal goals, and several action systems for defence (to avoid negative stimuli). The action systems determine how we behave, feel, perceive and think in a certain situation. Thus the same situation can be observed in very different ways. A man entering the room, for instance, can arouse fear from the perspective of the defence action system. But the same man can call up a feeling of security from the perspective of the attachment action system, or cause excitement from the sexuality action system. Within all action systems, two main categories are described. The daily life action system, with the purpose of adapting to and approaching attractive things in daily life with subsystems such as reproduction/sexuality, attachment, caretaking, energy management, exploration and play. The defence action system, with the purpose of avoiding or escaping from things that threaten our survival with subsystems such as hypervigilance, attachment cry, fear, freezing, fighting, flight and submission.

Van der Hart et al. (2006) describe that there is a balance and integration of activities that are necessary in daily life, on the one hand, and defence against danger, on the other hand: 'In mentally healthy adults action systems of daily life and defence are integrated [work together well]' (p. 32). Too much defence would prevent them from going out or driving a car at all. Too much daily life and too little defence could lead to reckless behaviour: 'For example, most people live daily life while also being aware of potential dangers: They drive carefully, avoid walking alone at night, and seek shelter during a major storm' (p. 32).

1.3.3 The stress system

To understand traumatized children, a brief explanation of the defence action system is necessary. When there is a threat, the reptilian brain signals this danger with the help of the amygdala (an almond-shaped nucleus of neurons in the brain), which can be described as an alarm bell. When this alarm bell starts ringing, the amygdala estimates the level of danger. The level of danger then determines the level of stress level and, if necessary, high activation of the defence action system. All of this happens automatically. This means that the perception of (supposed) danger by the body and the stress reaction happen before being able to think about it.

1.3.3.1 Window of Tolerance

When the amygdala perceives only a little danger, the stress level stays low and the defence action system does not have to become highly activated. The daily life and defence action systems can keep working together in an integrated way. A little bit of stress is good for us, as it improves the ability to learn because we pay more attention. Wilbarger and Wilbarger (1997) call this level of stress the 'optimal arousal zone'. This zone of stress, which the amygdala finds tolerable, is similar to Siegel's 'Window of Tolerance' (Siegel, 1999; Ogden & Minton, 2000) (see Figure 1.1).

If the stress stays within this Window of Tolerance, the three brains can be used together in an integrated fashion. A child is able to experience the emotions, physical sensations and thoughts that go with the experience without any need for the defence action system to be activated. Because the child's stress level is within the Window of Tolerance, he can effectively process the experience. This is very important information because that means that a child also needs to stay within the Window of Tolerance to process *traumatic* experiences (Wilbarger & Wilbarger, 1997).

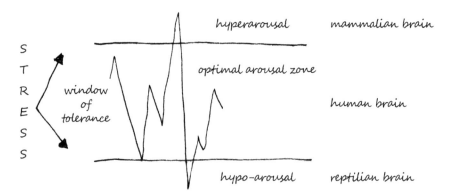

Figure 1.1

Source: Adapted from Ogden and Minton (2000); Ogden et al. (2006).

1.3.3.2 Hyperarousal

When the amygdala perceives a large threat, stress levels become higher until they become intolerable and the defence action system is highly activated. To deal with the danger, the body brings itself into state of hyperarousal, directed by the mammalian brain. The human brain then shuts down because the body has to respond immediately. The human brain would slow down the reaction by processing unnecessary information.

In a state of hyperarousal, our heart rate and muscle tension increase. The child becomes alert and watchful; everything is focused on the threatening danger. The senses become hypersensitive, so that the child is better able to smell, hear, see and taste the danger (Levine, 1997; Van Olst, 1972). This state provides for an active defence against danger, such as fight, flight or hide (see Figure 1.2). These active survival programmes are comparable to strategies an animal uses to survive: fighting to defeat the predator, or fleeing to stay out of the predator's reach. Hiding means keeping very still, disabling the attack response in the predator's brain, which reacts to movement, so that the predator leaves you alone. Children may have a preference, or use a mix of the fight, flight and hide strategy. If this works and the danger has gone, the body returns to its normal state.

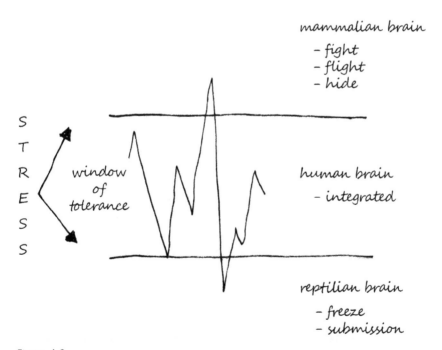

Figure 1.2

Source: Adapted from Ogden and Minton (2000); Ogden et al. (2006).

1.3.3.3 Hypo-arousal

When the amygdala judges a situation as very dangerous, and estimates that active defence will not be good enough, the brain switches to passive defence (Nijenhuis & Van der Hart, 1999). The body then prepares for serious injury by going into a state resembling that of shock, in which energy is preserved as much as possible. The body enters a state of hypo-arousal, directed by the reptilian brain. A state of hypo-arousal may be preceded by one of hyperarousal.

In a state of hypo-arousal, both the human brain and the mammalian brain are temporarily shut down, and only the reptilian brain functions. The brain temporarily loses the ability to scan for danger (an ability which is heightened during hyperarousal) and the ability to think and solve problems. A state of hypo-arousal involves a slow heartbeat and superficial, slow breathing, decreased blood flow and temperature. A stream of opiates (physical substances that work as painkillers) is released, sedating pain and creating a relaxed feeling (Perry & Szalavitz, 2007). Passive survival strategies include submission (Nijenhuis & Van der Hart, 1999) and freeze. Submission makes the body surrender to anything that may happen without resistance. The body becomes floppy and there is little muscle tension. Freeze means that the body feels paralysed and moving is difficult (Ogden & Minton, 2000). A similar strategy may again be seen in the animal world. Animals can 'play dead' to escape from a predator. Dead animals are floppy and when they are dead for a while, they become stiff. This works because most predators don't eat dead prey.

The term 'freeze' is used indiscriminately in the literature for three different strategies (keeping still in a state of hyperarousal, having limp muscles and being paralysed in a state of hypo-arousal), which is confusing. In this book the hide, submission and freeze are used to distinguish between the three.

1.4 How do the body and brain adapt to chronic stress and traumatization

1.4.1 Triggering

The amygdala can also signal a serious threat when something is not actually dangerous, but reminds a child of a traumatic experience. This is called triggering. The thing that reminds the child of the traumatic experience is called a trigger. Such was the case with Tim.

Ten-year-old Tim witnessed domestic violence from birth until he was seven years old. His father was an alcoholic, and was usually violent when he had had too much beer. His mother happily remarried, but when his mother and his stepfather are fighting he panics and demands them to stop.

Loud noises and screaming voices scare him and when children at school are fighting he runs off. Tim panics at the smell of alcohol and closes his eyes when there is a beer commercial on TV. His mother, who hardly drinks at all, cannot even have one glass of wine; merely the word 'beer' or the smell of alcohol is enough to trigger a hyperarousal reaction. Tim knows he is safe, but when he is triggered he *feels* unsafe.

1.4.2 Neural networks cause triggering

When we experiences something new or strange, the brain observes this in details and the memory starts searching for similar details. When the memory finds similar details, the whole memory is activated. A small detail can therefore trigger a complete image. This capacity enables us to assess a situation very quickly. To make this process as quick as possible, memories form neural networks in our mind (Folensbee, 2007). When there are similarities between memories such as the same location, feeling or thought, the experiences can become connected. One detail can then trigger a whole network of pictures and memories.

Because our memory plays an important role in the perception and interpretation of new situations, a neural network of traumatic memories can cause a detail to trigger the whole negative network of memories. A child with traumatic memories of domestic violence may develop a fear of everything that reminds him of it. Loud noises resemble the sound of father's hitting. But also an angry or flushed face, or even a bottle of beer, may be interpreted as a threat.

This can cause incorrect interpretations. A new situation that resembles the traumatizing one may be interpreted as a threat, when it is not. These negative networks can become larger and larger and new situations are wrongfully interpreted as threatening. When there are many triggers, the child may get hyper- or hypo-aroused easily in daily life. His Window of Tolerance is fairly small because there is a chronically heightened stress level.

1.4.3 Stress system dysregulated

Chronic stress can interfere with the cooperation between the 'three brains' and their automatic stress reactions. Children can need their survival states continuously.

1.4.3.1 Constantly in a hyperarousal state

The child can be in a constant state of hyperarousal unable to use their human brain. These children can no longer think or feel properly, are defensive and/or aggressive to others and themselves, are prone to uncontrollable fits of rage, and are hyper-alert, watchful and hyperactive (Ogden & Minton, 2000), as in Brian's case.

Brian is nine years old. He is fearful of loud noises and unexpected movements. He has trouble getting to sleep and is always watchful. He sleeps lightly and keeps getting out of bed. Brian is tired and easily irritated, but unable to relax. He keeps an eye on everything and remembers everything. When other children are fighting, Brian cannot continue what he was doing, he has to interfere. Often this will lead to him becoming angry as well. He does not do well at school because he is easily distracted.

David from the first case is also constantly hyperaroused.

1.4.3.2 Constantly in a hypo-arousal state

A child may also frequently be in a state of hypo-arousal. He then uses passive defence mechanisms such as submission or freeze. The child can adopt a submissive or helpless attitude. He obeys automatically, is unable to set boundaries, feels that he is a failure and keeps ending up in the victim position. These children may seem lifeless or robot-like, have little muscle tension in the face and express no emotion. They are unable to defend themselves and cannot detect danger or ask for help (Ogden & Minton, 2000). The child may also be confused and have the feeling that his own body is 'alien', or not really part of himself, as is the case for Dewi.

Dewi lives in her own world and fantasizes a lot. Because of her daydreaming she does not do well in school. She does not hear the teacher talking and she may have to repeat what she says four times, or touch Dewi. She seems to stare right through you. She does not talk about her feelings. She is 'always happy', she says. Her tolerance for pain is high. Recently she broke her arm during gymnastics, and this was only discovered after a few days. The doctor says she must have been in a lot of pain.

The question is whether Dewi actually felt the pain. She may have been paralysed by a state of hypo-arousal and felt nothing. Hypo-arousal is a more primitive form of defence that young children often use.

1.4.4 The body and brain adapt

A child can remain in this state of arousal for a prolonged time, or alternate between hypo- and hyperarousal. This consumes a lot of energy. The body does not return to its normal state and risks becoming exhausted. To prevent this, the body adapts, and changes in the brain or in the balance of certain chemical substances in the body may occur.

A chemical imbalance causes the amygdala to be over stimulated. When this is the case, it becomes impossible for the amygdala to determine what is dangerous and what is not. For some children the defence action system does not react to danger anymore and the child can no longer sense whether a situation is safe or not. Or the child feels always unsafe because the amygdala continuously signals danger and the defence action system is continuously active. Chronic traumatization disturbs the functioning of and the cooperation between the three brains. The child loses abilities he had before and is no longer able to do what he once could.

1.4.5 Delayed brain development

However, when the traumatization takes place at an early age, the three brains have not even matured, let alone learned to cooperate. In the first three years of a child's life, the prefrontal cortex (part of the human brain) develops rapidly and the child improves for example his attention, concentration, frustration, tolerance, emotion regulation, understanding cause and effect, and social skills.

The brain needs the proper sensorimotor stimuli for this development. The child's life must be predictable and the child needs safety, soothing and comforting. And this is exactly what is lacking in the case of early childhood traumatization and the result is that the brain cannot properly develop (Perry & Dobson, 2013). These children continue to be controlled by their reptilian and mammalian brains, just like very young children, and the development is delayed in many areas.

Chronic traumatization in early childhood thus, on the one hand, interferes with the functioning of and the cooperation between the three brains for as far as they have already developed, and, on the other hand, with their maturing and development. The child cannot properly assess new situations because he is constantly outside his Window of Tolerance and cannot use his control centre. The consequences of chronic traumatization at an early age, when the brain is still developing, are therefore more severe than those of traumatization at a later age or as an adult, when the brain is already fully grown when the trauma occurs.

'Traumatized people [children] frequently experience themselves as being at the mercy of their sensations, physical reactions and emotions' (Ogden & Minton, 2000, p. 4) without being able to use their control centre. Cognitions such as 'I am safe now' do not help them to reduce their physical sensations of insecurity. They are unable to suppress their needs and to delay their impulses, to predict the consequences of their behaviour, and to learn from their experiences. Traumatized children continue to have their activities directed bottom-up, comparable to young children (see Figure 1.3).

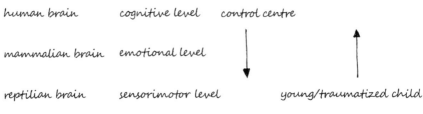

Figure 1.3

Still, these children have to go to school and are expected to take part in all sorts of age-appropriate activities. They children may also suffer failure of neuropsychological functions, such as memory, attention, concentration, planning, insight into causality and the integrative capacity. This is often expressed in a disharmonic intelligence profile. These children have learning disabilities and have trouble learning daily life skills. They may also have a deficit or surplus of certain hormones and neurotransmitters. The body may develop diseases of the immune system and become chronically exhausted, with growth disorders as a result.

1.5 Diagnosis

Chronically traumatized children can be diagnosed with posttraumatic stress disorder (PTSD). However a large group of chronically traumatized children does not meet the criteria for PTSD. A study with children placed in foster care showed that children that have experienced more complex traumatization exhibited fewer PTSD symptoms and significantly more severe trauma unrelated symptoms (Jonkman, Verlinden, Bolle, Boer, & Lindauer, 2013). The DSM-5 and ICD-10, manuals to classify psychiatric symptoms, unfortunately do not offer a classification to describe the broad consequences of chronic traumatization in early childhood because there is not enough research to support this. These consequences are now often regarded as separate symptoms and syndromes and they may be (mis) diagnosed with ADHD, anxiety or mood disorder, behaviour or learning disorder or autistic symptoms.

Van der Kolk (2005) has suggested a diagnostic construct for these children, Developmental Trauma Disorder. The term 'complex PTSD' (Herman, 1992, 1993) has also been used. Unfortunately there is not enough research (yet) to support this, as it is a promising construct, which would be extremely helpful for the diagnosis and treatment of these children (D'Andrea, Ford, Stolbach, Spinazzola, & Van der Kolk, 2012; Ford et al., 2013). Ten-year-old David from the earlier example fits the description of a Developmental Trauma Disorder or complex PTSD.

David (2)

David was abused by his father and witnessed domestic violence. His parents are divorced and he has lost contact with his father. David has learned at an early age that nobody can be trusted and that he must take care of himself. He therefore thinks mainly of himself and appears to be egocentric.

David has often felt like a coward because he did not protect his mother. He thinks his father beat him because he was a bad child, he deserved it. When his mother or teacher are angry with him, he can understand why: he is a bad child. But when they are nice to him, he becomes suspicious. That is not the way it should be, so they are probably planning something and this stresses him out (his defence action system is activated). It feels great, but feeling good is normally followed by beatings and pain and distress and the longer things are good, the more stressed David starts to feel.

At a subconscious level this is what happens: he cannot tolerate the stress that is building up inside and waiting for the bad things to happen, because it makes him feel powerless. To feel in control again, David will start a fight. 'Let's get it over with,' he thinks, 'and if I start it myself I can protect myself better because I am not taken by surprise and I don't let it hurt me so much.' When his mother gets angry with him, he calms down: this is familiar territory, I can understand this. When David hurts himself, the world is once more as he knows it. He deserves pain and he feels in control again. This is how David punishes himself.

But it is not very nice to feel insignificant and bad. David feels lonely and longs for someone who understands him (attachment system). He wants to be liked but he doesn't dare to trust anybody. He doesn't want to be alone and he wants attention from his teacher. When she talks to other children David feels awful: you see, she thinks I'm bad, she doesn't even want to be near me anymore. David cannot imagine (mentalize) that other children also need help or that teacher may like more than one child. It is all or nothing, black or white. He very easily feels rejected.

David misses his father and feels guilty that he hasn't seen him for so long. After all, his father is a good father. It is his fault that his father was violent and now he has caused his father pain because his mother has divorced him. David is also afraid of his father and angry with him because he beat David. His mother hates his father and he resembles his father, so she probably hates him as well. All these different feelings are confusing, and that is why he prefers to feel nothing and why he doesn't talk about it.

When David is busy he manages not to feel anything. As soon as he calms down he starts to worry. He prefers to keep busy all day. When he has to concentrate on his schoolwork for a longer period, his thoughts begin to wonder back to bad memories and he doesn't want that.

David feels threatened all the time, everyone is a danger to him. He is on his guard and pays close attention to everything around him. If he is not focused, he could get killed. As a result of the stress, David has to be constantly aware of every detail. It is as if he is in a war situation and there could be snipers anywhere. It is impossible to pay attention at the same time to details and to the situation as a whole, so David's perception is fragmented. He sees and hears separate parts of a situation and not the whole, and so he often misses parts. He is not good at integrating details into a whole.

Neither is he much good at generalizing and inferring. Generalizing is very dangerous when there is a threat. If one tree has been inspected thoroughly and no sniper has been found, that doesn't mean all trees are safe. They must all be studied and scanned one by one. That is exhausting. This is why he is not very good at reading comprehension and arithmetic.

New situations are difficult to assess because they are potential danger. David has to be alert to everything at once, and this wears him out. David likes routine and a regular schedule. This allows him to predict to a certain extent what will happen, and so he is less stressed. When there are exceptions to the rule, David feels unsafe. He has lost control and has to do all there is in his power to regain it. He gets irritated and tired. That is why he is compulsive and rigid in his behaviour. Warm and friendly situations are new, and therefore stressful to him. The stress increases and, to regain control, he will pick a fight to create a situation he is familiar with.

Understandably, David is bad at remembering names and often forgets things. The question is whether he has actually heard them. When someone is introduced to David, he is too busy scanning for danger to remember an unimportant detail like a name. David is also chaotic and constantly loses things. There is chaos in his mind, making it hard for him to order the outside world. However, he does like surroundings that are well ordered and tidy and finds them relaxing.

David often does not know what time it is, or what day or what month. He lives (or rather survives) in the present, and such details are not important enough to remember. Moreover, David is often outside his Window of Tolerance and therefore unable to learn from his experiences. Outside his Window of Tolerance he is unable to use his memory and previous experiences to assess situations. He is surviving and does not play or explore.

David enjoys violence; this gives him a pleasant feeling of power. It makes him feel just a bit less stupid and insignificant. But others disapprove and call him bad and weird. This confirms his belief that he is a bad child, undeserving of love. When David loses his temper, it is like a volcano erupting inside him. He gets so angry that he could almost kill somebody. He feels like hurting and humiliating others, and is unable to think.

Sometimes he is disoriented and his mind is flooded with memories from the past. Anything that makes him feel powerless makes him angry. The teacher tells him that he is angry over nothing, but to him it is important. When he is unable to control the situation, he is at the mercy of another, who cannot be trusted. Not being in control is a life-threatening situation. So when teacher tells him not to talk or walk around the classroom, she is trying to gain control over him. When his mother tells him to turn off the TV, she is in control. These aren't 'minor things' to David: they make him feel alone, bad and unwanted.

Five-year-old Demi (see p. 9), who was abused by her grandfather, also suffers from Developmental Trauma Disorder or complex PTSD. But she expresses it in quite a different way.

Demi (2)

Demi was abused at a very early age, which was painful and scary for her. Demi was constantly afraid to be abused again and often wondered: when is it going to start again, when will the pain come? She started to watch her surroundings very carefully for signs that predicted this so she could protect herself (dissociate) and be in control. The brain needs predictability. This made Demi go to her grandfather herself, to get it over with. After that she could relax. Demi thinks this is normal, that all men will have sex with her. She will approach unknown men and 'flirt' with them. Abuse me, she thinks, get it over with.

Demi acts out what has happened to her with her cousin and her Barbie dolls. She has a dominant role now, and that is a pleasant feeling. She identifies with the perpetrator; that is much better than being the victim. She does not know that this is not normal. The chronic stress makes her unable to determine what is OK and what is not. Her alarm system does not function anymore.

Mother, who was herself abused by the grandfather, is not very good either at picking up the signs. Her alarm system is off as well. She has failed to protect her daughter, because she is convinced that she herself deserved what her father did to her in the past. Because it was her own fault, there was no reason to suspect he would do the same to her daughter. If her father would turn out not to abuse her daughter, this would be definitive proof that he was a good man, that she had a father who could take care of her. This would give her a feeling of security. But when the abuse did in fact take place, mother could not pick up the signs. She had lost her sense of what was not OK.

> Socially, Demi is maladapted. She hasn't got time to learn from the interaction with other children, because she is constantly surviving. Besides, her brain has not developed properly because of the stress and she has learning difficulties.

1.5.1 No posttraumatic stress symptoms?

Some children seem to be doing well and do not display any symptoms. Professionals or caregivers argue they are not traumatized and do not need treatment. There are several reasons for caution with this conclusion.

Whether or not a child displays trauma symptoms needs to be assessed by an experienced clinician. Attachment difficulties, internalizing trauma symptoms, personality problems, overadjustment and dissociation can be hard to recognize, especially when the child tries to hide them. Extreme unsafety can make children not display any symptoms. A quarter of the children that are sexually abused do not display any sexual abuse symptoms.

Even though traumatization may not be visible on the outside, the impact is visible on the inside. A review of fMRI studies showed a relationship between maltreatment and neurocognitive functioning and neurobiology, visible on fMRI even with children who do not display any symptoms (Teicher & Samson, 2016). These changes seem to represent their vulnerability to develop psychopathology later in life (McCrory, Gerin, & Viding, 2017).

The consequences of untreated traumatization in childhood can be huge. In the Adverse Childhood Experiences study (ACE) (Felitti et al., 1998) 17 000 adult patients visiting a hospital, reported the number of childhood traumas (ACE) they had experienced. The study showed there is a strong relationship between the number of categories of chronic traumatization in childhood and having health, social and behavioural problems in adulthood. Chronically traumatized children were 7× as likely to be alcoholics, 6× as likely to have sex before the age of fifteen, 2× as likely to have cancer and heart disease, 4× as likely to have emphysema and 12× as likely to have attempted suicide. Overweight and obesity turned out to be one of the long-term consequences of untreated childhood trauma. In a study in a Bayfield Child Health Centre San Francisco, 51 per cent of the children (N=701) with an ACE score of four or more, had learning or behaviour problems (Burke, Hellman, Scott, Weems, & Carrion, 2011).

So even when the impact of traumatization is not visible or chronically traumatized children do not meet the criteria for PTSD, it is important to try and address their traumatic memories and wake up their 'sleeping dogs'. It is normal to provide preventative treatment for women with a breast cancer gene, even though they do not display any symptoms yet. Why do we withhold from children a chance to heal from their trauma simply because the damage is not visible to us (yet). Chances of traumatization disappearing without treatment are very small. The younger the child is and the longer the child goes without treatment, the greater the chance of permanent damage (Cohen et al., 2010).

A child must be able to stay within his Window of Tolerance to process traumatic experiences (Wilbarger & Wilbarger, 1997).

A new situation that resembles the traumatizing one may be interpreted as a threat, when it is not.

On the one hand, chronic traumatization in early childhood interferes with the functioning of and the cooperation between the three brains, insofar as they have developed, and, on the other hand, with their maturing and development.

Chapter 2

Why children become avoidant and resistant

The Sleeping Dogs method is developed for treatment of chronically traumatized children who display severe (trauma-related) symptoms and are not (yet) able to process their traumatic memories. They are avoidant or are resistant to talk about their memories. They have forgotten or deny their trauma. This chapter describes the normal development of the personality and how children adapt to try and survive traumatization.

2.1 Chronic traumatization and the development of the personality

In his article, Schore (2001) gives an overview of the research that has been done on infants and the effects of early relational trauma on the developing brain of these infants. Van der Kolk et al. (2009) describe the concept of developmental trauma. Both articles describe how trauma in early life impacts the development of the capacities of maintaining relationships, coping with stress and regulating emotion. The following paragraphs provide a simplified summary of this.

2.1.1 Stress regulation

A baby's brain is chaotic and disorganized and the infant's amygdala does not have many memories to assist in judging new situations. The infant's amygdala signals danger quickly and the infant becomes stressed. The primary caregiver needs to regulate the infant's stress and calm and soothe them by being an external regulator of the infant's nervous system. The parent watches over what the child can handle and makes sure that dose and timing are correct. When the parent's brain is calm and organized, the baby's brain will tune in to its parent's brain. It synchronizes at an unconscious level and also becomes calm. In this way, the adult brain regulates the infant brain. If all goes well, the brain will develop the skills to regulate itself in the first few years and will no longer need its parent for this. The baby uses the adult's control centre to develop its own mammalian and human brain.

However, when a parent enters a state of panic (a state of hyper- or hypo-arousal) both brains will panic. The parent may try to hide his panic, but the baby feels physical changes or changes in the heart rate. If this problem turns out to be structural, the baby's brain will remain chaotic and will not learn to regulate stress by itself. Brain cells or the connections between them may die when they are not stimulated in the right period, in the right way. A child therefore needs a parent with a calm brain in order to learn to regulate stress.

Secure attachment is also needed for this synchronization process. The child must feel safe with the parent in order to learn something. If the parent is also harming the child, the source of stress for the child becomes the same person he depends on for stress regulation. Then the child does not calm down and cannot learn. Chronically traumatized children lack the two conditions necessary in order to learn how to regulate stress themselves – a calm parent and a secure attachment relationship with that parent.

2.1.2 The attachment system shuts down

Every child is born with the desire to attach to adults. The attachment action system, also known as the attachment system, makes children seek support and form attachment relationships with other people. This is a survival mechanism, because the adults provide safety and keep the child alive.

Negative experiences with the attachment figure, the parent, can make the attachment system less active, or even make it change its strategy. The child will develop attachment anxiety, the fear of forming attachment relationships. Actions aimed at attachment will then at the same time activate the defence action system. These children will be torn between their fear of being close to other people and at the same time a strong need to be near others. Hedges (1997) has a beautiful way of describing this: 'Contact itself is the feared element because it brings a promise of love, safety, and comfort that cannot be fulfilled and that reminds (the patient) of the abrupt breaches of infancy' (p. 114).

When these children start to attach themselves (attachment action system) to foster parents or to caregivers, they start to feel threatened. That feeling can become so strong that the defence action system takes over from the attachment system by distancing the child from this adult for safety.

Since these children have built up a lot of negative experiences, their fear can be so strong that they seem to have no attachment system anymore. They seem to enjoy being on their own and not needing anyone. Caregivers say the relationship is functional and the child is unable to attach. For most children this is not true. They are able to attach, but their fear, caused by traumatic memories, is in the way. These children still long for attachment and closeness, but this need is masked by defence behaviour.

2.1.3 Strategies to control fear of attachment

Children may develop different strategies to cope with this conflict between the need for and the fear of attachment. The child may cling to the adult (ambivalent attachment) to avoid having to learn to regulate stress himself, since the adult does this for him. He may withdraw and try to calm himself down when there is stress (avoidant attachment). In order to control his fear of attachment, the child avoids contact and shows anger and resentment when he feels threatened. He does this to feel powerful and to cover up his fear of dependence.

Some children have no strategy and they can cling and avoid at the same time, sending out a mixed message to the caregiver (disorganized attachment). The alternation between sub-action systems that are active can explain the changes in mood and behaviour of children with a disorganized attachment style. The sub-action system *attachment cry* clings to the caregiver, and the sub-action system *fight* generates aggression. The child may then 'switch' to the 'defence part' of the personality. Such a switch is not always clearly visible, but can usually be recognized if close attention is paid. These children can also switch abruptly from dependence to aggression and, after a while, back to dependence again; from anger to seeking comfort, and back again to anger. This is very difficult to manage for caregivers.

But these rapid changes in mood and behaviour can also be caused by structural dissociation, the more extreme strategy to control this dilemma. If the child is in fact suffering from a dissociative disorder, he will also alternate between parts. The difference, compared to children with only a disorganized attachment style, is that children with a dissociative disorder generally fail to recall that they have been aggressive. They can barely talk about it later, because they don't remember.

2.2 Attachment is the basis for development

As discussed, the child must feel safe with the parent in order to learn something. Children then learn to regulate stress, to regulate emotions, to understand

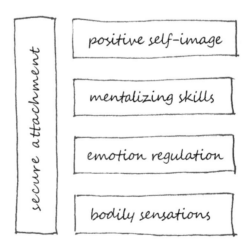

Figure 2.1

their own intentions and the intentions of others (mentalize), and to view themselves and the world from a realistic perspective (see Figure 2.1). When the child does not have that safe attachment relationship, this undermines the child's whole development. The next paragraphs explain this.

2.2.1 Development of emotion regulation

When a baby is born, it can only feel whether things are OK or not OK. There is as yet very little differentiation; he either cries or sleeps. The baby learns about what is going on inside because the parents talk to him: 'You are hungry', 'You are angry', 'You are frightened.' This is called mirroring (Kohut, 1977). Through the parent mirroring the child's inner world, the child learns to recognize his bodily sensations and learns to reflect on them. Later on the child learns to recognize and name his emotions and talk about them. The parent then teaches the child to regulate these feelings.

Emotions can be seen as important helpers in life. They give direction, motivation and strength. They warn us of danger by becoming afraid and they signal pleasurable things by feeling good. Emotions serve as a compass in life. For a person who cannot make proper use of his emotions, life is hard. It becomes difficult to choose and decide. In order to learn to recognize, articulate and regulate emotions, it is necessary for children to have a secure attachment to a parent figure who can mirror them.

2.2.2 Learning to mentalize

As a child grows older, they need to develop their skills to mentalize. The ability to mentalize is the ability to reflect on one's own intentions and those of others. Fonagy, Gergely, Jurist, and Target (2002) describe mentalizing as the permanently present, unconscious process by which people are able to see their own actions and those of others as being motivated by internal cognitions, intentions and convictions. Children who can mentalize can describe why they want something. They can explain why they became angry. They understand that when the teacher told them their answer was wrong, he was trying to teach them something, not to make fun of him.

The child learns to mentalize through that same mirroring process. Mirroring enables a child to learn to think about his inner world and his own intentions: he learns to mentalize his inner world. The next step for the child is to learn to think about the inner world of others and their intentions, mentalizing the inner world of others. Because the adult has to be able to imagine what the inner world of the child might be like, a child can only be mirrored by someone with adequate mentalizing skills and someone who is able to use his human brain (stress level within the Window of Tolerance).

Again, both a parent who is able to mentalize situations for the child and a secure attachment relationship with that parent, are prerequisites for the development of a mentalizing capacity. In addition to secure attachment, predictability and continuity are necessary in order to learn to interpret experiences and to experience how cause and effect are connected.

2.2.3 Trust and a positive self-image

In the first years of life, the child already forms core beliefs or core cognitions about life, others and himself. Based on his memory, the child constructs an internal working model (Bretherton & Munholland, 1999) of what he may expect from others and what others expect from him. This working model forms the basis of his trust in others and in himself. A child bases his core beliefs on the experiences he has with his parents, through that same mirroring process. The child sees himself through the eyes of his parents and his parents' behaviour towards him. The child develops self-confidence because he experiences that his signals are being taken seriously and that he is worth existing. He can put things in perspective and knows not everything is about him. For young children it is mainly the relationship with the parents that determines their self-image. As a child grows older, relationships with others and with the peer group begin to play a greater role. These relationships with others then also have their influence on their self-image.

2.2.4 Conclusion

So, in conclusion, secure attachment, stress and emotion regulation, and self-image are closely related concepts. That is why the consequences of a disruption in the early parent–child interaction are so devastating. Chronic traumatization in early childhood can result in deformation of the personality and lifelong, far-reaching problems with establishing stable relationships with others (Van der Kolk, 2005).

2.3 The child's underdevelopment

Chronic traumatization in early childhood can have serious effects in several areas of development. These children have difficulties in connecting with others, are insecurely attached, have trouble regulating their emotions and have limited impulse control. They have a chaotic brain, limited mentalizing ability and negative cognitions about themselves and others. All these elements are closely interrelated. Secure attachment is a prerequisite for regulating stress, for learning to regulate emotions and developing mentalizing skills and all are important building blocks for the child's development (see Figure 2.1). When one building block is missing, this will disturb development in all other areas.

2.3.1 Abusive parents

The child needs to feels safe and calm to be able to learn; in other words, stress levels need to be within the Window of Tolerance. This is generally not the case for traumatized children. If the parents are the source of trauma, they do not mirror the child enough because they are busy with their own inner world. When they hurt the child, they do not verbalize the child's physical feelings. When they scare or hurt the child, they do not verbalize how the child feels scared and calm him. When they abuse the child, they may verbalize the wrong things ('you ruined my life, you are bad. You enjoy having sex with me'), or do not mirror the child at all.

If the parent's mentalizing ability is underdevelopment as a consequence of their own traumatic experiences, the child's behaviour can frighten the parent, or make him angry. If a parent has been physically or sexually abused himself, the inner world of the child may bring up old memories of the parent's own traumas. For example, a child who is angry with his parent because he wants candy and the parent said 'no' might say: 'I hate you.' For the parent, this can bring up memories of being abused and humiliated in childhood, which can be so overwhelming that the parent's stress level takes him out of his Window of Tolerance.

2.3.2 Mirroring the wrong things

The child then triggers the parent and becomes a source of stress for the parent. The parent is then not able to react to the child adequately. This can result in the parent – outside his Window of Tolerance – saying to the child: 'You're trying to boss me around, you're trying to make me mad, you're doing it on purpose.' This, however, reflects the inner world of the parent much more than that of the child. The parent's mentalizing skills are a protective factor for the child. These skills help the parent to stay within his Window of Tolerance and to realize that it is only logical for the child to be angry because he wants candy and that does not mean he is a terrible parent. Mentalizing skills help the parent to be a safe attachment figure for the child in spite of his own trauma (Fonagy et al., 2002).

2.3.3 The child's lack of mentalization skills

If the wrong things are mirrored to the child, the child does not learn to recognize bodily feelings and emotions and it does not learn to mentalize. Because traumatized children have a limited capacity for mentalization, they cannot see themselves in the perspective of the larger context. They think they are the centre of the universe. They cannot think about themselves as 'who am I and what do I want' and they cannot think about what others want. They are seen as egocentric but from their own point of view everything that happens actually does refer to them. If mother is in a bad mood, it does not occur to them that she may have slept badly. Their conclusion is that they have caused it.

2.3.4 Negative self-image

The child may start to believe these ideas about himself and his own intentions, such as 'I am a bad child who torments his parents on purpose', 'I am scary, it is my fault, I am worthless'; or about the perpetrator, 'He is almighty.' Children often believe that abuse is their own fault, because perpetrators and others have said this to them and because they cannot think of any other reason why the – in their eyes – good parent is hurting them (Salter, 1995).

Besides, their impaired mentalizing ability makes it hard for them to imagine other's intentions. So it is not surprising that traumatized children draw the wrong conclusions about themselves, about others and about the world. The child evaluates every new situation with safe adults of children on the basis of the incorrect working model that 'you can't trust anyone and I am worthless'.

The perception and interpretation of events is also determined by the child's memory. Negative memories determine how a child perceives himself ('I am usually a bad child, so I'm probably bad now too'). Traumatized children will find it easier to remember negative experiences, because these can be connected to an extensive network of similar experiences. Positive experiences are new to them and have little connection to similar experiences, which is why these children may not easily notice or remember them.

This underdevelopment and damage reduces the child's capacity to deal with stress and survive. The lack of emotion regulation, attachment and mentalizing skills makes them more vulnerable for traumatization. The following paragraphs describe how psychological survival mechanisms can help children to survive.

2.4 Psychological survival mechanisms

There are many different ways in which children try and survive their traumatic experiences. In Chapter 1 the stress system and the biological survival programmes fight, flight, hide, submission and freeze were discussed. In addition to this, children can also use psychological survival mechanisms to cope. These are described in the following paragraphs. All these mechanisms serve to protect the child. In the long term, however, these mechanisms cause even more internal stress and difficulties in connecting with others (Van der Hart et al., 2006).

2.4.1 Loss of connection to the parent

When the child is being abused or neglected by the parent, the child loses connection with the parent. The person that is supposed to be safe becomes a threat. Threats need to be avoided, but the child cannot avoid the parent because children need connection with their parent to survive. Humans survive by living in groups. When a child loses the connection with his parent, he loses 'the hand that feeds him' and he end up alone and risks dying. That should be avoided at all costs. Psychological survival mechanisms help the child to solve this problem.

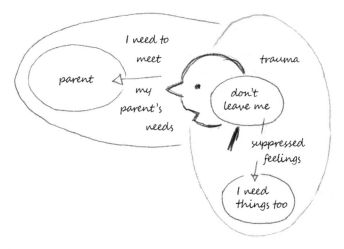

Figure 2.2
Source: Adapted from Knipe (2018).

2.4.2 Connecting with the perpetrator

The child tries to adapt his behaviour to restore this connection to the parent. Children can do this in different ways. Jim Knipe (2018) has developed a toolbox for working with avoidance, defence and dissociation in complex traumatized adults. With images, he illustrates how children survive (emotional) abuse and neglect by different ways of staying connected to the parent.

2.4.2.1 Connecting by meeting the parent's needs

When the child's needs and behaviours and feelings are not acceptable to the parent, the child can try to meet the parent's needs, instead of the parent meeting the child's needs. The child focuses on what his parent wants and pushes his own feelings and needs away. The child cares for the parent, which can be emotionally and physically, and there is role reversal. Children with a parent with a mental illness or disability often use this strategy. The child then learns to push his feelings aside: 'I must never be angry. I must never (or always) need. I must never (or always) be weak. I must not remember what was done to me' (see Figure 2.2).

2.4.2.2 Connecting through fighting

If meeting the parent's needs does not lead to connection, the child can try to connect by trying to win, fight and dominate the parent. Fighting with the parent is a way of keeping connection with the parent, to be seen by the parent. It is then said that the child draws 'negative attention' however this is not about getting attention. Survival is at stake.

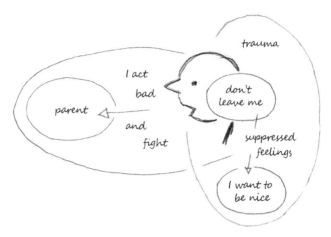

Figure 2.3
Source: Adapted from Knipe (2018).

They do not want to fight, but they need to make sure they are cared for. The fighting can be done by openly expressing anger or passively and more hidden. The child's real feelings, longing to be seen and heard, need to be pushed away. The child then learns: 'I have to be aggressive or passive aggressive. I have to withdraw or not tell my parents. I have to do the opposite of what the parent wants.' Instead of fighting the child can also use fear to try and connect. They need to be scared and afraid to connect to the parent, they have no other way. Children with separation anxiety disorders can have this interaction pattern (see Figure 2.3).

2.4.2.3 Connecting through becoming perfect

Children naturally idealize their parents. They want to make their parents happy and proud and they need their parents to feel how much they love them. Narcissistic parents sometimes have trouble feeling the child's love. The child then feels he is a failure and disappointment.

To stay connected the child needs to try harder to show the parent his love, to make sure the parent will not abandon him. These children try and fulfil their own need to make the parent happy, opposed to children in the first example who try and connect by focusing on the parent's needs. The child then learns: 'I have to be the perfect child. I am bad because my love is not good enough. I cannot make my parent happy.' These children want the parent to notice their love. Instead of making the parent responsible, they blame themselves so they can continue to idealize the parent. They can feel disgusted with themselves. They learn: 'I want to think it is my fault because it is too sad to think and feel how alone I was.' They use shame to deal with their self-blame. In order to act perfect, they need to push away all negative feelings (see Figure 2.4).

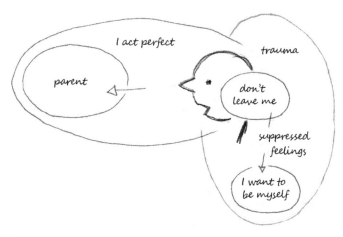

Figure 2.4
Source: Adapted from Knipe (2018).

2.4.2.4 Connecting to two different caregivers

When their parents fight, children can get stuck between their parents, especially when there is a high conflict divorce. Parents can be so distressed that they are unable to think about their child's needs. Then the child needs to adapt. When the child has two parents with different needs to connect, the best way to survive is to develop two different responses and three parts of the child: 'I need to be weak and needy and tell mum I like her best. I need to be tough and never cry

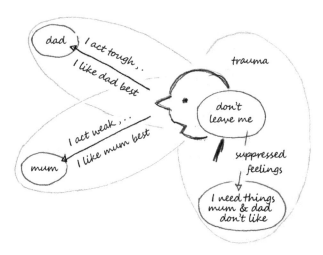

Figure 2.5
Source: Adapted from Knipe (2018).

and tell dad I like him best. I can never show the parts of me that mum and dad don't like.' Both parents think they know the real child while in fact nobody knows the child's real wishes. When professionals side with one parent, they risk being involved with only one side of the child, which is misleading. In court cases children can be asked for their views on decisions around contact. However a child who is stuck between his parents cannot afford to express his own wishes because he is busy trying to stay connected to both. Everything he says can be used against him by the other parent (see Figure 2.5).

2.4.2.5 Connecting by adapting to parent's emotional state

The same can happen when one parent has different responses. With the normal dad: 'I am normal and compliant.' With the drunk and angry dad: 'I am angry and defiant.' With the sexually perpetrating dad: 'I numb myself and I do "bad" things and feel disgusting feelings. By myself I can feel my real needs and be my real self.' These children's wishes and needs become fragmented and separated instead of integrated, which can lead to structural dissociation (see Figure 2.6).

2.4.3 Continue to use these ways of connecting

These interaction patterns were useful to survive the abusive relationships. However when the abuse has stopped, these children continue to interact in this way. Even though the child is safe in a new foster family, he continues to take care of his foster father, continues fighting with his foster mother or continues to act perfect. Or they continue to be totally different when interacting with the foster parents or the biological parents.

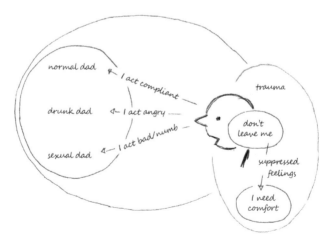

Figure 2.6

Source: Adapted from Knipe (2018).

2.4.4 Pushing away own needs

The child can only stay connected to the parent by pushing away all or part of his own needs. Since children need to have their needs met, this has serious consequences. Children can lose contact with what they really need, or they can feel empty, depressed and sad. The threat of losing the connection can make them feel anxious, without knowing what they are scared of. They can feel angry without being able to describe why. Because their real needs are not met, they can feel unloved or unworthy.

2.4.5 Shame

These feelings can be so intolerable that the child needs other psychological defences to cover them. Guilt can be managed by shame. When you feel shame, you do not feel the guilt so much. Children can feel ashamed of what they have done during traumatization. Shame and guilt are closely related. Children can feel guilty about something they have done: I have *made* a mistake. They did not help their parent or sibling, or were made to harm them. They enjoyed harming them and those feelings disgust them. Children can feel guilty for being sexually aroused during sexual abuse, even though involuntary sexual arousal is very common. They can feel guilty about their submissive or freeze reaction. They were not assertive when they were being bullied. When guilt turns into shame, they feel I *am* a mistake. They have become a disgusting, unworthy and unlovable person. Shame is a normal and healthy emotion, but for traumatized children shame can become a huge problem. Problematic shame has negative self-blaming thoughts, often a lowered head, feelings become flat and negative and they have less physical energy (Nathanson, 1994).

2.4.6 Idealization

It is better for the child to think that it is all his own fault than that his parents are doing something wrong. Guilt and shame can help the child to continue to see his parents are good and idealize the parents. From a survival perspective it is imperative not to risk being rejected by 'the hand that feeds', otherwise you die. Children are therefore programmed to see their parents as 'absolutely good' and 'always knowing best' and idealize them. If their parents hurt them, they will first try to find out what they have done to cause this, which is logical and advantageous from a survival perspective.

2.4.7 Avoidance

All these feelings and thought and survival mechanisms are connected together and add up to a perfect wall. The child needs to continue to idealize his parents. They avoid discussing anything bad about their parents and cannot risk learning

Figure 2.7
Source: Adapted from Knipe (2018).

the wise lesson. They avoid talking about how they feel because the shame is too painful. They avoid discussing how they think about themselves because they feel too guilty. They avoid connecting to their loneliness and pain because it is intolerable. They can only hold that together by avoiding talking about their memories at all. The memories become sleeping dogs.

2.5 Behaving like a perpetrator

Traumatized children may display cruel, violent or sexualized behaviour towards others and become perpetrators. For the adults surrounding them, this is difficult and they can react strongly to this, calling the child mean or dirty. However many of these children are not even aware of why they are doing this, they do not intend to be mean or cruel. There may be several reasons for children to demonstrate this kind of behaviour.

2.5.1 This is normal

They may not be aware that sexual and physical abuse is not normal; because they grew up with it, it seems normal to them, and so they will also do it to others. Fourteen-year-old Jody said the following about this:

> I used to hit other children and was really nasty to them. That is how my parents treated me and I thought it was normal. I often wonder why I did not tell someone sooner that I was being abused. But I thought it was normal, that all children were abused. When I heard that parents are not supposed to abuse their children and that this does not happen to all children, I was shocked. Apparently something really bad had happened to me.

2.5.2 Imitating the abuser

Children learn new things by imitating adult behaviour. Imitating is a biological survival mechanism that helps children to survive. For children, for example, their father, the perpetrator, can seem to be an exceptionally good survivor. Much better than their mother, who is the victim, whose life is threatened and is powerless. It seems to be much smarter to imitate dad's behaviour than mum's. This is often seen in even very young children, one, two, three, who are violent, aggressive, sexualized and imitate what they have experienced.

2.5.3 Identification with the perpetrator

When this imitation gets to a deeper level, and the behaviour is driven by how the child experiences this behaviour and how it makes him feel, there can be identification with the perpetrator. Abused children have experienced an overwhelming sense of powerlessness. They were hurt and harmed and could not do anything. They blame themselves for what happened and feel weak, helpless, like worthless wimps. These feelings can be very difficult to tolerate.

Some children, during abuse, pretend to be the perpetrator, identify with the perpetrator, instead of themselves, the victim. Pretending to be in control and overpower the victim can make them feel good about themselves again. In daily life, these children often feel weak, stupid and out of control. To compensate for those feelings, they can use the same mechanism and become a perpetrator by hurting others. These children are violent and controlling. They abuse others to feel powerful and strong. They can hurt other children or animals 'on purpose', abusing them physically or sexually or threatening them, and enjoy doing this. This compensates for their damaged self-image because the strong, powerful feeling is the opposite of the powerlessness and insignificance they feel inside.

This strategy works during abuse, but in daily life it can become problematic. For some children this causes an internal conflict. Violence gives them a powerful feeling, but they also strongly reject violence and do not want to feel like that or are ashamed of those feelings. They solve the conflict by expressing the violence not openly but becoming passively aggressive. They secretly steal or damage things, bully other children. When this passive aggression is still it causes an internal conflict, the child can split that part of the personality off through structural dissociation. This is called a perpetrator part and the child has amnesia for the violent things that he has done. In this way the child can believe that these feelings are not his.

2.6 Dissociation

In the previous examples the child uses psychological defences to survive. The child has different aspects of himself and can react differently, but there is no amnesia for these different reactions. However, when the internal conflict between the needs of the different aspects of the child becomes stronger, the child can resolve this with structural dissociation and amnesia. When the child cannot remember behaving in a certain way, these parts have become separate parts of the personality and structural dissociation has occurred.

2.6.1 Dissociation to survive abuse

In this book the term 'dissociation' is used to indicate a way to cope with overwhelming stress by withdrawing emotionally. The experience is too intense to regulate, the child cannot make sense of it or deal with it. When a child dissociates during such an experience, he withdraws inside himself and is 'absent' for a short time. The experience is disconnected from normal consciousness. If a child is dissociated during an event, he usually does not have a conscious memory of the event, he has amnesia. He does not know that he has actually lived through it.

Dissociation is a smart survival tactic to deal with difficult circumstances. Even though the child experiences terrible things, he is still able to function and go to school and take part in daily activities because he does not remember. The experience has not been integrated and the child can pretend it never happened. A child can also partially dissociate; he will, for instance, experience the event but without emotions or bodily sensations, looking at himself from a distance. The child can remember the event afterwards, but does not remember the traumatic feelings and sensations. They can tell horrific stories of what happened to them without any emotion, without being affected by it at all. This can be seen in refugee children who have experienced war.

Dissociation during trauma means that the traumatic experience has been wholly (complete dissociation) or partially (partial dissociation) disconnected from personal consciousness (Van der Hart, 1995). Many chronically traumatized children experience dissociation during the traumatizing event. Very young children in particular often have no other means than to dissociate to cope with the stress.

2.6.2 Dissociation as a trauma symptom

Unfortunately, dissociation during trauma is not very effective in the long term, because the dissociated experiences often return as flashbacks. When the child has a flashback, it feels like it is reliving the traumatizing event as if it happens. A flashback can be triggered by something, a detail, that reminds the child of the traumatic event and through the neural network the child re-experiences the memory of the danger and feels like it is in danger, even when there is no actual danger present (see also section 3.1.3 Filing Cabinets).

During a flashback the child gets into a state of hyper- or hypo-arousal again that then reinforces the need to dissociate again. The re-experience can be so real that the child actually 'goes back in time' to the abuse situation and thinks that, for instance, the parent or therapist is the abuser. The child's perception can be so disturbed that another person's face actually changes into that of the abuser. Such a flashback can be very frightening. Jill said to the teacher who corrected her:

> Wow, you gave me a fright. For a minute I thought you were my father. Your face looked just like him.

Dissociation occurs within a state of hyperarousal when the stress and emotions are too overwhelming for the child to stay cognitively conscious. The child then remains in a state of hyperarousal, but is no longer consciously present. This phenomenon can, for example, be observed in children who have fits of rage and do not respond anymore. Nine-year-old Emil's mother describes the following.

> When Emil is really angry his facial expression changes, as if there's a mist before his eyes. He can no longer be reached and his gaze is empty, as if he looks straight through me. Whatever I say to him, I cannot get through to him. Because I really do not know what to do at such times, I once put him under the cold shower. That was awful, but it did help. When he has calmed down, often he does not remember what happened and denies it. When Emil is angry, he does not notice what is happening around him.

Dissociation occurring within a state of hypo-arousal presents differently. The child feels paralysed, cannot feel anything anymore, cannot think or feels as if he is leaving his body. Such children look frozen, stiff or robot-like.

Besides dissociation, reduced awareness in a child can also indicate other problems such as absences, epilepsy, exhaustion or a low blood-sugar level. Some of these children have been assessed for or are even diagnosed with such medical problems.

2.7 Structural dissociation

Once the brain becomes accustomed to dissociation, this can remain the preferred strategy in later life. This prevents the children from learning to cope with emotions or stress, and will cause them to dissociate in relatively harmless circumstances. They are so defenceless that merely being introduced to an unknown adult and shaking his hand can cause the child to use the ultimate protection of dissociation.

When children at a young age are forced to survive through dissociation for a prolonged period, their integrative functions can become compromised to such an extent that, according to Van der Hart et al. (2006) *structural dissociation of the personality* occurs. The personality and consciousness are divided into two or more parts to solve the contradiction between the goals and the desired actions of the different action systems. To this day there is disagreement as to whether structural dissociation exists and what it is exactly. There has been insufficient scientific research to give an unequivocal answer, however the theory of structural dissociation has some research support (Schlumpf et al., 2013; Vissia et al., 2016). Since this theory offers a useful framework for treatment, a brief and simplified explanation of the theory is described with some comments based on practical experiences.

When children are forced to survive through dissociation for a long time, both action systems (daily life and defence) have to be active simultaneously. They counteract each other: the daily life action system wants to make contact, play, explore, while the defence action system wants to keep its distance, to have as little change as possible, to trust no one. Play and exploration are far too dangerous. When a child has to defend himself for a short time, the daily life action system can be shut down temporarily. But when traumatization is prolonged, as in chronic traumatization in early childhood, the daily life action system has to be active too.

When simultaneous activation of both systems is necessary for a prolonged period, then the solution lies in a strict separation of those two systems: a structural dissociation of the personality. Because a compromise can no longer be found between both systems, the personality is divided up into different parts, which is called structural dissociation of the personality (Van der Hart et al., 2006). The fundamental reason to develop structural dissociation is the problem of the attachment to the abuser. In order to survive the child needs to attach to the person who is hurting them. They cannot escape. The only way to keep the attachment system active and stay connected to the parent is to block the traumatic information coming in through the senses. The reality needs to be dissociated (Ross, 2007).

2.7.1 Dissociative disorders

Children who have used structural dissociation as a survival mechanism, may meet the criteria of a dissociative disorder, such as Dissociative Disorder-Not Otherwise Specified (DD-NOS) or Dissociative Identity Disorder (DID) and there is structural dissociation to a greater or lesser extent.

2.7.2 Division of the personality

Structural dissociation can lead to a division of the personality into two or more systems, the main division occurring between the daily life and defence action systems (also called the apparently normal part (ANP) of the personality and the emotional part (EP) of the personality by Van der Hart et al. (2006)). This main division occurs between the two main action system categories because they are most opposed to each other. Within these separate systems, further divisions may occur, usually in the defence action system.

These children often show their emotions in a very clear and unadulterated way; because of the rigid division of the action systems, their feelings are very strong and they are totally frightened, or angry, or detached. When the child's personality is divided into several parts by structural dissociation, there are usually different kinds of parts, such as:

- parts that appear to function normally (daily life action system);
- parts that are very aggressive and identify with the abuser – these parts of the personality use aggression to cover up their fear;
- parts that seem emotionless and detached (defence action system in the state of hypo-arousal);
- parts that are very dependent and young (defence action system, attachment cry);
- parts that are very anxious and avoidant (defence action system, flight);
- parts that experience themselves as still being in the abuse situation in the past;
- parts with thoughts about themselves such as: I am a bad child, I am an animal, I am Satan, I am my father.

Children alternate between different states, depending on what happens around them and what action system has to react. A child can switch from the part of the personality with the daily life action system (the daily life part) to a part with the defence action system (the defence part) while he is being abused, and back to the daily life part after the abuse so he does not remember the abuse.

To a greater or lesser extent there may be amnesia between these parts; one part of the child does not know that there is also another part, let alone what this part experiences. The part which experiences the abuse does not know there are also other situations in which the child is not abused. This part only knows abuse situations and interprets all other situations from that perspective. Therefore the child can also alternate between parts of the personality for example in a fight at school and the child feels threatened. The defence part then becomes active to protect the child. Because the daily life part has amnesia for the defence part which has experienced the abuse, it can continue to take part in 'normal' activities such as playing, going to school and inter-acting with parents. This part of the child does not know about the terrible things the parents are doing to him, and can continue to believe that they are good parents. More parts can develop, which all are part of the same child but seem to be separate persons.

2.7.3 Phobia for parts of the personality

The amnesia for the trauma is important to keep functioning in daily life. However some children have flashbacks or nightmares and the daily life part then receives images, bodily sensations and feelings of traumatic experiences, which were formed when a defence part was active. This is very frightening to the child. The daily life part does not know that he himself experienced the events. The child does not want to know, for this is a very threatening thought. Flashbacks only reinforce the necessity for a strict separation of the parts, that is, the structural dissociation. The child does not and cannot realize what he has gone through.

A phobia is formed for the traumatic experiences and emotions, a phobia for a part of the child's own personality. The child may even experience the parts of his personality as different persons. If a child believes that the part, which lived through all these terrible experiences, is another person, he can believe that it did not happen to him. Some adolescents and adults with dissociative disorders even give different names and describe different appearances for the parts (blond hair instead of brown; old/young; male/female). These appearances are often very different from their own because the bigger the difference in appearance, the greater the probability that it is indeed another person and that it really did not happen to the child himself. My experience is that usually at a young age, there is still little differentiation between the parts of the personality. As a child grows older, the structural dissociation develops, increasing the phobia for the parts and hence their differentiation.

2.7.4 Downside of structural dissociation

This division of the personality is an effective survival strategy, but it also has its drawbacks. The defence parts, for instance, can be aggressive because they act on their fight response, whereas the daily life part knows nothing about this. One part of the child's personality is confronted with behaviour of another. When another part has been active, the child may feel that time has been lost. The child does not know what he has done in the time, which has passed. For instance, the child may be accused of shamelessly lying and denying that he has broken or stolen other children's toys. But the child denies because he really does not remember. There is a gap in the child's memory, he has 'lost' time.

2.7.5 Hiding structural dissociation

There is a difference between children who do not want to know what they have done and children with a dissociative disorder who really do not remember. The latter feel they are being punished and accused when they have done nothing wrong. However, they try to hide their problems as best they can: 'Dissociative patients attempt to compensate or cover for their sudden memory deficits in a variety of ways. Some of their deceptions are clearly bogus and contribute to the "phony" character of their behavior' (Putnam, 1997, p. 82). They often will not say that they have 'lost time' and have no idea why they are being accused. They are continually in a state of defence, in which they distrust others. They dare not tell what is going on inside them or to ask for help. Naturally, they feel misunderstood and lonely. This isolation cuts the child off from support and help in coping with stress. He has to do this alone, which reinforces the need for structural dissociation. Seven-year-old Sandra, who lives with her foster family, the Smiths, is such a girl with a dissociative disorder.

Sandra (2)

Sandra grew up in unsafe family circumstances. When she first came to stay with her foster family, the warm and nurturing environment scared her. She had not experienced this before and was suspicious of it. Sandra could not believe that this family were really kind and kept wondering when they were going to hurt her. She tried to adapt as far as possible. On the outside, she seems to function reasonably well now, but inside there is chaos. Sandra keeps her distance and trusts no one. She is very alert to anything 'suspicious' such as a raised voice, sudden movement or being alone with another person. These things signal danger to her. Sometimes she moves very cautiously and stiffly. Her heightened stress and flashbacks interfere with her perception. At school and at the dinner table, some things will trigger flashbacks. This frightens her and 'transports' her to the past. 'I thought you were my brother', she will say. She does not seek comfort or support, but she longs for it. She is lonely, but mistrusts everybody.

Her foster parents and her teacher often reprimand her. They tell her that she hurt her foster brother, that she broke something, that she is aggressive. But Sandra herself is completely unaware of this. This makes her insecure, because she wants to do things right. She is afraid of being sent back to her parents. Sandra denies the accusations because she really has no idea. Sandra often 'loses' time. When her foster parents tell her it's time to go to bed, she is startled. 'So soon? I just came home from school and I haven't eaten yet', she thinks. 'Is it evening already? What have I done all this time?'

Sandra 'forgets' things. She forgets names and does not remember what her teacher explained in class; one day she is able to do something, and the next she is not – for instance, tying her shoelaces or doing mathematics. Her teacher is irritated and thinks that Sandra is daydreaming. She should pay more attention. Sandra's handwriting is very neat but sometimes she writes very messy. When her teacher asks why her writing is so sloppy, Sandra does not know. She is convinced that someone else has written in her exercise book, but she is afraid to say this because her teacher won't believe her. Her teacher might think she is crazy, and send her back to her parents. Sandra had extremely irregular scores on her intelligence test. The results say she has an intellectual disability, but she does not come across as if that is true.

Sandra hears voices in her head. She does not talk about this because 'they will think I'm crazy'. Sandra has a friend, but her foster parents say he is imaginary. She doesn't understand, because to her he is real and she talks to him. Could she really be crazy? Sandra sometimes talks in a growling voice, or like a baby. Sometimes she crawls on the floor like a dog. When asked by her parents why she does this, she does not know what they are talking about. She laughs it off and says she was joking.

2.7.6 Always in defence

The brain and body of children with a dissociative disorder are continually in a state of defence, because of their extreme feelings of insecurity and stress. These children trust no one, have a great fear of attachment and usually do their best to hide that they are dissociating. They feel unsafe everywhere, which includes their new foster family. They may live in a safe environment for years while their attachment behaviour does not change. They tend to give other people the feeling that they are exchangeable. This is because they partly live in the past and are continually re-traumatized. The separation of the action systems prevents integration of experiences and adapting. Even if the daily life part of the personality experiences safety, this does not reduce the defensive reaction because the experience is not shared by the defensive part of the personality and so cannot be integrated. The defence action system remains active even when there has not been any real danger for years. These children are wholly geared to fitting in and not attracting attention. They try to hide anything that might give away their dissociation and will not report their symptoms, even if they are explicitly asked about them. It is not surprising that a dissociative disorder is also a severe attachment disorder because of the structurally dissociated personality.

The fluctuation of knowledge and skills, which is often observed in traumatized children, as well as trouble with learning from experiences (Putnam, Helmers & Trickett, 1993), could be related to the alternation of dissociative parts. Putnam (1997) writes: 'Fluctuations in the level of basic skills, in habits, and in recall of knowledge are classic forms of memory dysfunction in dissociative patients' (p. 82). This is how Sandra's teacher wearily puts it:

Sandra (3)

Sometimes she really frustrates me, she just does not listen. First I explain how to add numbers bigger than ten, and she does the first row of sums correctly. Five minutes later she comes to ask me how to add numbers bigger than ten, and claims that I never explained it to her. She is playing games with me.

Unfortunately, very little is known about dissociative disorders in children and these children often struggle a long time before getting diagnosed.

2.7.7 Risk factors to develop structural dissociation

Clinical experience shows that children with dissociative disorders are often prone to dissociation; frequently there is a family history of dissociative disorders. When a parent has a dissociative disorder, he can be unpredictable to a child. The best way for a child to anticipate a parent's alternating states (angry, nurturing, childlike) is to adapt to them, and vary his behaviour as well: with an angry parent he keeps quiet, with a nurturing parent he seeks attention and with a childlike parent he offers comfort. When the child also experiences the extreme stress of chronic traumatization in early childhood, developing different dissociative states is an understandable adaptation

Research with adults with a dissociative disorder shows the circumstances with the greatest chance of leading to structural dissociation are those that are experienced as life threatening such as choking or smothering combined with sexual abuse, being locked in a confined space, and being threatened with a weapon or with abandonment. The abuse is inflicted by multiple perpetrators, including one or both parents, occurs over a number of years and the child does not have adequate time to recuperate between episodes. The abuse, which is often physical, emotional and sexual, is often witnessed, but the witness is unable or unwilling to effectively intervene. If child protection is notified, most often the abuse did not stop as a result. The abuse occurs against a backdrop of a negative family life, including an insecure attachment to the parents, and one or both parents being the perpetrator or playing a negative role in the abuse, such as enabling it to occur or blaming the child for the abuse (Kate, 2017).

2.8 Conversion

Conversion disorder (Functional Neurological Symptom Disorder in the DSM-5) or Dissociative Disorder of movement and Sensation (ICD-10) in children is very rare but chronically traumatized children can display symptoms of this disorder. When an overwhelming stress level exceeds the Window of Tolerance, the child goes into a hypo-arousal state. The stress causes the body to shut down certain bodily functions to release the overwhelming stress, for example by partial paralysis, fainting, deafness or blindness. Conversion can be seen as a desperate measure by the brain to reduce stress in a state of hypo-arousal, a form of somatoform dissociation.

Children have no conscious control over the failure of certain bodily functions or body parts. It may seem that way because the failure of their body may occur at very convenient moments for the child, when they need to do something challenging or difficult. However conversion is a way of coping with stress, not an act of manipulation by the child. Most children with conversion problems have trouble perceiving stress; they think they are relaxed. Without them being aware of it, stress levels can rise so high that their brain enters a state of hypo-arousal. Conversion occurs in traumatized children, but also in children with an autistic spectrum disorder. These children have difficulties perceiving or regulating stress and may become over-stimulated.

Because dissociation, structural dissociation, memory loss and conversion can block the processing of traumatic memories, they are indications for the therapist to further assess the child's situation and possibly use more stabilizing interventions. Chapter 14 describes the specific aspects of the treatment process for children with dissociative disorder.

> Dissociation can occur both during a traumatic experience and in daily life, when there is no stress or when the child is confronted with a trigger causing a flashback.
>
> The fundamental reason to develop structural dissociation is the problem of the attachment to the abuser. In order to survive the child needs to attach to the person who is hurting them. The only way to keep the attachment system active and stay connected to the parent is to block the traumatic information coming in through the senses. The reality needs to be dissociated.

2.9 Summary

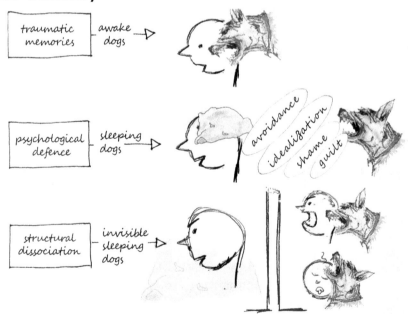

Figure 2.8

Source: Adapted from Knipe (2018).

Traumatic experiences can influence the development of the personality structure in three different ways. First, it can lead to dysfunctionally stored traumatic memories. Those memories can impact the child's development and create flashbacks. However, the child can still talk about these memories and the dogs are awake. Second, the child can use psychological defence. Psychological defence blocks access to the memories and makes children afraid to speak about them, deny or actually forget their memories. The dogs have gone to sleep and the memories are not accessible anymore. When the child uses structural dissociation, the sleeping dogs have become invisible (see Figure 2.8).

Chapter 3

What is needed to overcome resistance?

Once children have started to use psychological defences, motivating them to process their trauma becomes more difficult. Very young children do not have these defences yet, which makes their trauma more easily accessible. The older children get, the more difficult it can be to access their memories, as their strategies to avoid become better and better. This chapter describes what processing of memories entails and how problems in the child's life can form barriers to engage in trauma treatment. Then the key principles of the Sleeping Dogs method are described.

3.1 What is processing of traumatic memories?

It is important to have an understanding of the way the memory works, how traumatic memories cause problems and what is needed to process them into integrated memories. This information makes it easier to understand why some problems form barriers, and what can be done to overcome them. Section 5.2.3 describes how this can be explained to children.

3.1.1 Processing and integration of experiences

Human beings are able to survive because they are 'programmed' to learn from their experiences, so we can avoid dangerous situations and do more things we like or enjoy. From our experiences, we learn important lessons such as 'I like chocolate ice-cream, I don't like vanilla, and the fireplace really is hot.' After learning these lessons, the experience becomes vaguer and loses its details, colours, smells, images and feelings and changes into a memory, stored away in a memory bank. The experience is then integrated in our self-image, our memories and our life. When a child talks about an integrated memory, he can tell the story coherently without becoming overwhelmed. Proper integration of experiences offers the best chances of survival, because it teaches us what to avoid and which situations to seek out.

The brain does not want to remember the past as accurately as possible, but the brain stores memories so it can predict the future.

Figure 3.1

3.1.2 Temporary memory bank

However, when an experience is very overwhelming, such as experiencing violence or sexual abuse, the body automatically enters a state of hyper- or hypo-arousal, before we have had a chance to learn the lesson or we avoid thinking about it and try to push it away. From the brain's point of view this is a dangerous situation, because our survival depends on learning from experience. Therefore the experience is stored away in a temporary memory bank and brought back into consciousness later to evaluate and learn the wise lesson.

3.1.3 Re-experiencing traumatic memories

The memory is stored and presented back to re-experience the event. Because the chances we learn the wise lesson are the greatest if the recalled experience is exactly the same as the real experience. This re-experiencing is done with as much detail as possible, including behaviour, emotions, physical sensations and cognitions. So the purpose of having flashbacks, intrusions or nightmares about traumatic experiences is to enable the child to evaluate these experiences, learn wise lessons such as 'It was not my fault, I am lovable', and to integrate the experience.

Unfortunately that usually does not happen. The child becomes overwhelmed again and pushes the memory away instead of learning from it. This becomes a repeating cycle. Every time the child has a nightmare or flashback, the stress levels exceed the child's Window of Tolerance and the child goes into a hyper- or hypo-arousal state. Because we feel exactly the same physical sensations and terror, the stress caused by a flashback is re-traumatizing. If a child dissociated during a traumatic situation, he often dissociates again during a flashback, which reinforces the need to continue to dissociate, and a vicious circle is established. When the child eventually processes the memory during trauma processing, this circle is broken.

3.1.4 What is needed to be able to process a traumatic memory?

In order to process a traumatic memory, the child needs to stop avoiding and re-experience the traumatic memory while tolerating the strong emotions and learn a wise lesson. Then the memory can be stored in the long-term memory bank. The memory become vague and loses its emotional content. We need our human brain, our ability to think and evaluate to be able to learn this wise lesson. This means that while processing the traumatic memories, the child's stress level needs to stay within his (often very small) Window of Tolerance while re-experiencing the memory. This is the work that needs to be done in the preparation phase.

3.1.5 Unprocessed memories block safety on the inside and attachment

Unprocessed traumatic memories can prevent a child from benefiting from a safe placement. Some children have been in a safe and stable foster placement for years, but continue to be afraid of being hit or do not attach to foster caregivers. Their foster parents don't understand why the child still doesn't trust them enough to relax, as the traumatization has stopped, they should know better. Even though the child is safe on the outside, the traumatic memories continue to make them feel unsafe on the inside, until he processes and integrates these memories. This demonstrates the importance of waking up sleeping dogs.

> Fifteen-year-old Paul was placed in a foster family when he was five after experiencing severe physical abuse. For ten years Paul suffered from nightmares and flashbacks but refused to talk about his memories. When the foster parents got angry at Paul, he would always say: 'please don't hit me'. The foster parents said Paul did not seem to have formed a relationship with them and they were very angry, as Paul should know by now that they would not hit him. They were his parents already for ten years.

> Paul's example demonstrates how traumatic memories can block learning from new experiences and continue to make a child feel unsafe on the inside, even though the child is perfectly safe.

3.2 First-line treatment for traumatic memories

For children with PTSD, psychotherapy focusing on processing traumatic memories is considered first-line treatment. The Practice Parameters for the Assessment and Treatment of Children and Adolescents with PTSD state:

> Trauma-focused psychotherapies should be considered first-line treatments for children and adolescents with PTSD. Among psychotherapies there is convincing evidence that trauma-focused therapies, that is, those that specifically address the child's traumatic experiences, are superior to nonspecific or nondirective therapies in resolving PTSD symptoms.
>
> (Cohen et al., 2010, p. 421)

For children, TF-CBT or EMDR therapy are both evidence-based treatments recommended by international guidelines (Cohen et al., 2010; de Roos et al., 2011; de Roos et al., 2017; Diehle, Opmeer, Boer, Mannarino, & Lindauer, 2015; Rodenburg, Benjamin, de Roos, Meijer, & Stams, 2009; World Health Organization, 2013). In order to participate in these therapies, the child needs to come to therapy and talk about his memories. Both are problematic for these children. They deny having traumatic memories or become dysregulated when thinking or talking about them. It all happened a long time ago and they have found ways to live with it. Some children refuse to even come to sessions or to engage in any form of therapy: 'Going to a psychologist? No way, I am not a psycho!'

3.3 Barriers to engage in therapy

Caregivers and family can be reluctant to address the trauma out of fear making things worse, which was the case for Cynthia who engaged in therapy but after each session tried to strangle herself. Her therapist decided Cynthia was not ready to work on her trauma and ended therapy, leaving her alone with her guilt and self-blame without anyone to help her overcome those feelings. Therapists can get stuck and say 'it is better to let sleeping dogs lie' meaning, the traumatic memories should not be addressed. But these children continue to have severe symptoms damaging their development, feeling lonely and bad about themselves. Some, as a consequence, grow up going from one foster or adoptive family to another because of their problematic behaviour.

Children refusing to participate in therapy are often perceived as being not motivated or resistant. The word resistant or not motivated implies wrongly that there is fault in the child. The barriers to engage in therapy are created by the child's current social environment and by what has happened to him in the past.

3.3.1 Lack of safety

Chronically traumatized children have experienced many unsafe situations in their lives. Many are removed by child protection services, or have returned to their (unsafe) families. When they are referred for trauma treatment, it is not uncommon to find that abuse or neglect and therefore traumatization is still ongoing (Potter, Chevy, Amaya-Jackson, O'Donnell, & Murphy, 2009; Zeanah, Chesher, & Boris, 2016). Even when they are physically safe, they might still feel threatened or afraid of being abused again.

Being or feeling unsafe can be one of the reasons for chronically traumatized children to be unable to talk about their traumatic memories. They are trying to survive and cannot afford to become more vulnerable by talking about their traumatic memories. They can be afraid their parents will get angry or punish them for talking about what happened. For Joy this was a barrier and she refused to come back after talking about a few of her memories. She said, 'I feel bad now. I am afraid my mom and dad will hit me when they find out that I told you.' Children can also no feel emotional permission from their parents. Simona who was very loyal towards her parents who abused her before she was removed said: 'I don't want to talk about my memories, because you are not supposed to talk bad about your parents behind their back.'

Children need to feel loved by adults they are attached to and safe with in order to grow and develop. Many children in foster care have had several different foster parents caring for them and they might not be sure whether they can stay in their current placement. Some children end up in residential facilities with little or no contact with their parents and family, and caregivers rotating on a roster. Child protection services are their legal guardian, and their parents passed away, are in prison or have abandoned them. They do not have a consistent attachment figure to support them during therapy.

A child without love is like a plant without water, it will not grow. Growing up without someone loving you, holding you in mind and making sure you are taken care of, is very unsafe. From a survival perspective you can die without protection and these children need to be in a survival state permanently. They become cactuses and build a strong wall around their heart so they cannot get hurt. They push everyone away and seem to only care about themselves, without empathy or compassion. Or children without love will start looking for water (love) by attaching themselves to residential staff, therapists or by developing unhealthy relationships with friends or partners.

Not feeling loved, supported and being noticed can be a barrier for these children to discuss their traumatic memories and relive their fear, anger and

Figure 3.2

abandonment. They do not have anyone to do it for them and no one to rely on to support them while doing so. These children need an attachment figure to love them, water them. Fertilizer such as expensive treatment programs or medication will not provide a solution.

For children in out of home care, child protection workers decide on the arrangements for contact between the child and their parents. Decisions on these contact arrangements can either support or undermine treatment by forming another barrier for these children. Children in out of home care can be reluctant to talk about their memories of traumatic events, because they may be afraid that their disclosures will reduce contact with their parents or minimize chances to be reunified. Children can also have unsupervised contact visits with their parents during which traumatization is ongoing or the parent pressures or threatens the child not to talk.

3.3.2 Unstable daily life

Chronically traumatized children can experience many problems in daily life, at home, in school and with their friends. Their posttraumatic stress symptoms, behaviour and/or learning difficulties can create problems in school as well. Being placed in foster families or a residential care facility, they go from one foster placement to the next especially when their behavioural or attachment problems are too difficult for caregivers to manage. Foster children in the United States have on average three different foster care placements (Childrens Rights, 2015) and in a study profiling children in out-of-home care in South Australia, Delfabbro, Barber, and Cooper (2002) reported that almost a quarter of all children had experienced ten or more placements during their time in care.

They worry that talking about their traumatic memories will increase their nightmares, anger, depression or anxiety and create even more problems than they already have. They can be afraid that when they become even more difficult, their caregivers cannot handle that and they will have to move or they will be expelled from school. Surrounded by threat and chaos, these children need all their energy to protect themselves and survive their daily lives and they cannot afford to become more vulnerable by talking about 'forgotten' and suppressed memories.

3.3.3 Unsafe attachment relationships

As discussed previously, children need to have an adult that loves them and supports them when they process their traumatic memories. When a parent is traumatized as well, or has mental health issues, it can be difficult for the parent to support their child processing their traumatic memories. When a parent is traumatized by the same events as the child, as in domestic violence, the child for example can trigger the parent's own traumatic memories. Parents or caregivers can become angry or so overwhelmed, they cannot comfort the child, but need comfort themselves. The child may then choose not to talk about his memories and take care of their parent as a defence strategy. Some children are so disappointed and hurt by their caregivers that they do not to attach themselves anymore. They have a safe and calm attachment figure, but their internal attachment system is not activated enough. Because of their traumatic memories, they are too afraid to go to that person when they are distressed and they try to regulate themselves by dissociating or avoiding contact.

3.3.4 Lack of emotion regulation skills

Chronically traumatized children can have difficulty tolerating, expressing and regulating their emotions. They can be afraid to talk about their traumatic memories because of the strong feelings they might feel. Some say they do not want to talk about their traumatic memories because they will become too scared or angry and start to feel 'really bad'. The shame can make them feel so bad and passive, that they almost feel paralysed in those feelings. Caregivers or professionals can be afraid the child may dissociate or become dysregulated. Caregivers can be afraid the child ends up injured or dead, when children use maladaptive ways to cope with strong feelings such as drugs or alcohol, self-harming or attempting suicide, dangerous behaviour or violence.

3.3.5 Negative core beliefs

As described, children can develop negative cognitions about themselves as psychological survival mechanism. They can blame themselves for abuse or neglect, or feel they do not deserve to be treated well, or are unlovable. They can feel ashamed and as a reaction to their shame avoid, withdraw, attack others or themselves with self-hatred (Nathanson, 1994). These strong negative cognitions about themselves (for example 'It's my fault') related to the traumatic memory ('I see dad beating up mum and I do nothing') can be based on what their parents have told them ('It's your fault, because if you had called the police, I would not have broken my nose'). Parents can reinforce these negative ideas, for example, by denying the abuse took place, minimizing the impact or even blaming the child for it. The child's defensive, aggressive behaviour can then lead to more rejection by their parents, caregivers, friends or teachers, which reinforces their negative ideas. The negative cognitions around events in the past add up and can eventually generalize and lead to the child forming a negative core belief, such as 'I am a bad person'.

When the child's parent does not acknowledge the child was innocent and continues to holds him responsible, the child risks the parent getting angry for believing these wise lessons. Making this shift seems dangerous and they would rather not talk about their memories and feel guilty or bad, than talk about them and risk being rejected. Jeremy got stuck on this barrier when he refused to continue during a trauma-processing session. He said: 'I am getting such awful thoughts about my mother. If she has left my dad earlier, my life would not have been so ruined. That makes me feel so bad, I don't want this anymore.'

Children who have experienced trauma often do not realize that their symptoms are trauma related and are actually normal reactions to an abnormal, frightening situation. They can feel hopeless that their behaviour or feelings will ever change. They don't understand why it would be beneficial to them to talk about their traumatic memories. They can be distrustful of the therapist's intentions in the therapy process. When these children would try and process their traumatic memories, they would have to learn wise lessons, such as 'It was not my fault and I am lovable'. They would have to make a cognitive shift from the negative ideas to positive ideas.

3.4 Key principles of the Sleeping Dogs method

The Sleeping Dogs method is originally developed as an adaptation for children of the Three Tests method for chronically traumatized adults by Joany Spierings (2009) The Three tests are used to assess the level of stability in chronically traumatized adults and to develop a customized treatment plan to increase the adult's stability in order to proceed with trauma processing. These principles are adapted for children into the Sleeping Dogs method.

3.4.1 The phased model

To be able to process traumatic experiences, a child must stay within his Window of Tolerance while exposed to the traumatic memory. Children who have had a single traumatic experience are usually able to do this. They are treated with EMDR therapy or TF-CBT and process their memories. Children who have been chronically traumatized in early childhood have such high chronic stress levels, that they have only a very small Window of Tolerance. Talking about their traumatic memories quickly takes these children outside their Window of Tolerance and, as a result, they are re-traumatized without processing their trauma. The fact that these children have such high chronic stress levels and are so easily upset is why it is essential for them to process their trauma to improve their functioning, but they are unable to do so, due to their poor functioning. This is a difficult dilemma.

For chronically traumatized children it is recommended to use a phased model (Child and Adolescent Committee of the European Society for Trauma and Dissociation, 2017; International Society for the Study of Trauma and Dissociation, 2004). In the first phase, the stabilization phase, the child needs to get enough control over his symptoms to remain within his Window of Tolerance. This can be accomplished by working with the child or by stabilizing his environment. In the next phase, trauma processing, the traumatic memories are processed. During this phase, children need to seek out situations that they avoided before practising new behaviour. In the final phase, integration, the child works on better ways of handling stress to prevent traumatization in future. This is not a linear process and after trauma processing or integration takes place children can go back to the stabilization phase or go through several cycles.

3.4.2 What is meant by stabilization

In literature, the word stabilization is used to describe different things, which is confusing. The word 'stabilization' in the Sleeping Dogs method means the preparation phase with all interventions focused on overcoming the barriers for the child to start processing traumatic memories. Stabilization interventions can focus on improving the child's internal stability such as skills for self-regulation and emotion regulation, but more often on improving his environment such as family relationships, living environment, school or the child protection context.

3.4.3 Meeting the child's basic needs – autonomy, competence and connectedness

The Sleeping Dogs method uses the principles of the Self-determination Theory (Deci & Ryan, 2002). This theory describes autonomy, competence and connectedness as the three basic needs determining human motivation. When these basic needs are not met, we become less internally motivated and as a result less persistent to reach goals. This view is also used in the treatment of drugs and alcohol abuse or overweight with a technique called Motivational Interviewing (Miller & Rollnick, 1991).

Most chronically traumatized children feel helpless, incompetent and disconnected from their families. They do not have these needs met at all. It is no wonder they present as unwilling or unmotivated to engage in trauma-focused therapy. The Sleeping Dogs interventions focus on increasing the child's feelings of competence, autonomy and connectedness. Professionals using the Sleeping Dogs method interact with children in a respectful and equal manner. Children are in charge of their own treatment and by providing them knowledge about themselves and treatment, through psychoeducation, they become competent to make their own decisions. A large part of the Sleeping Dogs interventions is focused on improving the child's relationships with family and caregivers to make them feel more connected as the relational environment is the major mediator for therapeutic change (Perry & Dobson, 2013).

3.4.4 Structured assessment

The Sleeping Dogs method uses a structured assessment of the child's barriers to determine a customized treatment plan.

3.4.5 Collaboration with child protection services

The lives of children in care can be complicated by decisions made by child protection workers. These decisions can either support or undermine treatment and strengthening ongoing partnerships across disciplines can ensure children have the best chances to have their needs met (Greeson et al., 2011). The Sleeping Dogs method uses active involvement and collaboration with child protection services to engage children. Child protection workers can make or review decisions that form barriers to the child. They can inform the child of the possible consequences of what they tell the therapist about their memories.

Collaboration between therapist and child protection services can be time consuming and sometimes difficult and frustrating. However, in many cases it is not fantastic therapeutic work, but these decisions that make the child participate in trauma treatment. The Sleeping Dogs method invests in this collaboration, in sharing information, using psychoeducation to speak the same language, analysing the child's barriers together, so that everyone becomes partners instead of opponents.

3.4.6 Collaboration with the child's network

As the child is not willing or able to participate in treatment at the start, collaboration with the child's current and past network of family, caregivers, previous foster families or caregivers, other professionals such as therapists, teachers and child protection workers, is necessary. Key figures from the child's network who have already established a relationship with the child, are identified and encouraged to participate either by attending sessions, or by phone or video conversations, by making stories or messages for the child. Child protection workers, teachers and foster parents are taught Sleeping Dogs interventions which they can use to explain things to the child in daily life. In this way, the child does not have to attend therapy sessions and treatment starts indirectly. When the child is ready to start with therapy, the number of sessions can be kept to a minimum.

3.4.7 Involving the child's biological family including the abuser-parent

Many of the barriers concern the child's biological family, including the abuser. To overcome these barriers and motivate the child, they need to be included in treatment, provided this is safe. Biological parents are not judged or criticized, but they are invited to assist their children to heal from the trauma they have (unintentionally) caused. This often forms a powerful tool to overcome the child's barriers. Even for children in out of home care who are not returning to their families, involvement of the child's family is important. In some cases, a lot of motivating and psychoeducation for child protection workers, caregivers or other professionals is required to make this possible. However the Sleeping Dogs method is only for children with severe symptoms, who are stuck and desperately need treatment but refuse to do so. When all else fails, this approach provides an opening for the child.

When interventions focus on the biological parent's responsibility for the abuse, the terms abuser-parent and non-protecting parent are used for clarity purposes. Obviously every parent is more than just an abuser-parent or non-protecting parent. The pronoun 'he' can also be read as 'she'.

3.4.8 Minimal sessions with the child and not office based

To engage resistant children it is important to keep treatment short and focused. The number of therapy sessions with the child is kept to a minimum. That is possible because of the collaboration with the child's network. They can do intervention with the child, without coming to therapy. The Sleeping Dogs treatment is not only office based but also outreaching. Interventions are not only done by professionals, but also by the child's network.

3.4.9 Structured treatment interventions

The sequence of the chapters follows the order of the interventions. When the child is resistant to become vulnerable, there need to be some prerequisites first. The child needs to be safe and calm, before relying on an attachment figure. After that, the child can start to feel and recognize and discuss his thoughts. Then the child can become vulnerable by talking about traumatic memories, anger, fear, sadness and negative feelings about himself. The neurosequential model of therapeutics (NMT) (Perry & Dobson, 2013), an approach to clinical work informed by neuroscience, is based on the same principle. NMT provides a framework to sequence the application of interventions in a way that is sensitive to the principles of neurodevelopment: start with the lowest undeveloped/abnormally functioning set of problems and move sequentially up the brain.

3.4.10 Sleeping Dogs method combined with other methods

The Sleeping Dogs method is *always* combined with a treatment to process traumatic memories, preferrably an evidence-based treatment for children with PTSD such as EMDR therapy or TF-CBT. These structured methods have a clear-cut phase to process traumatic memories.

As discussed, many chronically traumatized children do not report having flashbacks or nightmares and they display fewer PTSD symptoms but more general problems. They can engage in psycho-therapy or family therapy focused on attachment or relational difficulties, improving emotion regulation and mentalization, reducing depression, suicidality or anxiety or behavioural problems. These methods have a less structured and more indirect approach, where traumatic memories are processed when they come up when for example discussing daily life situations, emotion regulation difficulties or relational problems.

The separation between the stabilization, trauma processing and integration phase and the Motivation and Nutshell Check are not applicable for those methods. The interventions in these chapters can be adapted to fit those approaches if needed. The analysis with the Barriers Form can be used in addition to these treatments for example to analyse situations where treatment is stuck or not effective, children do not engage or drop out, or when the child's situation is too unstable to start treatment.

3.5 Other similar methods

The Sleeping Dogs method describes interventions for the stabilization and integration phase of treatment and some to support the child during the trauma processing phase. The Sleeping Dogs method describes mainly interventions that are new or different from other methods, since there are many other great methods with comprehensive descriptions of interventions for these children which can easily be incorporated into the Sleeping Dogs method's plan. There are methods for the treatment of chronically traumatized children (Adler-Tapia & Settle, 2017; Blaustein & Kinniburgh, 2010; Gomez, 2013; Greenwald, 2002, 2005; Lanktree & Briere, 2013; Saxe, Ellis, & Kaplow, 2012; Wesselmann, Schweitzer, & Armstrong, 2014) and some are specifically focused on dissociative children (Silberg, 2013; Waters, 2016; Wieland, 2015). Most of these treatment methods describe an extensive stabilization phase in which some of the barriers mentioned earlier, such as safety, self-regulation, attachment, psychoeducation, motivation, emotion regulation and core beliefs, are addressed. The comprehensive description of interventions and tools in these methods are very useful for clinicians working with these children.

The brain does not want to remember the past as accurately as possible, but the brain stores memories so it can predict the future.

Children need to be safe on the outside by stopping the abuse, and safe on the inside by stopping the flashbacks and nightmares.

Trauma processing can be seen as integration of traumatic experiences in our self-image, our memories and our life. Trauma processing can only take place if levels of stress are within the Window of Tolerance.

Chapter 4

The Sleeping Dogs method

This chapter describes the Sleeping Dogs method illustrated with case examples.

4.1 The Sleeping Dogs method

The Sleeping Dogs method provides a framework to make a structured analysis of the possible barriers creating resistance. This including decision-making by child protection services and the relationship and interaction with the abuser-parent. With this analysis, the clinician drafts a customized treatment plan with a selection of interventions focused only on overcoming these barriers. The interventions reduce the child's need for psychological defences. Psychoeducation and interventions to improve safety, stability in daily life and attachment reduce the need for avoidance. When the child idealizes his parent, has strong feelings of shame and guilt or dissociation blocking him, further interventions around attachment, emotion regulation and increasing acknowledgement for his innocence are needed to overcome those defences. After the child's barriers are removed, the child participates in trauma processing. In the integration phase a selection of interventions is planned to improve the child's situation and functioning so treatment can be ended.

4.2 Mapping out the case

The Flowchart illustrates all options for trauma-focused treatment and assists clinicians to clarify at what stage they are in treatment (see Figure 4.1) Information is needed to be able to decide whether the child needs Sleeping Dogs treatment. These children often have thick files with a lot of information. It is important to pick out only the information that is needed to make decisions. It needs to be clear which traumatic circumstances the child has or may have experienced, what the child's symptoms are, how these symptoms are related to the traumatic clusters, and whether the child has awake, sleeping or preverbal dogs. Then it is important to know details about the child and his network. The Case Conceptualization Form (see Appendix 1) is used for this.

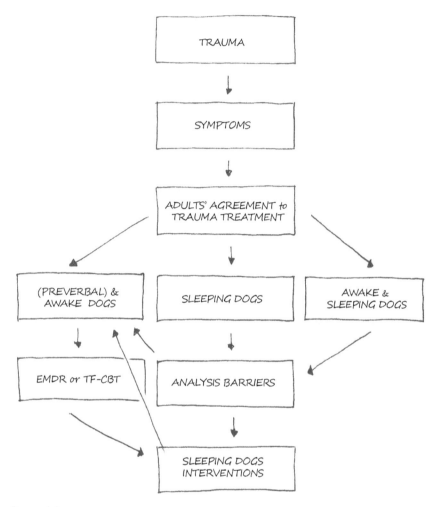

Figure 4.1

4.2.1 Case Conceptualization Form

This form focuses only on trauma treatment, not all other problems in the child's life. All information that is irrelevant to this goal is left out. When this form is filled in it should consist of a maximum of one or two pages. The form is filled in with the professionals. When the child is in out of home care, the child protection worker, foster care worker and residential staff are included. By mapping out the child's symptoms, the traumatic experiences and how these symptoms can be related, the team can get a better understanding of the child's inner world and the reasons behind the child's behaviour.

Often it becomes clear that there is a lot of information on the child's current symptoms, but hardly any information on the traumatic experiences in the past or the child's network. This information needs to be gathered. The child's symptoms are briefly described. Elaborate descriptions of problem behaviour in school or on the streets can only distract the focus on trauma. This form can also make clear what symptoms are likely to change through treatment and which symptoms may not. As described chronically traumatized children can have a wide variety of symptoms including non-specific symptoms. Treatment will hopefully reduce these symptoms and enable the child to develop further. Children can also have symptoms related to co-morbid disorders, disabilities or damage caused by their mother using alcohol or drugs during pregnancy. These symptoms will obviously not change after treatment.

Then the team discusses which traumas are awake dogs and which are sleeping dogs.

4.2.2 Sleeping dogs, awake dogs or mixed

When the child wants to talk about his traumatic memories, he has so-called 'awake dogs'. The rest of the Sleeping Dogs method is skipped, as the child is then ready for trauma processing and has no barriers. The Motivation and Nutshell Checks can be done when unsure whether the dogs are awake.

When the child does not want to or cannot discuss his memories, the child has so-called sleeping dogs. Children can have several clusters of traumatic memories, such as witnessing domestic violence, neglect and sexual abuse. The child might refuse to discuss some of those clusters, such as sexual abuse, which are then considered 'sleeping dogs', but be more open about memories of domestic violence, which are then considered 'awake dogs'. Children can also have different barriers for different clusters of traumatic memories. Then the barriers are analysed separately for each cluster.

4.2.3 Preverbal dogs

When children are unable to talk about their traumatic memories because they have experienced trauma at a very young age (between zero and three), they do not remember because they were too young. These memories are called preverbal and are usually stored in bodily sensations and feelings. These memories are not *sleeping dogs* because these children will never be able to talk about them, so the interventions are pointless. Young children have preverbal memories, but also older children or adults can have preverbal memories. Children with preverbal trauma can start with trauma processing, without stabilization.

Children can also have both. When children have preverbal trauma and sleeping dogs, the analysis of the barriers for the sleeping dogs needs to be done first.

4.2.4 Difficult circumstances versus trauma

Children can have traumatic memories and difficult circumstances in their life. When a child struggles with difficult circumstances, such as being a foster child, having a father who died, not having contact with a parent or having parents who divorced, these are *not* traumas and trauma processing with TF-CBT or EMDR therapy will not provide relief. They need help to deal with grief, mixed and conflicting emotions and thoughts, and make a plan on how to manage these circumstances. This is a very important distinction. However when children struggle with traumatic memories about these difficult circumstances, such as having flashbacks of being removed by the police and mum screaming, or having flashbacks of seeing dad drive off with his car promising to be back but he never returned, or seeing a father suffocate, these are indeed trauma and the child can benefit from TF-CBT or EMDR therapy. These can be sleeping or awake dogs. The difficult circumstances are ideally dealt with in the integration phase.

4.2.5 Agreement with the adults on trauma treatment

To be able to start trauma treatment the child's legal guardian and the professionals working with the child need to have at least some agreement on the hypothesis that the child's symptoms are related to traumatic experiences and treatment is going to focus on overcoming traumatic memories. Eventually the child also needs to agree with this as well, but at the start of treatment children usually deny symptoms and traumatization. They may not understand this, which could be solved by psychoeducation, but more often the denial is a result of barriers in the child's environment or history. After analysing and overcoming the child's barriers with the Sleeping Dogs method, children usually come to understand there is a relationship between their symptoms and traumatic memories and agree to treatment of their traumatic memories.

4.3 The Motivation Check

Children need to consent to trauma treatment before being able to start. Obviously very young children, under the age of two-and-a-half or three, do not have to consent because they do not actively refuse to do so. However in many cases, it is *assumed* that the child will not want to talk about his memories but it is not *explicitly* asked. The child never talks about his memories, but his network never brings it up. If this is the case, the network or the therapist needs to ask the child first to determine whether the child's dogs are indeed asleep. Chapter 11 describes the Motivation Check that can be used for this conversation. The child needs to be informed about the possibility that his symptoms are related to his traumatic memories, about treatment options and be given a choice to engage in trauma processing. When the answer is no, the child has sleeping dogs.

Tony (1)

(Source: Struik, 2018)

Upon referral Tony (six years and ten months) was hyperaroused, anxious, oppositional and experienced nightmares. He did not express emotions and had trouble socializing with other children due to dominant behaviour. Tony stayed at a residential facility in a group of six children with rotating staff. Most children went home on weekends but Tony did not. In school Tony had difficulty concentrating and was defiant. His school hours were reduced to one hour a day. Tony was diagnosed with ADHD and was medicated with methylphenidate.

Tony grew up with his parents until age four, when his father stabbed his mother to death in his presence. Tony's father took him to his brother's family and turned himself in. The police interviewed Tony and, since he was crown witness, he was placed with a foster family. Tony's father pleaded not guilty, but was sentenced to eight years' imprisonment. Child protection services denied the paternal family's requests to care for Tony, because it was believed he needed to be placed in a neutral foster family. Tony's extreme violence led to the placement breakdown after three months, and he was placed in the residential facility.

The paternal family's request to have Tony was denied again and visitation was limited to once every two months supervised at the facility. Tony's father sent him postcards and letters weekly. After a few months child protection services decided to withhold the mail because the child protection worker thought it made Tony scared and upset. The residential staff had taken Tony to visit his mother's grave and he had photos of her. The maternal family were not interested in contact arrangements. After eighteen months in the residential facility, without trauma treatment, Tony was placed in a new foster family, which broke down after a few weeks due to Tony's behaviour and a mismatch with the foster caregivers. The paternal family again asked if Tony could live with them, but child protection services placed Tony back in the residential facility. Tony started to visit respite caregivers monthly for a weekend.

The referring psychologist requested EMDR therapy for Tony to process traumatic memories of his mother's death, as she believed his behaviour was a consequence of posttraumatic stress and grief. It was expected that trauma processing would decrease problematic behaviour, and lead to successful foster family placement, and increased school attendance. It was stated that Tony normally refused to talk about his father or his mother's death. Tony was considered a stuck case, as the child protection worker had not been able to find him another foster family.

Since it was unclear whether Tony would be willing to participate in EMDR therapy, residential staff were instructed to discuss EMDR therapy with him. They explained in simple language the relationship between his symptoms and trauma with the Volcano metaphor and the process of EMDR therapy, and how this would potentially help him overcome his traumatic memories. Halfway through the explanation Tony said: 'I don't want to talk about that' and he ended the conversation. Tony had indeed sleeping dogs

4.4 The analysis of barriers

When the adults agree on trauma treatment and the child has sleeping dogs, an analysis of the barriers needs to be made. The previously described barriers are translated into a checklist, the Barriers Form (see Appendix 2), with five items each with a set of questions to assess whether this item could form a barrier for the child and requires focus in treatment. Professionals fill in this form since it guides clinical decisions. The Barriers Form is not discussed with the parents or caregivers. The Barriers Form is filled in with information from reports and child protection services documents. If needed, additional information is acquired from caregivers, parents or other professionals. The answers are based on clinical judgement and reflect the current status of the child, e.g. the way things are now, not what is hoped for in the future, or what the child did in the past. In the following sections the questions are explained in detail.

4.4.1 The answers do not reflect the child's functioning now

Children can display severe symptoms, function very poorly in daily life in many areas and grow up in challenging circumstances but that does not mean all these items form barriers to discuss traumatic memories. They can be physically unsafe, have problems at home and in school, and struggle with attachment and emotion regulation. Caregivers want assistance to discipline the child, school demands meetings, the police are involved and the child protection worker wants something to be done *now*. Professionals tend to focus on symptom management, addressing challenging behaviour and deal with crises, especially when there are many people involved, all with their own interest. However focusing on the behaviour often does not lead to an improvement, when the underlying traumatic memories are not addressed.

The questions in the Barriers Form focus only on whether or not this item from the child's perspective potentially forms a barrier and does not reflect the child's daily life functioning. The Sleeping Dogs method differs from other methods as it focuses treatment initially *only* on overcoming the barriers, not all the other problems. Overcoming the barriers enables the child to then process his traumatic memories. This needs to be done as fast as possible, because it will decrease the child's trauma-related symptoms and improve daily life functioning. After that, in the integration phase, all the remaining problems become the focus of treatment. These problems need to improve for the child to grow up safe and healthy.

In some settings, it would be helpful to be able to assess the child's functioning. In section 15.4, an adaptation of the Sleeping Dogs method is described that assesses the child's functioning as well as the barriers.

4.5 The Barriers Form

Name child: DOB: Date:

Who is/are the child's main attachment figure(s)? ....

Who is/are support person(s)? ....

Which parent gives the child permission to talk about memories? ....

Sleeping dogs	Child's negative cognition	Shift to positive cognition

Fill in for which sleeping dogs the barriers are analysed, which dysfunctional cognition the child may have and which shift the child needs to make.

Instructions
The questions in the Barriers Form focus only on whether or not this item from the child's perspective potentially forms a barrier and does not reflect the child's daily life functioning. The goal of this form is to find out what could be the main reasons for the child not wanting or being able to talk about his/her traumatic memories. The questions are numbered 1a, 1b, 1c etc. The questions are answered from the child's perspective, what would he/she think or feel. Tick the box as yes or no. Focus only on the main barriers so do not tick nearly all. Interventions are planned in the stabilization phase on the Barriers Action Plan. These interventions have priority.

Motivation and Nutshell Checks

Ⓨ Ⓝ The child has passed Motivation Check. If yes, discuss whether to fill in this form.

Ⓨ Ⓝ The child has passed Nutshell Check. If yes, discuss whether to fill in this form.

Barrier 1 Safety

1a Is not being or feeling safe because the abuse could happen again a barrier?

Ongoing abuse, being or feeling threatened can form a barrier when the child is afraid that the abuse *from the past* will continue to happen in the future. The adults may know the child is safe, but the child has not been explicitly informed about the safety measures that are in place. If this forms a barrier, not all abuse needs to be stopped in order to overcome this barrier. For example, it may be possible to process memories of domestic violence in the past, even when emotional neglect is ongoing, or to process the memories of dad hitting mum without being able to address 'mum not protecting the child'. The child can be currently unsafe because of problem behaviour or fighting in school, or bullying, but those only form a barrier when the child is constantly terrified and outside his/her Window of Tolerance.

1b Is not having an attachment figure or not being sure who is an attachment figure a barrier?

This can form a barrier, when a child does not want to talk about his/her memories mainly because he/she does not have anyone who thinks of him/her and supports him/her. Why would he/she do it, for whom? In the Sleeping Dogs method, an attachment figure is defined as someone who loves the child and who wants to stay in the child's life. The attachment figure would want to be informed when the child for example would get severely injured, moves elsewhere or when a placement ends. When the child would get married, the attachment figure wants to come to the wedding and sit in the front row. When children are born, the attachment figure will want to know. The child does not have to live with the attachment figure or have intensive contact. Most children have one or both of their parents as an attachment figure.

The primary focus here is the quantity 'is there an attachment figure?' The quality of the relationship does not have to be good and the child does not have to be attached to that person, as this is addressed in barrier 3. The attachment figure can even be a father in prison, a grandmother who visits every two years or mother with a borderline personality disorder who lives in a psychiatric hospital and has, once every two months, two hours supervised contact with her daughter. She loves her and wants the best for her. Sometimes she is too unwell and the visits are cancelled, but the daughter knows mum still thinks of her and approves of her talking to the residential staff.

Children in residential care with staff on a rotating roster without any contact with family, mother died and father in prison, can have this barrier.

They do not have anyone to do this difficult therapy for. More often than one would think, lack of an attachment figure is a reason for depression in children (manifesting itself as problem behaviour). For those children an attachment figure needs to be found in order to wake up sleeping dogs.

1c   Is not having regular contact with that attachment figure, or not being sure that contact is guaranteed to continue, a barrier?

This forms a barrier when the child's main reason not to start talking about his/her painful memories is that he/she cannot rely on the attachment figure to continue to be there for him/her. The child needs to be certain that the attachment figure will stay in his/her life and cares about his/her wellbeing. Contact does not have to be regular or intensive, as long as the child has another temporary support person to talk to and the attachment figure has approved that. Some parents can be unpredictable and say they never want to see the child anymore during fights, even though they do not mean it. If the child knows that, that is good enough. Contact is not guaranteed when the parent is capable of refusing contact with the child for months until for example the child apologizes. When the parent would then not come to the hospital to see his/her injured child, because he/she is angry, this attachment figure is not good enough and the child needs another attachment figure in addition. This can form a barrier for children in foster care who may not know whether their foster parents want to have a life-long relationship with them, or are only daily caregivers until the placement breaks down or the child becomes eighteen. They need to be informed about that. The child may live with grandparents who are very old or sick and he/she cannot be sure he/she will not end up alone. They need another attachment figure to wake up the sleeping dogs.

1d   Is being afraid that disclosures will have legal consequences and/or that contact arrangements will be changed, and/or that the child will be removed or not reunified a barrier?

This forms a barrier when the child is worried that talking about his/her memories will have consequences for people outside the family. The child can be afraid the police will be informed, and his/her parents or he/she him/herself will be convicted. Children can refuse to talk because they fear the legal guardian will reduce contact arrangements, not reunify the child or make contact supervised. Children can also fear the opposite, that the legal guardian will intensify contact, make contact unsupervised or reunify him/her with his/her parents because his/her problems are solved. Besides traumatic memories of incidents that were already disclosed or are known, the child may also have secrets or think he/she has secrets, which would be *new* disclosures. Reassurance needs to come from people outside the family. The possible consequences need to be clarified to the child, so the child can decide what to do based on this information.

1e   Is not having permission from the biological parents to talk about the memories and being afraid of being punished a barrier?

This forms a barrier when the child is worried that talking about his/her memories will damage the relationship with one of his/her parents or both. He/she is afraid of his/her parent's reaction. The parent may have threatened him/her or the child is not sure if his/her parent approves of him/her talking. Many children do not know what their parents think and they need to be explicitly told by their parents. To overcome this barrier, the child needs reassurance from his/her parent. Parents can also fear consequences from outside the family, which can be the reason for them to tell the child not to talk. Reassurance from outside for the parents can also help to overcome this barrier.

When the child fears abuse as a repercussion, barrier 1a is analysed, as reassurance from the parent is not enough to overcome that barrier. The child needs a Safety Plan. When the child does not really care about what his parents think, this does not have to form a barrier. Or when the child has one parent who gives him permission and he lives with this parent, and does not really care about the other parent not approving.

Barrier 2 Daily Life
Processing traumatic memories requires the child to be calm enough to focus on doing this. It can temporarily increase the child's symptoms. What could be the main reason why the child wants to avoid this?

2a   Is having too many problems at home, and/or the child being afraid to be removed from home, a barrier?
With 'home' is meant where the child currently lives. This forms a barrier when the child has too many problems to deal with and he/she refuses because he/she does not have the headspace to also dig up old memories. Or the child does not want to talk about his/her memories because he/she is afraid he/she will get more difficult to handle and his/her (foster) parents or the residential staff will be unable to handle that. The child's placement can be under pressure, staff can be exhausted and this can even be discussed with the child. The child rather keeps 'a lid on his/her traumas' than risking being removed. Or the child absconds so much that the caregivers, attachment figure or others cannot talk to the child to motivate him/her, provide psychoeducation or eventually make sure the child attends therapy sessions.

2b   Is having too many problems at school, and/or the child being afraid of getting expelled from school, a barrier?
This forms a barrier when the child is barely managing at school and refuses to talk because he/she does not have the headspace to also dig up old memories. Or the child does not want to talk about his/her memories because he/she is afraid he/she will get more difficult to handle, and the school will be unable to handle that, or the child needs to pass exams. The child may have been expelled several times and been given a last chance, and this can even

be discussed with the child. The child rather keeps 'a lid on his/her traumas' than risking being expelled.

2c Is the child or caregivers being afraid the child does not have enough distraction because the child does not have a daily routine a barrier?

This forms a barrier when the child does not go to school, has no job, lies in bed all day or hangs around with too much time to think. Waking up sleeping dogs can be difficult and the child needs to have some distraction. The child does not have to go to school or have a job, a schedule with activities can be good enough.

2d Is the child or caregivers being afraid of not being able to handle an increase in flashbacks and/or sleeping problems a barrier?

This forms a barrier when the child has so many flashbacks and sleeping problems, that he/she can barely function. Or the child's caregivers are exhausted, and they fear that talking about memories would cause more flashbacks and sleeping problems and they would not be able to handle that. They can fear not being able to take care of the other children, losing their job or failing at work. However, in most cases this does not form a barrier and flashbacks reduce significantly and sleeping problems become less after processing traumatic memories.

2e Is the child or caregivers being afraid drugs and alcohol abuse will increase and/or lead to serious problems a barrier?

Children use alcohol and drugs to numb their feelings, they 'self-medicate'. In most cases bad feelings reduce significantly after processing traumatic memories and the need to use drugs and alcohol also reduces. It becomes much easier to stop afterwards. This only forms a barrier when the child or his/her network fear that the child cannot come to the sessions sober, and when they fear that that talking about memories would increase the child's need to numb bad feelings with alcohol or drugs and this would lead to an overdose, serious injuries or death.

Barrier 3 Attachment
The child needs to feel supported to process trauma. What could be the main reason why the child is not supported enough?

3a Is the child being afraid of upsetting the attachment figure who would not keep a calm brain when the child would process the traumatic memories a barrier?

This forms a barrier when the child fears the attachment figure will become upset *when he/she would talk about his/her memories*. For example when the attachment figure is traumatized, overwhelmed, has experienced the same trauma such as domestic violence or has become upset in the past. By avoiding traumatic memories, the child cares for the attachment figure.

This does not form a barrier if the parent has severe emotion regulation problems in daily life, but is able to stay calm when the child talks about the traumatic memories and the child is aware of that. Barrier 3a assesses whether the quality of the relationship forms a barrier because the child does not have enough emotional support, whereas barrier 1b assesses whether not having an attachment figure forms a barrier, the quantity. Barrier 3a assesses whether the child thinks that the attachment figure can handle 'talking about memories', whereas barrier 2a assesses whether the attachment figure can handle the child's behaviour.

Question 3b is only relevant when 3a forms a barrier.

3b   Is not having a support person with a calm brain in daily life who can compensate for the attachment figure with his permission a barrier?
This forms a barrier when the child's attachment figure does not have a calm brain and the child does not have anyone else to talk to, or the attachment figure does not allow the child to talk to this adult, or the child is not sure if he/she can. This does not form a barrier when the child's parent allows the child talk to the other parent, a grandfather or aunt, foster parents or residential staff.

3c   Is being afraid that the child cannot stay in contact with the therapist during trauma processing a barrier?
This forms a barrier when the network or child itself fears that the child will dissociate or run away during the trauma-processing sessions. Many children dissociate or avoid in daily life situations and in therapy sessions where their bad behaviour is discussed, but are very capable of staying in contact during a trauma-processing session. Then this does not form a barrier. Symptoms and daily life are like big clouds of suffocating smoke, while the traumatic memories are the fire causing this smoke. Children can find it easier to get to the fire directly, than talking about the smoke session after session.

Barrier 4 Emotion Regulation
During trauma processing the child needs to tolerate the old feelings. Is the child able to do that?

4a   Is the child not being able to feel and tolerate bodily sensations during trauma processing a barrier?
When bodily sensations are not tolerated and they need to be dissociated or blocked, this can form a barrier, for example with children with a dissociative disorder or conversion. The child needs to learn to tolerate these first. However, in most cases this is not necessary and children become more aware of their bodily sensations after trauma processing. When barrier 4a is identified, 4b also forms a barrier.

4b   Is the child not being able to feel and regulate the feelings during trauma processing a barrier?
When feelings are not tolerated and they need to be dissociated or blocked, this can form a barrier, because trauma processing can overwhelm the child,

for example with children with a dissociative disorder or conversion. Children can be afraid they will become violent and harm someone or themselves, or self-harm or be suicidal. If this forms a barrier, the child can make a plan to control this temporarily, so he/she can get through the trauma-processing phase, after which these feelings often reduce. However, in most cases this is not necessary and children become more aware of their feelings and can express them better after trauma processing.

Barrier 5 Cognitive Shift
These questions are only relevant when the abuser is a parent or someone the child will maintain close contact with. Experience shows that with a stuck case, this is very often one of the identified barriers.

5a Is the child fearing that the mother blames him/her for the abuse or neglect and will reject him/her when the child would believe he/she was innocent, and the child does not want to risk this a barrier?
This can form a barrier, when the child's mother blames the child and the child finds her opinion important, or when the child thinks his/her mother blames him/her but is not sure. When the mother blames the child, this does not have to be a barrier. The child can have his/her own view and know he/she was not to blame, or have the father, or foster parents acknowledge his/her innocence. With help, most parents can acknowledge that the child was not to blame for the past. That is good enough, even though they continue to blame the child for his/her current behaviour.

5b Is the child fearing that his/her father blames him/her for the abuse or neglect and will reject him/her when the child would believe he/she was innocent, and the child does not want to risk this a barrier?
This can form a barrier, when the child's father blames the child and the child finds his opinion important, or when the child thinks his/her father blames him/her but is not sure. When the father blames the child, this does not have to be a barrier. The child can have his or her own view and know he/she was not to blame, or have the mother, or foster parents acknowledge his or her innocence. With help, most parents can acknowledge that the child was not to blame for the past. That is good enough, even though they continue to blame the child for his or her current behaviour.
        If applicable otherwise skip:
5c Is the child fearing that .... (other person) blames him/her for the abuse or neglect and will reject him/her when the child would believe he/she was innocent, and the child does not want to risk this a barrier?
This can form a barrier, when for example the child's sibling, stepmother or grandfather blames the child and the child finds their opinion important, or when the child thinks they blame him/her but is not sure. When the child's sibling, stepmother or grandfather blames the child, this does not have to be a barrier. The child can have his or her own view and know he/she was not

to blame, or have the father or foster parents acknowledge his/her inno-cence. It also does not have to form a barrier when the child's sibling, step-mother or grandfather is no longer part of his/her life and he/she does not have to have a relationship with them. However, with help, most people can acknowledge that the child was not to blame for the past. That is good enough, even though they continue to blame the child for his/her current behaviour.

Question 5d is only relevant when 5a and 5b both form barriers.

5d   Is the child not having an alternative attachment figure acknowledging the child's innocence and the child not wanting to risk ending up alone a barrier?

This can form a barrier when both parents continue to blame the child and threaten to reject the child when the child would claim innocence, and the child does not have someone else to rely on. To maintain the relation-ship, the child then chooses to continue to take the blame. This does not form a barrier when the child lives with foster parents who do not blame him for the past and who guarantee to maintain the relationship and will be guests at the child's wedding.

Tony (2)

Tony's main barriers seemed to be aspects of Safety (1) and the Cognitive Shift (5). Tony did not have an attachment figure (1b) to support him during therapy, and it was unclear for him whether his father gave him permission to talk about what had happened (1e). Tony also seemed unable to make the cognitive shift (5b). The police interview showed that Tony had refused to talk about what happened and, after this interview, Tony was taken into care. Tony may have perceived his removal as punishment for something he had done wrong, and he may have even felt responsible for his mother's death. During EMDR therapy, Tony would have to think about his memories and formulate a negative cognition in relation to the target image. During desensitization Tony would have to make a cognitive shift towards believing he was innocent. If Tony believed his father and family held him responsible for his mother's death, he would not be able to make that cognitive shift (5b, 5c).

Unfortunately, case files did not provide information about family rela-tionships and context leading up to the incident, such as ongoing domestic violence or drug or alcohol abuse. Without this information, it was unclear if there was additional trauma and whether Tony would be willing and able to discuss those memories, 'whether these dogs were awake or asleep', and what could be possible barriers for him to discuss this. Therefore, after this information became available the treatment plan would need to be revised.

4.6 Treatment plan

A customized treatment plan is made to overcome the identified barriers. The professionals draft the plan. This plan is then discussed with the therapist, the child's family and network, and other professionals such as the child protection worker or residential staff because they can all conduct interventions contributing to the treatment. To keep an overview of the interventions, the Action Plan (see Appendix 4) can be used.

4.6.1 Action Plan

It is the easiest to fill in the Action Plan while making the analysis. When a barrier is analysed the interventions are selected. Concrete actions and the person responsible for these actions are noted. The Action Plan consists of two parts. The first part describes actions to overcome sleeping dogs barriers in red and trauma processing. The second part describes actions for the integration phase in green. The plan is evaluated and adjusted regularly. The integration phase is usually unclear at the start, and interventions are selected only after the child has done trauma processing. When the child has sleeping dogs and awake dogs, the awake dogs preferably are addressed, before waking up the sleeping dogs. If this can be done safely, it relieves part of the child's symptoms and increases the child's competence to address the sleeping dogs as well. When the child has different barriers for different traumatic memories, a choice is made which cluster of sleeping dogs, and therefore which barriers, are addressed first. The sequence (top-down) of the Action Plan provides a guideline for the sequence in which interventions should be conducted.

4.6.1.1 Instructions

The child's name, date, evaluation date and current owner of the plan are filled in. Then the identified barriers are circled. Examples of interventions are listed. These can be ticked if applicable. Describe concrete actions with the numbers of the barriers that are addressed by the action (e.g. 1b and 1c, 3a and 5b) or only one (e.g. 1e). Fill in who is the owner of the action (e.g. foster care worker Sonja) and with whom this action is going to be done (child protection worker Tina, biological mother and child). Several interventions can be combined into one action. Note an evaluation date. When evaluating this Action Plan, tick 'OK' for the completed actions. Describe new or altered actions. Note an evaluation date. Continue until all barriers are removed. Then describe actions for the Motivation and Nutshell Checks and trauma processing. Note an evaluation date. Evaluate the child's symptoms, set goals and describe actions for the integration phase. Note an evaluation date and evaluate until goals are reached.

4.6.2 Metaphors to explain the phased treatment plan

It can be useful to explain the different treatment steps of the Sleeping Dogs method to professionals or caregivers, who do not understand why the child cannot participate in treatment of his traumatic memories and how the Sleeping Dogs interventions can contribute to improve the child's motivation. When the child wants to know why he has to do some of the interventions, this can also be explained in the presence of the child. This can increase the child's feeling of control over treatment and engage the child in the therapeutic plan.

4.6.2.1 The Fairy Tale

The 'Fairy Tale', by Greenwald (2005, pp. 30–34) is a very useful metaphor, which incorporates nearly all the elements of the Sleeping Dogs treatment. Below is an adaptation of this fairy tale, modified to suit this book's purposes.

Once upon a time there was a prince who fell in love with a princess (=motivation) from another kingdom. Her father tells the prince that in order to marry the princess he must first slay the dragon (=the trauma) that lives in the kingdom. The prince is afraid that he is not strong and skilful enough. He asks the king to provide him with a coach (=therapist or professional or team of coaches) to teach him how to slay dragons. During the training the dragon keeps chasing them and the prince asks the king for some people to protect him. They build a fence around the training field so the prince can train safely (=safety) and there are no other problems to distract him (=stability in daily life). When the training becomes difficult, the prince wants to give up. He rings his mother and father who encourage him to continue (=attachment figures). They remind him of the princess (=motivation) he wants to marry.

The coach teaches the prince dragon slaying techniques (=emotion regulation skills). The coach talks to the prince's parents when they start to deny and minimize the dragon. He asks them to acknowledge that from the prince's perspective, the dragon is real and scary (=cognitive shift). Then the prince feels ready and the coach arranges a test fight (=nutshell). All goes well until he is caught in a corner and asks for a time-out. The coach teaches him some more skills and he is ready. They prepare the day of the fight together and the prince invites his family and friends, the princess and her parents.

The prince starts the fight (=trauma processing) and it is going well until he gets caught in the same corner. The prince panics and wants to run off. Then he sees his beautiful princess (=motivation) for whom he is doing this. He hears his parents (=attachment figure) encourage him, and the coach (=therapist) reminding him of the things he learned and he slays the dragon. Everyone is happy and proud and he marries the princess (=memories processed). When he becomes the king, the prince makes sure the kingdom is better protected against new dragons coming in the future (=integration phase). The prince and princess live happily ever after.

This metaphor can also be helpful to explain lack of progress in the treatment. For example, a common reason for lack of progress is absence of motivation – there is no princess to fall in love with.

4.6.2.2 Other metaphors

There are other metaphors that can be used if they suit the child more, such as the metaphor of the Boggart, which features in *Harry Potter and the Prisoner of Azkaban* (Rowling, 1999, pp. 146–147). Harry Potter has to learn control his fear of the Boggart, so it does not control him anymore. He practises with Professor Lupin to achieve this. The film version of the book can be watched with the child or this part of the book can be read. Harry shows clearly how frightened he is and how difficult it is. However Harry manages to get control over his own fear and slay his dragon,

Simpler metaphors can be used, such as practising to playing football in the national team, a boxing match or horse racing, climbing a high mountain. It does not matter which metaphor it is, as long as it contains the following elements: wanting to achieve something; a difficult challenge; practising; a contest; evaluation afterwards, learning from mistakes and practising in order to be ready for the following contest and avoid making the same mistakes again. What is wrong about these metaphors is that the child chooses a contest or challenge. Trauma has happened to the child against his will, and the child does not have much choice than to try and overcome the consequences. Most children do not think that deeply and these metaphors explain the basic elements of phase-oriented treatment. If children do indicate that something is wrong, the story of the prince, or Harry Potter can be used. During treatment, the elements of the metaphor that apply at that point can be referred to. These metaphors may seem childish but Greenwald originally developed his metaphor for adolescents.

4.7 The Sleeping Dogs interventions

4.7.1 Motivation and psychoeducation

It is usually necessary to motivate the child before treatment can start. Like the prince, the child needs to have a reason for wanting to fight the dragon. The child has to fall in love with a princess. Psychoeducation plays an important role here.

Motivating a child, however young, is an essential part of treatment. Nevertheless it is often given too little attention. Traumatized children have often been forced to do or undergo or watch things. Sometimes they have survived by resisting or running away. If these children are forced, they will be provided with a fresh experience of having to do something under duress. And that is precisely what one wants to avoid. It is also possible that children do not openly resist, because their defence strategy is submission or dissociation. They may then seem to undergo the treatment obediently, but they do not learn anything because they are outside their Window of Tolerance.

Through psychoeducation the child increases his knowledge and therefore his competence. The child can begin to realize the necessity of trauma processing and understand what he will gain from it. The child's autonomy is increased, because he can understand what is happening to him and how the treatment will proceed. Chapter 5 describes various metaphors and ways to provide the child with an explanation on different topics.

4.7.2 Safety

When Safety is analysed to be a barrier, the child is either unsafe or the child feels unsafe. It is clear that trauma processing is of little use if new traumas are still being created: it would be a waste of time and effort. But, in addition to this, trauma processing is simply not possible if a child does not feel safe. When the brain experiences danger, it will focus on the external world in order to protect itself. Trauma processing, however, requires the brain to focus on the inner world – a very vulnerable position. Since the brain cannot focus on the inside and the outside at the same time, it can only take this position if the external world is not threatening. The child needs to feel safe physically and emotionally.

The first treatment recommendation in the practice parameters for children with reactive attachment disorder is 'providing the child with an emotionally available attachment figure' (Zeanah & Gleason, 2015), which is why this is the first item. 'Social support is a biological necessity – not an option, and this notion should be the backbone of all prevention and treatment' (Van der Kolk, 2016, p. 269). Developing these safe, secure, supportive relationships, in addition to other stabilizing interventions in the Sleeping Dogs methods allows for trauma therapy, and memory processing to occur with chronically traumatized children, who otherwise have been unable to engage in the treatment they have needed to recover and heal. The prince in the fairy tale could not train properly because the dragon kept threatening him. That is why he could not concentrate on his training. To become strong and learn to fight well the prince must be able to exhaust himself and be really tired. If, however, the dragon is around, it is dangerous to be exhausted and vulnerable. The child needs adults who are responsible for protection. Chapter 6 describes possible interventions to overcome the barriers on Safety.

4.7.3 Daily life

When the instability in daily life is identified as a barrier, interventions focus on reduction of the daily life stress or a plan to deal with this stress. By making the problems in daily life more manageable, the brain can focus on the inner world. This is why this is the second item. The aim of working on these aspects is for the adults to build a fence around the training field with the child, enabling the child to train without having to fear a surprise attack by the dragon. Chapter 7 explains interventions for the child or the child's network to make the problems in the child's daily life more manageable.

4.7.4 Attachment

Interventions may focus on increasing the child's support and the child's ability to connect to regulate himself. The child's attachment system has to be activated in such a way that the child is prepared to take risks and de-activate his defences. Attachment is the third item because the child needs an attachment figure (1b) before being able to work on the quality of the relationship. It needs to be clear for the child who is going to stay in his life, before attaching to that person (1c). In order to be able to become vulnerable by working on improving the attachment relationship, the child needs to be safe (1a) and not have too many problems in daily life requiring attention (2). The child needs support when he gets scared or it is too painful: supporters who encourage him to see it through, who tell him that he must listen carefully to the coach, that the coach is teaching him useful techniques. He also has to stay in contact with the coach during the fight and to act on his instructions. Chapter 8 describes interventions to work on these barriers.

4.7.5 Emotion regulation

For some children fear of intense emotions such as rage, fear and shame form a barrier. The child or his caregivers are afraid that the strong emotions will cause the child to shut down and lose contact with the therapist during trauma work. This is the fourth item, as attachment is a prerequisite to learn emotion regulation. Traumatized children block out their feelings for a good reason: they are too difficult. Working on emotion regulation, without providing the necessary safety and attachment relationship can be dangerous. When these children start to feel how abandoned and sad and hurt they are, while still being alone, this may increase self-harm or suicidal ideation or even lead to suicide attempts. The skills needed to regulate emotions are the fighting techniques the prince needs to defeat the dragon. The dragon may breathe fire during the fight, or corner the child. Even then the child must be brave and not run away. Chapter 9 describes interventions to overcome this barrier.

4.7.6 Cognitive shift

Interventions on this item are only necessary when the child's parents or a close family member with whom the child continues to have a relationship, has traumatized the child.

To enable these children to make this cognitive shift, it is necessary that the child can openly say he was innocent or, even better, put the responsibility on the abuser (usually the parent), without the risk of losing 'the hand that feeds'. Interventions focus on working with the abuser to acknowledge to the child that he did not have the responsibility for the trauma and that the parent will not reject the child when it would come to that conclusion.

If the parents continue to blame the child for the trauma in the past and this is a barrier for the child, then the child needs to be able to rely on another attachment figure to take care of him. The child needs to have another 'hand that feeds', so he can safely risk rejection by the abuser parent. From the point of view of survival, there is then another 'hand that feeds' and that is safe. That is why interventions on the Cognitive Shift are done after Attachment. However, this is a very difficult step for a child. Children can be extremely loyal to their parents and once disappointed they will not easily trust someone else. Experience shows that with a stuck case, this is very often one of the identified barriers. Unfortunately it is often not recognized. The child is thought to have trouble regulating feelings and emotion regulation skills are taught, without success. Everything seems stable but the child is still resistant to talk.

The Cognitive Shift does not quite fit in with the metaphor of the prince and the dragon, since the parents of the prince are not responsible for the existence of the dragon. But this can be explained as follows. For the dragon to be defeated it is important that the parents acknowledge that there is a dragon and that fighting the dragon is difficult for the child. Parents who minimize traumatic experiences send their child a complicated message saying that the dragon is not dangerous at all, whereas the child is terrified of it. The prince must also be certain that the support figures will still be there for him after the fight with the dragon, that they will not be disappointed in him and leave him to fend for himself. The prince has to be quite sure that they approve that he is fighting the dragon. Chapter 10 describes interventions to overcome this barrier and prepare the child so he can make cognitive shift during trauma processing.

4.7.7 Evaluation

Treatment for these children can be very challenging with new problems arising, chaos in families and changing circumstances, children moving from placement to placement, or changing child protection workers. Treatment can very easily lose focus and divert to symptom management and crisis interventions. In order to stay on track it is important to have a structured and concrete treatment plan that is evaluated and adjusted regularly. During the evaluation the team discusses which barriers have been removed successfully and which barriers still remain. The plan is adjusted to address the remaining barriers and, if needed, new interventions are planned. When all barriers for a cluster of sleeping dogs are removed, this should result in the child being willing and able to discuss the traumatic memories from that cluster and to participate in therapy focused on processing these memories. The child's caregiver, residential staff or family can discuss and assess this with the child.

4.7.8 The Motivation and Nutshell Checks

After having worked on the identified barriers, the child's sleeping dogs become awake and the child is ready for trauma processing. This is a final check to see if the child is stable enough to proceed with trauma processing.

The child is asked whether he wants to talk about his memories and what his princess is, in the Motivation Check. In cases of chronic traumatization there will obviously be very many traumatic memories and it can feel like a minefield. To keep the stress levels manageable, the mines must be detonated in small clusters and not all at once. With the Nutshell Check, it is assessed whether the child can make an overview of his traumatic memories (explain in a nutshell) without being overwhelmed.

These checks are the test fight in which the child mentally goes over the whole fight and prepares for it. If the child cannot do this, there are still barriers that need more work. The Motivation and Nutshell Checks are described in Chapter 11.

Figure 4.2

4.7.9 Trauma-processing interventions

Within the Sleeping Dogs method, any directive therapy to process traumatic memories can be used. The Sleeping Dogs method provides interventions to support the child and family during this phase, as it can be quite challenging for children. For children who have suppressed their memories or dissociated, processing these memories could lead to a temporary worsening of symptoms. The prince has to slay the dragon, which can be very scary. The prince needs to keep in mind the reason why he is doing that, his princess (the motivation) and he needs his network to support him. Chapter 12 describes interventions to support children and caregivers during this process.

4.7.10 Integration interventions

After the trauma processing has finished a new treatment plan is made with a selection of interventions from the chapters on safety, daily life, attachment, emotion regulation and cognitive shift. The Integration part of the Action Plan can be used for this.

The remaining problems in the child's life that were ignored in the stabilization phase, can be addressed. It is important to continue treatment and increase the child's resilience to prevent future traumatization. The aim of the integration phase is to teach the child how to minimize the chances of being traumatized again and make him more resilient. The child makes the transition from '*surviving life* to *living life*' (Van der Hart et al., 2006, p. 339). The child learns that he no longer has to keep the surrounding world under control; he is now able to control himself. The child can adapt to the circumstances when these do not adapt to him. After slaying the dragon and marrying the princess, the prince also wanted to protect his kingdom against any new dragons. Dragons follow each other's tracks so the prince has to erase these tracks and learn how to keep his kingdom safe. Chapter 12 describes interventions for the integration phase.

4.7.11 Back to the stabilization phase

Chronically traumatized children can work through their traumas in layers. After stabilization, they can process a series of memories. They need time to integrate these memories into their life and personality. They may become more attached and their emotion regulation improves. After this a new series of memories can start to bother them. They can become distressed and dysregulated and need another stabilization phase, preceding processing of these memories. Joan Lovett (1999) describes treating chronic traumatization in children as a zigzag process from strengthening attachment to processing traumatic memories to strengthening attachment to processing traumatic memories. When it is high tide memories are processed, when it is low tide the child integrates and stabilizes to build up another high tide. Treatment can be paused or ended in between these phases of processing or continued if possible.

Tony (3)

It was necessary to provide Tony with an attachment figure (1b and 1c). Tony had a large paternal family, who seemed willing to take that role. However, previous decisions by child protection services would need to be reconsidered. Tony's respite caregivers could be considered as an attachment relationship. Tony also needed to be informed about whether his father would give him permission to talk about his memories, and whether he blamed him. More information was needed to be able to plan additional interventions to address the other possible barriers (Safety and Cognitive Shift).

The child protection worker was contacted to explain the impact of the decisions forming barriers for Tony to move forward with treatment. In several meetings the clinician explained, with the analysis, why Tony's case was stuck, and how contact with paternal family could help Tony move forward. The child protection worker approved an initial meeting to gather more information and contact with the respite caregivers.

The paternal family provided important information about Tony's history. In their opinion, Tony's mother had mental health issues, and had maltreated and neglected Tony since birth. Tony's father had been the main caregiver. His paternal uncle and his wife often cared for Tony, when his father worked, and Tony's aunt was like a second mother to Tony. They stated that Tony's father had had ongoing conflicts with his wife, mainly over her maltreatment of Tony, resulting in domestic violence incidents, and eventually leading to her death. Even though it was obvious that the domestic violence dynamics between Tony's parents were far more complex than the one-sided description provided by the paternal family, this information was important. It meant that during EMDR therapy, additional target memories regarding domestic violence, maltreatment and neglect needed to be addressed, and it provided a new insight into Tony's perception. The loss of contact with his father and the paternal family may have been more traumatic for him than believed up until now.

Tony's respite caregivers were willing to become attachment figures for him as well, they guaranteed ongoing contact with him, but stated Tony could not live with them (1b and 1c).

Sleeping Dogs session 1 (Tony and residential caregiver)
The first Sleeping Dogs session focused on increasing Tony's feeling of control and knowledge. The clinician explained to Tony why he was referred for EMDR therapy, and that his refusal to talk about his traumatic memories would be respected. The plan for treatment was discussed. Tony thought increasing contact with his family was a great idea. The clinician explained

that a Trauma Healing Story was going to be made with his father and family over the next months to explain why he was taken into care (5b and 5c). The clinician informed Tony of her intention to visit Tony's father, and asked Tony if he had questions about his history. The residential caregiver was asked to pass on any questions that Tony might think of later.

Interventions with the paternal family and father
The clinician visited Tony's father in prison to discuss his views on the treatment plan. Tony's father was able to see his son's perspective, but kept stressing how abandoned Tony must feel, and that placing him with paternal family should be a priority, instead of talking about traumatic memories. Since the analysis also concluded that reconnecting Tony to an attachment figure was the first priority and Tony's father was unable to reflect on his own responsibility and actions at this point, the clinician decided to postpone discussing this topic.

With the new information the clinician explained to the child protection worker again Tony's stuck position and the requirements to be able to continue treatment. The child protection worker increased contact with paternal family and assessed them as a potential foster family. Tony responded well and within three months he was spending a fortnightly weekend with them (1c). Tony became calmer and more open towards the staff.

The clinician visited Tony's father several times and made a Trauma Healing Story with him and the paternal family (1d and 1e, 3a, 3b and 3c, 5b and 5c). Tony's father was very relieved to hear his son was doing better. He acknowledged for the first time killing his wife and took responsibility for his violence, because he realized his son had a right to know the truth. Tony's father was able to tell some positive stories about Tony's mother, their family life, holidays and activities, which were also included to provide a balanced narrative of Tony's history. The child protection worker and mother's family were contacted, to describe all perspectives, the mother's, the father's and child protection services, in the story. On his request, therapy was arranged for Tony's father.

Sleeping Dogs session 2–4 (Tony and residential caregiver)
In subsequent sessions, Tony asked more questions about his father, such as 'What does he look like? What kind of work did he do? Do I look like him? What kind of food does he like?' The clinician answered those questions with information from his father. After each session the Safe Deposit Box exercise was used to container all the 'bad pictures and feelings'. With Tony's permission, his family and respite caregivers were informed about sessions and asked to refer to this information during the weekends.

Crisis in the team

As treatment was progressing, unfortunately the referring psychologist and child protection worker became increasingly worried about the responsibility they carried for this plan to 'wake up sleeping dogs'. They feared that addressing Tony's traumatic memories would trigger violent behaviour and residential staff would not be able to manage him. In order to continue with the plan and to decide on reunification, they required Tony be placed in an inpatient psychiatric child hospital and an intensive assessment on the family's parental capacities. This was arranged and Tony was moved to an inpatient unit with eight children under twelve and rotating staff, which delayed treatment by four months as the plan had to be re-evaluated with new referring clinician and team.

Sleeping Dogs session 5–6 (Tony and paternal family)

In a family therapy session the family told Tony stories from their own childhood and they looked at photo albums, mentioning Tony's father in stories told. In a subsequent session, the paternal family told stories about Tony's mother and how his parents met (3c). They looked at photos and Tony stated he did not remember his mother at all, and therefore did not miss her. He asked hesitantly whether that was strange. Tony became increasingly curious about his father and asked why his father had stopped sending him letters, stating this led to him feeling rejected.

Child protection worker's intervention

The child protection worker gave Tony a box of mail from his father (3d). He explained that he withheld them from Tony because of his initial strong reactions, which he had assumed to be fear based. Tony said: 'Well, you were wrong. I was not afraid, I just missed him so much.' Tony then wanted to visit his father to see what he was like now. The clinician discussed this with the child protection worker and explained that the last memories Tony had of his father were around the death of his mother from the perspective of a nearly four-year-old. That it could be beneficial for Tony's recovery to create new memories of his father in the present, to reduce his fear. The child protection worker granted Tony permission to visit his father with his uncle (1c). Tony then requested regular contact visits, which was granted.

Sleeping Dogs session 7 (Tony and residential caregiver)

Since the sessions in which the Trauma Healing Story was going to be read could be stressful for Tony, these sessions were prepared with him. Tony was curious and scared.

Sleeping Dogs session 8 (Tony, paternal family and child protection worker)

The next week, the story was read in the presence of Tony, his aunt and uncle, his five cousins, a residential caregiver and the child protection worker (1d and 1e, 3a, 3b and 3c, 5b and 5c). Tony was excited to have so many people there for him. Tony asked questions, but was quiet, and sat on his uncle's lap when the story was read about his mother's death. He was surprised to hear why he was removed from his family. Tony had believed they did not want him because he had been naughty.

Sleeping Dogs session 9 (Tony and his father, paternal family outside the room)

The clinician arranged for the father to attend at the treatment facility escorted by prison guards. The same story was read, and Tony's father confirmed the story's content (1d and 1e, 3a, 3b and 3c, 5b and 5c). Tony suddenly asked his father why he had not stabbed him as well, or whether he intended to do so upon release from prison? He was the crown witness after all? Tony's father stated in tears that he would never consider that, because he loved his son very much (1a). He said that his mother's death was not Tony's fault and he could not have done anything to prevent it, as he was only four. He gave permission to talk about all of his memories. The paternal family and respite caregivers were informed about this session and instructed to discuss EMDR therapy as an option again with Tony. They emailed the clinician that Tony had nightmares and he wanted to start EMDR therapy.

Sleeping Dogs and EMDR therapy sessions 10–11 (Tony)

Tony confirmed he was ready for EMDR therapy and made an overview of his traumatic memories (Motivation and Nutshell Checks), without becoming overwhelmed. In the same session, he processed the first and second memory with EMDR therapy. During desensitization, Tony expressed fear, confusion and anger, after which he felt relieved and stated the memories were fading and it was a long time ago. The session was concluded with the Safe Deposit Box exercise. Two weeks later, Tony processed the other two memories.

The clinician contacted the paternal family by phone and respite caregivers via email and they viewed Tony much calmer, happier and more talkative, without having any nightmares.

Sleeping Dogs session 12 (Tony and residential caregiver)

Two weeks later, upon review with his caregiver, Tony stated that all his 'bad pictures' were gone and did not have any more nightmares, felt much calmer and relieved. He believed he did not need more therapy. The clinician emailed this outcome to the paternal family and asked them to evaluate with Tony as well. After three weeks, both stated Tony was still doing well.

Results

The referring clinician evaluated Tony's case in the residential team, with the child protection worker and clinician present. The clinician advised the child protection worker to place Tony with his paternal family as soon as possible. After four months of debating within child protection services, they decided to reunify Tony with his family under the condition that the clinician would continue supporting the family and Tony. In the meantime Tony had increased to full-time school attendance and his school results were excellent. The clinician made arrangements for Tony to visit his mother's grave regularly, and to continue to visit his father. The Sleeping Dogs treatment was ended.

Parental support was continued for eight months. Tony was transferred to a local school without any problems and he stopped using medication. Tony was happier, had friends in school and started karate. The paternal uncle became legal guardian and child protection services withdrew, after which treatment ended. Two years later the clinician received an email that Tony was doing well, had started high school and was an A-grade student.

Chapter 5

Psychoeducation to increase motivation

This chapter describes several psychoeducation interventions. Psychoeducation allows the child to discover what his 'princess' is (i.e. what motivates him) and to fall in love with that princess. Psychoeducation is preferably given to the child in the presence of his parents or daily caregivers. They can repeat the explanations and continue to motivate the child in daily life situations where his problems occur.

5.1 Psychoeducation can increase motivation

Psychoeducation can increase the child's inner motivation. Competence, autonomy and connectedness are the three basic human needs that increase internal motivation (Deci & Ryan, 2002). Psychoeducation about the impact of trauma, the child's trauma reactions, why that is happening and what the child can gain through treatment increases the child's competence. Sharing the explanations with the child and parent or caregiver, provides them with language to discuss what is happening. The child can feel more understood by and connected to his parents and caregivers. Parents or caregivers may want to proceed faster than the child. They often insist on trauma processing even if the child is not yet ready for it. This can cause the child to panic and freeze. It is essential for the child to be in control. The child decides what is talked about and whether he wants to discuss his traumatic memories, this increases his feeling of autonomy. Initially this may cost the therapist a little more time and it may even mean spending several sessions just playing card games, but, if this means that the child does not give up during trauma processing, it is worth the effort.

5.1.1 Find a reason (princess)

The child needs to have a reason to dig up all the bad memories that he has stored away so well, he avoids or even does not remember. Why on earth would he do that? The child needs to know what he can gain from this. It is better to spend too much time on motivating a child than to spend too little and thereby run the risk of losing the child. This conversation is a standard Sleeping Dogs intervention.

The first step is to discuss with the child what they experience as a problem (see worksheet 'Motivation'). This is their life and the focus of treatment should be on what they want. It can be called a 'princess', when the prince story has been explained. Some children want to be less angry or to get rid of their nightmares and fears or feel happier. Those can be good princesses. Some children want to go home to their parents. This cannot be a princess, as they cannot influence that. The princess should be something realistic, something the child can influence and that is linked to traumatic memories. They can become less angry and have fewer fights with mum and dad, which may increase the chances of going home. Besides that mum and dad also have to work on their issues. If the children themselves do not feel they have a problem, the therapist can try to motivate them through their parents or caregivers. They can indicate what may change for the child and why that would be beneficial. Or they may want their child to be happier or have more friends.

When children cannot find a princess, there are often barriers that need to be removed first before continuing this conversation and finding a princess. Psychoeducation however can still be provided.

5.2 Psychoeducation about why memories create problems

If a child can indicate what symptoms he would like to get rid of, that is, what his 'princess' is, the reason for having these symptoms needs to be explained to connect those symptoms to the traumatic memories. Several metaphors can be used to explain this.

5.2.1 The Volcano

Children are often unaware of the connection between traumatic memories and their current symptoms. After assessing the child's problems, the next question is whether the child understands the relationship between his memories and these symptoms. The following explanation can make them more aware of that. The angry outbursts in the following example can be replaced by fear or sadness if that is the child's main problem.

> Right, so you want to get rid of your angry outbursts? Do you know why you get so angry? You do not know? Well, I am not sure either. Shall I tell you what I heard from other children about their anger? Do you want me to explain what they discovered? Maybe it can help you figure out why this is happening to you? OK.

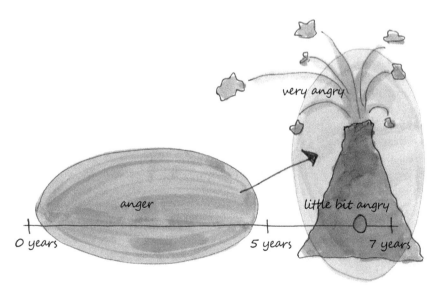

Figure 5.2

Some have told me that their anger had something to do with the bad things that happened to them when they were little. Maybe it is the same for you. To explain, I am going to draw it for you. Let's draw a line, the line of your life, from zero to seven years. Between zero and five lots of bad things happened to you. But when this was going on you couldn't feel angry about it. All the anger from that time is still there, like lava bottled up inside you (draw a pool of lava full of anger between zero and five on the timeline). Those bad things don't happen anymore, but the anger is still there in your body.

Now, when something makes you angry, like when you want to do something and you aren't allowed to, you get angry just like anybody else would (draw a small pool of anger at seven years). But then, the old anger wants to get out too (draw a line from the old pool of anger to the new pool and turn it into a huge angry pool of lava) and the anger becomes bigger and bigger until you explode like a volcano (draw a volcano). Is that how it works for you? Do you feel like the anger just gets bigger and bigger and you cannot stop it, without understanding why? And others don't understand it either. They don't see the volcano inside you until you suddenly explode.

Now what we can do is make a plan on what to do when you get so very angry and the volcano explodes, how to make yourself calm again. This can help you a bit. However, the old anger will still be there and you will still explode. If you really want to get rid of those explosions we would have to get rid of the old anger. We can empty the lava out of the volcano, so that it cannot erupt anymore. But the thing is, to really get rid of it properly we will have to talk about all those bad things, and you may not feel like doing that. Just give it some thought.

With more resistant children this explanation has to be presented more carefully by, for example, referring to other children and what they discovered about how things worked for them, without referring to the child at all (see Figure 5.2).

5.2.2 Bruises

A shorter explanation is the Bruises, described by Ricky Greenwald.

It is as if you have a bruise on your arm that really hurts, but nobody sees it under your sweater. But if someone accidentally grabs you exactly in that spot, it hurts you badly. That can make you mad and you start screaming. The other person doesn't understand why, because they can't see your bruise and they don't know that it hurts (Greenwald, 2005, p. 13).

After this explanation some children will choose to start with processing trauma at once. Others take longer. In any case they will now have a better understanding of what the effect of their choices will be, and the child himself will be in control.

5.2.3 The Filing Cabinets

The Filing Cabinets metaphor explains the way memories are stored and why traumatic memories can cause problems, such as nightmares or flashbacks. The following explanation can be used.

Figure 5.3 Filing Cabinets.

To survive, we need to learn from our experiences. When things happen, we need to think about what happened and learn a wise lesson, so we make sure we do things that we like and we avoid danger. When you eat a great ice cream, you learn wise lessons, such as 'this was very yummy ice-cream' or 'I don't really like vanilla flavour, next time I will get chocolate again'. After learning this wise lesson, the experience is stored in drawers of a filing cabinet in your head. When you want to get an ice cream next time, you can open the drawer, bring out the wise lesson and choose better. Then you put the memory back and close the drawer.

Memories are stored in drawers with the wise lessons. We throw away the details and smells and colours of the memory to make the memory smaller, and it becomes more and vaguer over time. However, when really nasty and bad things happen, we do not want to learn a wise lesson. We do not want to think about what happened at all. Then the brain starts to worry a bit as we do need to learn from those bad things so we can survive. The brain then stores those memories in a different temporary filing cabinet. Then later, the brain brings that memory back to our mind so we can learn from it.

Bad memories are stored differently from the normal memories because the brain wants to make sure we learn the wise lesson. The brain stores the memory with as much details and colours and smells, so when the memory comes back to our mind, it is exactly as if it is happening again. This is what we call a flashback or it can happen in a nightmare. That is smart of the brain, because in that way the chances that you learn a wise lesson are the greatest.

Unfortunately these flashbacks can be so scary, that we do not want to think about it again. We try and push it away again without learning the wise lesson. Then the brain keeps giving you flashbacks or nightmares, until you learn the wise lesson. Only then can the memory can be stored in the other long-term filing cabinet and the details and colours and smells disappear. So even though these flashbacks can be very scary and yucky, your brain is actually trying to help you and warning you to learn something.

Because these bad memories have so many details, they are too big for the drawers of the filing cabinet, and the drawers do not close. Then when you are looking for a wise lesson, for example in school, your foot can bump the drawer with the yucky memory and this memory can pop out and you have a flashback. Or something a little bit similar to the yucky memory happens (a fight at school can remind you of the fights that there always used to be at home), and the yucky memory pops out. This is called triggering, which is very annoying. You do not have control over when the memory pops up because the drawer cannot close.

Now there is a way to solve this problem but I don't know if you want to do that. To get rid of these flashbacks, the memories from the temporary filing cabinet need to be stored in the long-term filing cabinet so you can close the drawers and have control over when you want to think about them. Those memories will then not frighten you so much, or make you angry or upset. They will be vague and in the past. However, to do that we will need to talk about those memories a bit and I am not sure if you want to do that. You would have to come for a few sessions of about an hour to do this. Would you want to do that? Just think about it and maybe talk about it with your parents (caregiver).

The child can then be explained what trauma processing would look like and what is expected of him. Building a filing cabinet in wood or with matchboxes, drawing the different filing cabinets can support this explanation. The child does not have to discuss which memories are in the filing cabinet yet, as that would activate his traumatic memories.

5.2.4 Splinter in the foot

Some children or their caregivers argue that it is not necessary to process trauma, because the child does not have any symptoms. The following metaphor can be used.

Have you ever had a splinter in your foot? Traumatic memories are like splinters in your foot. They can hurt a lot, but after a while, the pain and swelling can get less. The splinter is still there, but you only feel it when you make a certain movement. It is not so invalidating and you can manage it. That is how it seems to be now. The trauma is there, but it does not cause any problems. The thing is, splinters can get infected any time. They can start to hurt a lot and become a big problem. You could get gangrene and your leg could be amputated. It also seems OK now, when you try and avoid using your foot. However if you would start to train for a marathon, your foot would start to hurt a lot. Children have to run marathons when they are in school or in social situations. They need to use their foot all the time. When they avoid school or social situations, they do not feel the splinter, but it is there. That is why it is important to remove the splinter. The longer you wait to take the splinter out, the more damage it will do. You will start to avoid using your foot. Your knee and hips will get sore and you may get a hernia.

Removing the splinter may hurt. You may not be able to walk for a while. Maybe you will need to recover or do physiotherapy. Or maybe it is not that painful at all and you will be able to walk on it the next day. We don't know until we operate. After the operation (trauma processing) you will need to recover and then you can train for marathons and fully use your capacities.

5.2.5 Knee reconstruction

Some professionals of caregivers may have the wrong impression that trauma processing is easy and a quick fix. Then the following explanation can be used.

Trauma processing is relatively easy when there is only one traumatic memory. It is like a leg that is fractured. It is a stable fracture that needs to be set. With a few weeks in a cast, the fracture is healed. It is different with chronic traumatization. This child does not have just one stable fracture. He has many complicated fractures all over his body and needs a knee reconstruction. There may be several operations needed over a longer period of time, with periods of recovery in between. This child needs a safe place to recover with sufficient support that knows what to do and what the child needs. The fractures may heal, but scars may be visible and the child may have metal plates in his legs. Together with the child and his network we need to make a plan on how to make these operations successful.

5.3 Psychoeducation about the stress system

Parents often think that their child is tormenting them deliberately, and children may believe this themselves. For children and parents it is good to know that they are not just annoying children who misbehave, but that their behaviour is caused by automatic stress reactions of the brain and body. Explaining this can relieve the tension between parents and their child, as six-year-old James said.

> So it is really not my fault that I get angry so often. My brain does that automatically, do you hear that, mum?

The child's tantrums, anxieties and strange behaviour are suddenly normalized as reactions to the things the child has experienced. Apparently other children experience such things too, and they have been studied scientifically. Traumatized parents get a better understanding of their own reactions and the interaction with their child. The children themselves gain a better understanding of why they react as they do, and their parents and caregivers can become more accepting of their behaviour. They are provided with language for what is happening inside the child, which makes it easier to communicate.

5.3.1 The Window of Tolerance

This explanation is illustrated by drawing on a flipchart or whiteboard. The animals can be adapted to the native animals in the child's country. A simplified version of the Window of Tolerance can be used for children from about the age of six. For children who react mainly from the mammalian brain, the last part of this box about the reptilian brain reactions can be skipped. For children who react mainly from the reptilian brain, the use of the example of a mammalian brain reaction is skipped.

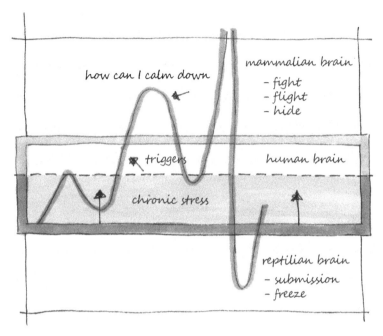

Figure 5.4
Source: Adapted from Ogden and Minton (2000); Ogden et al. (2006).

Our brain has three parts: the human brain, the reptilian brain and the mammalian brain. The reptilian brain takes care of the automatic systems in our bodies, such as our heartbeat and breathing. We don't think about these things, we just do them. The mammalian brain is the part of the brain that takes care of the instinctive reactions when we are in danger or under stress. Humans' instinctive reactions are the same as animals' reactions. Let's see what animals do when there is danger. What do deer do when they are grazing and they suddenly see a lion? They run away, because they can run very fast. They run until there is no more danger. Running away is an instinctive reaction. And what does the lion do when it has caught a deer and is enjoying its meal and suddenly another lion arrives? They fight, because lions are good at fighting. This is also an instinctive reaction. And what do rabbits do when they are in danger? They sit very still and hope that nobody sees them. They hide and wait very quietly until the danger has gone. That can also be an instinctive reaction.

Humans have the same instinctive reactions: flight, fight and hide. The mammalian brain takes care of all these reactions. Which one of them do you use most? I heard about what happened last week in school and I think you were a good lion then right? Are you always like a lion, or sometimes like a deer or rabbit? And mum, what do you normally do?

Then we have the human brain, which enables us to talk, think, organize and plan things. And the box around the human brain we call your 'Window of Tolerance', the 'window' of stress that you can tolerate. When we are relaxed and there is no danger, all the parts of our brain work together – for example, when you were watching television last week. This line is the line of the stress you felt at that moment (draw a line at the bottom of the window). But when it was bedtime and you wanted to go on watching but mum said no, you got a bit angry and the stress starts to rise (draw a rising line). This is the stress line, and it goes up like this. You told your mother that you really wanted to see the end of the show. Then mum said OK a few more minutes and your line went down and you were less stressed. Ten minutes later, mum turned the TV off and then you got so angry that the line went up and up, and your stress went outside the window (draw a line going up and out of the window).

When the stress gets too high our human brain switches off (draw a cross through the words 'human brain'). We can only use our reptilian brain and mammalian brain and our instinctive reactions are automatically activated. So when your stress went out of your window, your human brain was switched off. That means that you could not think or talk any more. That is the way our brain is programmed, because if you are in danger it is more dangerous to take the time to talk about things. What if deer did that when they saw a lion? What would happen if they first discussed what they should do ... they would be eaten! So it's a good thing the mammalian brain reacts immediately when there is danger. Your instinctive reaction to your mum turning off the TV was to fight. You became so angry and hit your mother. After you calmed down you were sorry (the stress line goes down until it is no longer outside your window). Then the human brain was switched on again.

So when you are outside your window, you cannot think. That is why it's no use your mother or the teacher trying to talk to you when you are very angry, because then your human brain is switched off. They shouldn't do that anymore. You can only start talking again when you have calmed down (this is a very important conclusion).

For some children even those instinct reactions don't work and the stress gets more and more. Then the mammalian brain shuts down as well and you only have the reptilian brain that is working. Your body is then in so much danger that your brain reacts by preparing you for serious injury; you try to survive as if in a state of shock.

(The following part can be skipped if not applicable.)

There are two ways to react from the reptilian brain and they are similar to what animals do in great danger. Animals 'play dead', they pretend to be dead because a predator does not like dead prey and they hope the danger goes away. Humans, just like animals, use two ways to 'play dead'. Freeze is when your body become totally stiff and you feel frozen and you can't speak. Submission is when your body feels floppy and you just do whatever they tell you to do and do not resist. Both reactions from the reptilian brain, freeze and submission, happen automatically when stress levels become too high, you cannot stop that.

Some children blame themselves afterwards, when the stress has gone down and they can use their human brain again. They feel they should have done something or feel stupid. The problem is that while your body is in submission or freeze, the body responds automatically. You cannot use your human brain to think of things to do and you cannot stop it. It would be like trying to stop your heart from beating. Try to stop your heart! Did you manage? No, because we cannot stop our reptilian brain reactions. Only when the stress goes down, all the parts of your brain start functioning again and then we can think about what happened. Then we cannot change what happened anymore.

What we *can* do is try to get better at the mammalian brain reaction to protect ourselves. When you are better at fighting or running away or hiding, you can prevent the reptilian brain from taking over. This can be hard, because you might also feel more irritation or anger, or you could feel more anxiety and have more nightmares. But this is actually a good sign, because if you feel the stress, you can learn to avoid it and gain more control.

(Resume the explanation here.)

Now the thing is, children who have had a lot of very bad experiences have smaller windows than other children. The bottom line of the window is much higher, because there is still a lot of stress and feelings of danger left over from when you were smaller (draw this in). So even when you are watching TV you are near the top of your window. You need only a very little extra stress to be outside your window.

5.3.1.1 What can be done

Reacting from your mammalian or reptilian brain when you are outside your window is just the way our brains work, there is not much we can do about that. What we can do, is to find out what sort of things make you go outside your window. We call these things 'triggers'. They are often things that remind you of what happened to you, or that give you the same (powerless) feeling you had then. What are the things you can't handle? And is there any way you can avoid these things?

Second, we can make plans on how you can calm down when you are outside your window. For example, we could make a plan of things you can do when you are outside your window to release the anger without getting into trouble by harming someone or destroying things or to deal with your fear without running off. It is important to practise this plan every day around the same time so your brain and body get used to doing this and it becomes a routine. It will then be easier to also use the plan when you are outside your window and cannot think of the plan anymore (see 7.7.2 and 7.7.3 for interventions 'prevent triggering' and 'Within My Window' in chapter Daily Life).

However your window is still very small and it is hard for you to manage stress. We could also try and get rid of some of the old stress from your bad memories, so we make your window a bit larger. Then you would be able to deal with more stress without going outside your window and you would feel more in control. There is a therapy to get rid of the old stress. I am not sure if you would want to. If you would want to do that, you would have to talk a bit about your bad memories. Just think about it.

For mothers who themselves also go beyond their window the following can be added during the explanation.

But when you hit your mother, maybe she also went outside her own window. Is that right mum? Mum said some bad things that she did not mean, because she could not use her human brain. When she calmed down and she could use her human brain again, she was sorry for what she did. Maybe your mum also has a small window herself? Is that right? If both of you have a small window, that means both of you lions are outside your window very quickly.

The Window of Tolerance explanation helped ten-year-old Tim to gain more control over himself, and improve the understanding and connection between him and his mother.

Tim had witnessed domestic violence and had been a victim of abuse for years. He became violent very quickly and during the therapy sessions, he frequently walked out to get a glass of lemonade. His behaviour irritated his mother; she felt it was obnoxious. After the Window of Tolerance had been explained, Tim sighed that he did indeed have 'only a very tiny window', as he called it. We discussed how him walking out was actually an excellent solution for his anger. By leaving the room to have a glass of lemonade, he was able to get back inside his 'tiny window'. It was really a very clever idea of his. After this explanation, he got better and better at indicating when his stress levels were rising.

Tim and his mother made a plan together on how to handle his anger at home. They decide that, when Tim got angry, he would say: 'I'm just going outside to breathe different air.' His mother would leave him alone for a bit. Tim learned to puff away his anger by counting backwards from ten to zero and breathing deeply from the stomach. This exercise demands concentration and brainwork, which makes it easier for him to get back inside his window. After this, Tim and his mother would discuss the problem. He was also able to come back sooner, because he no longer needed to be afraid his mother would be angry with him. When his mother sometimes got angry herself and forgot to leave him alone, he told her: 'Mum, you are outside your window. Just count from ten to zero.'

5.4 Psychoeducation on conversion

Children with trauma-related conversion, somatic dissociation, react from their reptilian brain. The following psychoeducation can be used to explain this.

5.4.1 Trauma-related conversion

Children can develop conversion symptoms as a consequence of trauma, such as paralysis, epilepsies and blindness, as a way to cope with the stress and danger. Susan's case illustrates that.

Ten-year-old Susan was sexually abused by her uncle from when she was two until she was nine. Her parents were not aware of this abuse. When she was nine years old she started showing symptoms of paralysis in her legs. As a result, she was in hospital for several months, but no physical cause was found. The abuse had stopped during hospitalization. The paralysis gradually disappeared and Susan was allowed to go home. Susan indicated that she did not want to stay with her uncle anymore. Shortly after this the uncle was arrested for sexual abuse of another child, and he confessed to having abused Susan as well. When her parents confronted Susan with this, the temporary paralysis immediately occurred again. The doctors diagnosed Susan with conversion symptoms. After this, the conversion symptoms occurred more and more frequently, and at the moment of treatment her legs failed twice a day for 30 minutes, on average.

Trauma-related conversion can be added as a reptilian brain reaction while explaining the Window of Tolerance (see section 5.3.1).

> The reptilian brain can also make parts of your body switch off to release stress, just like how you cannot move your legs sometimes. When your brain estimates that the danger has gone, the human brain and the mammalian brain can switch on again. Then you come back inside your window, and you can use all the parts of your brain again, your legs, too. This is a smart way of your brain to deal with stress. The problem is that your brain often gets triggered and your brain then thinks there is danger and stops your legs from moving, when you are actually safe.

5.4.1.1 What can be done

> Now there are ways to help your brain to get back into your Window of Tolerance, so you can use your legs again (see Here and Now in section 7.7.5). We can try some of them to see what works for you. You can, for example, distract your brain by doing something that requires the human brain to think or react, and then your legs will function again. For example, you can catch a ball, count backwards from ten to one, hop on one leg or stamp hard while counting to ten, do a difficult calculation and so on. These are solutions to get your legs moving again.
>
> You can also learn how to prevent your legs to stop working. If there is too much stress you can't stop this happening, it's automatic. But you can learn to reduce the stress before it becomes too much and switches off your mammalian brain by practising the mammalian brain reaction. Once you get better at fighting or hiding or running away, you can lower the stress without getting into the reptilian brain.
>
> Right now your body does not feel so much because you needed that to manage when things were unsafe. When you start practising this, you might start to feel more stress than before, and that might feel weird or not nice. By practising the mammalian brain reactions, you will feel more in control and then you can learn to stay more in your Window of Tolerance. Unfortunately the only way to get rid of your conversion symptoms is by working hard and getting through this.

Learning to feel more, and to use the mammalian brain more effectively, is not very attractive for children with a dissociative or conversion disorder.

Dissociation and conversion is a solution that brings instant relief and is therefore easier. A great deal of energy will have to be invested in motivating the child to go for the long-term solution instead of the short term. This also goes for the parents, who will temporarily be confronted with their child seeming only to get worse and have more symptoms. In general, the motivation of these children and their parents will have to be refreshed every few weeks.

Fortunately, Susan's treatment had started at an early stage, so that she did not have much experience with the advantages of conversion. An adolescent boy with conversion symptoms, who had been in a wheelchair for years, had adapted his whole life to his 'handicap'. He participated in disabled sports at a very high level. A life without conversion disorder was very frightening for him. If he were to be rid of his conversion symptoms and no longer need a wheelchair, he would also lose his position as a top sportsman, which had become part of his identity.

5.5 Psychoeducation on a dissociative disorder

As described in section 1.3.3.1 the Window of Tolerance is a biological model to explain the way stress affects the brain and body. Dissociation is a psychological reaction to stress, which can coincide with these biological reactions. Children can dissociate while in a fight, flight or hide reaction, for example when they are very angry and afterwards do not remember what happened. They can also freeze or be in submission and dissociate. Those children can seem in a trance or epileptic and are not responsive.

5.5.1 The Matryoshka doll

Children with a dissociative disorder often feel weird or they worry they are going crazy. Explaining structural dissociation with a Russian Matryoshka doll (a wooden doll filled with several smaller dolls, one inside the other) can be a great relief for them and it can help them to get more control over themselves. This explanation can also help caregivers to understand the child's behaviour better and to understand why 'normal' parenting strategies do not work. They need to understand that these children can have amnesia and don't remember things they do. They are not lying, they really do not know.

The following explanation can be used by replacing the child's name and personality parts. It is a lot to explain at once. Providing parts of this explanation in different sessions helps the child to get used to the language and gradually lower his defences.

Sandra (4)

When you were very small a lot of bad things happened to you. That was so awful that you couldn't think about it all the time. Sometimes the brain then thinks of something really smart: it makes two parts in the brain. One part that remembers the bad things and one part that does not remember anything. We are wondering if your brain did that. It would be really smart, because in that way you didn't have to think about all those awful things all the time. Sometimes the brain even makes more parts. Those parts of you protect you and keep all the bad things that have happened to you away, so that you don't think about them all the time.

Maybe inside you it looks a bit like this Matryoshka or Russian doll. It looks like one doll, but inside this doll there are other smaller dolls. They are all separate dolls but together they still make one doll. You are one Sandra, but inside you there are a lot of different Sandras. This, for instance, is cheerful Sandra. And this is angry Sandra, this is sex Sandra, this is scared Sandra. Sometimes we see cheerful Sandra, like right now, and sometimes angry Sandra is here. She breaks things and can get really mad. Sometimes we see sex Sandra, who does sex things with other children. She is used to that, because your brothers did that too. And then we tell you what angry Sandra or sex Sandra did and you don't understand, because you don't know anything about all that, because you are this Sandra again. Is that maybe how it works for you?

When your teacher gets angry with you because you have broken something, you often think that it is not true and she is blaming you for something you didn't do. What has happened is that it was angry Sandra inside you who did it. And when angry Sandra does something, you don't remember that. That is not very nice for you, because they are angry with you when you don't even know that you have done anything wrong. If this is what is happening, that means you are not lying at all and we need to explain that to your teacher.

We are not going to say anymore that you are lying. If you say that you haven't done anything, and you have, then that means that you don't remember. Then you can say: 'Perhaps I did it, but I don't remember.' There will have to be consequences for what you did, because a part of you did actually do it, even if you don't remember. And you also have to learn not to do these things anymore; we will help you with that. But you will not be punished for lying, because you really don't remember. This is just the way it works with you, the way you are. And that is OK, you are OK. This behaviour is a part of you and all the Sandras inside you. That is something you still have to learn.

Do you know why angry Sandra gets so angry? She doesn't do that to get at you, she does it to help you and protect you. The angry Sandra inside you thinks that the teacher wants to hurt her. She thinks that the teacher is just like your brothers, that she has to be strong and defend herself. She doesn't know that the teacher won't hurt her. When you were smaller and not safe, this angry Sandra looked after you and protected you. This angry Sandra stored up all the bad things and kept them for you, and she is still very angry about that now. When you were smaller she defended you very bravely.

We are very thankful to her for that. 'Thank you, angry Sandra, for being so brave and defending Sandra with your anger. You are a hero!' But these days angry Sandra doesn't have to defend you anymore. Your foster parents do that now; they look after you. Angry Sandra doesn't have to be angry anymore, because you are safe now. You can learn how to tell her that, so that she doesn't have to get so angry. We must tell her that, many times. The same thing goes for sex Sandra. She thinks that everybody is like your brothers, that she has to have sex with everybody; that is what she was taught. Then, when you were smaller, it was wiser not to put up a struggle, but now that's all over. You can learn to tell her that there's no need for that anymore. We are going to teach you how to do that.

All those Sandras inside you have stored up all the bad things that happened to you then. Together with you and all those Sandras we are going to get rid of all those awful memories. Then all those Sandras will know that you are safe now, and then it will not be necessary to be different Sandras anymore, and you can become one Sandra again. One Sandra, who knows that she is safe, who can get angry herself when that is necessary, and who can also be sad and scared sometimes. And happy too, of course!

5.6 Psychoeducation on attachment

5.6.1 The Heater

Explaining the consequences of emotional neglect– of something being withheld – can be more difficult than explaining something that has been done to the child, such as abuse. Emotional neglect is more subtle and often less visible. That makes it even more important to explain and to provide child and parents with a non-blaming narrative. This understanding can make the behaviour easier to handle and can reduce feelings of being rejected or unloved for all. It can also alleviate the parent's guilt and shame.

Psychoeducation is most effective when the abuser-parent is willing to accept part of the responsibility for the unintentional attachment problems. Therefore the explanation of the Heater Metaphor is first discussed with the parents and caregivers, before involving the child in it. This metaphor can be confronting and at the same time relieving for parents who have been emotionally neglected themselves.

Figure 5.5

We all have a heater in our heart that keeps us nice and warm inside. When that heater is warm you feel good and happy. You feel that there are people who love you and you feel good about yourself. Children's heaters do not burn when they are born. Their mother and father need to light the heater and make it warm with their own heat. When the mother or father has a warm heater, they can make the child's heater be warm and burn well.

When the mother or father does not have a warm heater, it is very difficult to make the child's heater warm and the child's heater stays cold. Some mothers or fathers have a wall around their heart and the warmth of their heater stays behind the wall. The child's heater stays cold, no matter how the mother or father tries to make it warm. Or the mother or father are not around to light their heater, because the child is in a hospital or in an institution.

When the child's heater is cold, the child feels not happy, sad or empty. They feel that nobody loves them or that nobody even likes them, because they are not warmed up inside. They begin to hate themselves, or other people, or they have lots of fights with their parents.

Some children who are so cold inside want to be near an adult's heater all the time. They do not like to be alone because it makes them feel cold and unloved (children who are ambivalently attached). They have not yet learned to warm inside when the adult is gone.

Some children build a wall around their heart, so that they no longer feel the cold, that miserable, lonely feeling. Then they do not need anyone. They prefer to be by themselves (children who are avoidant attached). They don't like to feel the warmth of an adult's heater, because this makes them feel extra cold. But because of the wall around their heart they cannot feel any real pleasure, either. Nothing can reach their heart and it is very difficult to light their heater.

There are also children who switch; sometimes there is a wall so they don't feel the cold, and sometimes they go looking for an adult or a friend to warm themselves. This can be confusing, for them and for the adult.

That is what happened with you and why you feel sad and lonely. Your heater is not warm because your mum's heater is not warm either. She wants to light your heater, but it does not work. (If the child asks why this is so, the parent can say that this is because of things that happened in the past, but that the child does not need to know all the details; that is private.) Mum is now getting help to get her heater lit, so that she can then try to light yours. If that works, you will start to feel happier and you will have more confidence in yourself and others. You do not have to help your mother with this, she is going to do it herself, with the help of other adults.

This explanation can be shortened or adapted to the child's situation. For avoidant-attached children it is important that they permit contact. This can be explained as follows:

You can practise by lowering your wall a little, or letting down your drawbridge sometimes and let the warmth in. Then maybe you will feel a bit more sad and lonely, but at the same time you will find that you are having more fun.

5.6.2 How the heat lights the child's heater

For adolescents and their parents a more detailed explanation can be helpful. The following text can be used, and adapted to the situation.

Babies are completely dependent on their mother (or father). The only bodily signal they know is pleasant (OK) and unpleasant (not OK) which makes them cry. The mother reacts to this with what she thinks the child needs and she says something like: 'Yes, you're hungry, aren't you?

Here's your bottle.' This is how a child learns to feel his body (hungry, sleepy, cold).

When children get a little older, they start to feel angry and sad and afraid. Because the mother tells the child how he feels, the child learns what feelings are. In this way the child learns when he is angry, happy or sad. The parent's reaction teaches the child to recognize the feeling inside himself, to name and to express it and, still later, to have control over it.

By guessing and telling the child why he is angry or sad the child learns to reflect on his intentions. 'You're angry, aren't you, because you're not allowed to throw your food around.' That is how children learn to understand why they feel something, because they want things or like or don't like things: they learn to mentalize. Because the child feels that he is seen, heard and understood, he begins to trust others. He feels that others know what is going on inside him. They make him feel good, and they do not hurt him.

Then the child starts to realize that others have feelings and intentions too and the child can put himself in the other person's perspective. When children understand that not everything is about them and others have feelings too, they can put things that happen into perspective. When their mother is angry, that is not because she hates them, but because she got a parking ticket just before. The way you think about yourself is based on how you believe others think about you. If others treat you well, you must be OK, and this gives you confidence. By understanding the other person's reaction well, children become more confident and feel good about themselves.

As you see, this development starts with having a parent that can put himself in the child's perspective, understand the child and name the child's inner feelings. The parent must be able to read the child's mind. This can be very difficult if you are a parent and you are depressed or have your own bad memories, or you do not have control over your own emotions and need all your attention for yourself. If, for example, a child has ADHD, the reaction of that child's brain will differ from other children's. His brain will try to focus on the parent, but it will be distracted by other stimuli and it is difficult to concentrate on his own body. For the parents it is harder to guess what is going on in the child and figure out what made the child angry. Besides, it is difficult for the child to focus on the interaction with the parent. Listening to what the parent is saying and connecting that to the feelings inside requires quite a lot of concentration. Therefore forming an attachment relationship can be more difficult for children with ADHD.

If the mirroring process is disturbed, for whatever reason, a child feels misunderstood. Then the child does not develop a secure attachment relationship. This makes children distrustful of others, because in their experience others do not understand them. As a result they have problems with social contact. Consequently, they have little self-confidence. They often feel empty, depressed and lonely, without apparent reason. Also, these children do not learn to understand themselves. They have difficulty in understanding emotions and keeping them under control. This causes them to fall behind in their emotional development. It can be sad for a parent or a child to see that this is what is happening, but it is possible to do something about it. Children are never too old to get to know themselves.

Parents can help a child to become more aware of himself by mirroring their child. Therapy, in which the therapist functions as a mirror for the child, can also help the child to get to know his emotions and to learn to control them. But this is only possible if the child feels really safe and at ease, and therefore such a therapeutic process may take a long time

Chapter 6

Interventions to overcome barrier 1

Safety

When the prince feels unsafe and has to run for his life, he is unable to train. He needs adults to provide safety. This chapter describes interventions to overcome the child's barriers around safety. Most of these interventions are done with the child's network.

6.1 Barrier 1a: Not being or feeling safe

When children are referred for treatment, it is often assumed that the abuse has stopped. Parents say they do not fight anymore and they seem to be doing well. They have had therapy and their therapist is also positive. Of course that is great, but their therapist did not visit the house to make sure that even then the parents do not become violent on Saturday nights, when friends are over with beers to watch football. Even when the parents have stopped fighting, children can still be afraid it will happen again. How can they be sure that parents have changed their behaviour? Parents may be so used to the lack of safety, that they don't realize what safety means. This was the case for Rodin.

Case study

Eleven-year-old Rodin has DID. He was admitted for inpatient treatment. Six months later it becomes apparent that his mother also has DID. She had been sexually and psychologically abused by her own mother, Rodin's grandmother. She had been in treatment for years, but the DID was only diagnosed when her son started treatment too and other aspects of her personality came to light. They both had extensive treatment, and Rodin went home on the weekends. After another six months it turned out that the grandmother had been living in their house all this time, and was still terrorizing the family. The traumatization had been going on all this time, and it had never occurred to the mother to tell the therapist.

6.1.1 Contact with biological parents

When the child's parents are divorced, the child can still have contact with the parent who abused him. In this chapter the terms abuser-parent and non-protecting parent are used for clarity purposes. Obviously every parent is more than just an abuser-parent or non-protecting parent. The pronoun 'he' can also be read as 'she'. Contact with the abuser-parent is not a contra-indication for trauma processing. But the contact needs to be safe, which means that it should be guaranteed for the child that no abuse will take place. If there is still a threat in the perception of the child, understandably the child will not be prepared to speak of what he has gone through. The child is afraid of the consequences. Even when a child grows up in a foster or adoptive family, it can never just be assumed that the child is safe. The child's loyalty may be so strong that he may secretly go to see the abuser-parent himself. Adolescents can visit their parents against the child protection services' decisions. The abuse may then continue while the child, supposedly safe, lives in a foster family. Mieke (38) has DID and tells about her childhood.

When I was seven years old, I was placed in a foster family. Very sweet people who took care of me well. But do you think the abuse stopped? My parents did not live far away, and I just went to visit them after school. I did not dare to stay away; the abuse was how it was supposed to be. I was made for it, is how they put it. I used to say that I was going to play with friends, and pretended that everything was fine. The abuse just went on, and child protection services never knew about it. First my parents said they would kill my dog if I would not come. Then they said it was my own choice, not theirs. They said that if anyone would find out, I would go to prison.

6.1.2 Abuse starts again during treatment

With a change of circumstances, the abuse may start again during the treatment. A divorced mother who has unsupervised contacts with the children may start a relationship with the abuser-parent again without child protection services knowing. The parent who had stopped abusing may revert to his old behaviour. When treatment appears to be ineffective or if a child hardly ever says anything about the situation at home when one would expect otherwise, the child could be the victim of ongoing abuse.

6.1.3 Interventions to overcome barrier 1a

When 'the child not being or feeling safe' forms a barrier, interventions need to focus on increasing the child's safety and making sure, as much as possible, that the abuse from the past has stopped. By informing the child of the safety measures and including children in making a Safety Plan, the child can start to feel safer as well and more in control. This plan can also reduce the child's fear of threats from the abuser-parent, because he knows what to do.

6.1.4 Safety Plan

Safety planning approaches such as Signs of Safety (Turnell & Edwards, 1999) or Partnering for Safety (Parker, 2011) can be used to create more safety in families or to increase the child's safe feeling. The child and network are informed about the unsafe situations in the past by constructing a brief story with drawings in child language with the parents: a Words and Pictures story (Turnell & Essex, 2006). The brief story describes what happened, who is concerned and why, the parents' explanation (then and now), what happened afterwards and how the parents are going to make things safe. Providing the child, no matter how young, with a clear explanation about the difficult things that happened in the past, greatly contributes to building a sense of security for the child. The parents and their network identify the future danger to the children, and describing safety rules with the parent's new safe behaviour. Children are included in drafting this plan.

The parent's new safe behaviour needs to be demonstrated over time, to increase the child's safe feeling. The network checks whether the parents actually stick to those rules and advises on adaptions of the plan. By using their own resources and being an active participant in the process of identifying the worries and planning for future safety, families experience more control over the situation. Safety planning can lead to children feeling safer and enable them to talk about their trauma or it can even lead to children disclosing new abuse.

Safety planning can be used to prevent the child being removed or to prepare reunification after the child has been removed. Children in out of home care may have weekend or holiday visits with their parents. If the child feels unsafe and worried that the abuse may reoccur during these visits then this can form a barrier. Safety Plans can also be made for contact only to enable the child's network to supervise contact with their parent instead of professionals.

Safety Plans can be made for supervised contact so that the family know what to do to ensure the child's safety during contact and the supervisor knows what to do to support the family during the contact. The Partnering for Safety approach includes tools and processes that can be used to develop contact Safety Plans collaboratively with families and their networks (Parker, 2011).

Safety planning around contact reinforces the parent's safe behaviour. This could be the catalyst to new interactions with the child.

6.1.5 No contact with the abuser-parent

Children can still feel threatened or unsafe, even when the child does not have contact with the abuser-parent. They can be afraid their mum and dad will get back together, or be afraid they meet the abuser-parent unexpectedly. When there is no contact, the perception of the abuser-parent gets frozen in time. Whenever the child thinks of the abuser-parent, he will remember the last time he saw him or her, which is often a traumatizing situation after which contact stopped. Having contact with the abuser-parent can actually reduce the child's fear, provided contact can be done safely. Looking at photos, reading a letter the abuser-parent wrote, watching a video the abuser-parent made can make the child feel safer.

After nine-year-old Jody saw her brother, who abused her when she was four, she said: 'He is so small, I thought he was much bigger! I am not scared anymore.'

When contact has ceased, making a Safety Plan can assist in starting up contact again. New experiences with the abuser-parent enable the child to create 'new history' replacing the terrifying last memories of the abuser-parent. Not having contact may seem safe, but is only a temporary solution. Their parents are still their parents and when nothing has changed by the time they turn eighteen, the child is left to deal with the unsafety without support.

6.1.6 Safety Plan for meeting the abuser unexpectedly

Sometimes after a divorce one of the parents threatens or stalks the other parent or the children. The child can meet the abuser in the street or shopping centre, or he can wait for the child in school. For those situations a Safety Plan can be made with the child and network. School can be informed about the child's fear of the abuser. They can inform all the school staff and provide them with a photo of the abuser, so he can be recognized. School can make a plan with the child and parent of what to do if the abuser came to school unexpectedly. Other children can be included in this plan too. The child can feel more in control and safer when he knows where to go to, whom to inform, what to say to the abuser, to scream loudly, to blow a whistle, to run to the principle, to call out 'help', to ask other children or adults in the street to help, or to call someone. The same can be done at the sports clubs, with neighbours, parents of the child's friends and family members. When the threats are severe, the police can be involved in making a Safety Plan.

6.1.7 'Denied' or disputed abuse

Safety planning can also be used when parents do not acknowledge abuse. Resolutions (Turnell & Essex, 2006) is a specific adaptation of safety planning for 'denied' or 'disputed abuse', such as sexual abuse or fabricated illness. This approach has been shown to reduce chances of re-abuse (Gumbleton, 1997).

6.1.8 Medical trauma

Children with medical trauma may need ongoing medical procedures or painful treatments. Obviously this 'abuse' cannot be stopped. By making a clear distinction between which incidents were in the past, such as the operation when I was five and I woke up, and situations that are ongoing, such as having a needle every day, the incidents from the past can become safe and over. They can then be processed, which can make the child more resilient.

6.2 Barrier 1b and 1c: Attachment figure and contact

Children may not talk about their memories because they do not have an adult to do it for. When they have an attachment figure, they may not be sure whether they can rely on that person or they do not have regular contact. Seven-year-old Wesley, with whom I had made the mistake of initiating trauma processing too soon, demonstrated how this can form a barrier.

Wesley grew up with his mother till he was five years old. His mother abused her children daily, both physically and mentally. His father did not live with them, but he saw his children regularly. When Wesley was five he went to live with his father, because his mother was sentenced to six years' imprisonment for attempted manslaughter. Suddenly his father was responsible for four young children, in an apartment that was much too small. He managed to take care of them, but only kept going by taking drugs. When Wesley was seven years old, his father was also taken into custody for a minor offence. Child protection services placed all the children in foster families. His father had a year to meet the conditions child protection services had set for getting his children back.

During this period, Wesley and his sisters lived with different foster families. He saw his father sporadically and it was doubtful whether his father would manage to come through. During this year, Wesley's behaviour deteriorated. He was aggressive and picked fights with his foster parents. He was also anxious during the night and began to have nightmares. He talked more and more about the violence and abuse during the period when he lived with his mother. To relieve him of his symptoms EMDR was started, but during the second session he became angrier and angrier. He refused to go on and ran out of the therapy room. In the corridor he yelled and screamed, and threw toys around. The following session Wesley was already angry when he came in. He had been pressured to come by his foster parents, and on entering he immediately said that he did not want to continue. He said: 'I don't want to go on. EMDR doesn't help; those pictures won't go out of my head, anyway.' When he was asked why, he said: 'I can only get rid of those pictures if I live with my father again.'

Wesley was right, 1b and 1c formed a barrier to him. He could not process the traumatic memories, because this would make him much too vulnerable. His main attachment figure was still his father, and the uncertainty about his future prevented Wesley from forming an attachment relationship with anyone else. First he needed the support of his father to take on the fight. When this is identified as a barrier, an attachment figure needs to be found for the child and contact with that person needs to be guaranteed to overcome this barrier. For children between sixteen and eighteen who become independent, not having an attachment figure can become less of a barrier. They have their friends and their own life, they do not need to have someone to take care of them.

6.2.1 Find an attachment figure?

An attachment figure is emotionally involved with the child, loves the child unconditionally and feels responsibility for his wellbeing. The child can share important events with this person, such as a birthday or getting a diploma. And when the child, for instance, breaks his arm, this attachment figure wants to be notified and may come and visit him in the hospital or call. This connection is lifelong, in principle. The child needs a minimum of one attachment figure, but it is better to have more. The child does not have to live with the attachment figure. The attachment figure may have caregiving tasks but this is not necessary. They can be a parent whom the child visits in the weekends, or a foster family where the child goes for weekends, a grandmother overseas who visits once every year. A parent in prison, in another country or in a mental hospital can still be an attachment figure. As long as there is a way to communicate and another daily caregiver to support the child.

When the child does not have contact with a parent, that parent can still become the attachment figure. Contact can be resumed and the parent can express his wish to continue contact. Obviously the child needs time to build up trust in that parent again. The child does not have to be attached to this person or like this person or have a good relationship with him. The safety barrier arises from a survival perspective. The child needs at least one adult to feel protected and survive. The quality of that relationship is addresses in the barrier attachment.

6.2.2 Biological parents as attachment figure

The child's biological mother and father are the first option to be the main attachment figure, even when they have abused or harmed the child. Many children are still very loyal to their parents, despite what they have done to them. Only when the parent is still dangerous, does not love the child, does not care about his wellbeing or rejects the child, is he not safe enough to be an attachment figure.

6.2.3 Plan to guarantee continuity of contact attachment figure

Parents can easily become overwhelmed with their own emotions. The child's behaviour can trigger their own sore spots and they can reject the child and say things like: 'I never want to see you anymore. You are no longer welcome here. Go find another father, I don't want you anymore.' Most parents say these things, but do not act accordingly. They may regret saying it. When a parent cannot control himself, he can explain to the child that even though he sometimes says these things, he does not mean it. That the child can trust the parent is always going to be there. When the child believes that, then contact is guaranteed enough. The same plans can be made for foster or adoptive parents.

Sophie's mother explained to Sophie that she had a lot of bad memories herself. Sometimes those memories would make her so angry and upset, that she would start to yell at Sophie on the phone. She would say things she really did not mean. Sophie's mother said she wanted to make a plan with Sophie on how to manage this. Together they decided that Sophie would hang up the phone. She would not answer her mother's calls, until the mother send her a photo of the two of them hugging.

6.2.4 Foster parents or adoptive parents as attachment figure

When both of the child's parents cannot be attachment figures, foster parents or adoptive parents can take that role. They need to be able to commit to loving the child unconditionally, to feel responsible for the child's wellbeing and to give the child a permanent place in their family. They do not have to guarantee the child can stay with the family permanently, because this is not always possible. Sometimes the behavioural problems are too difficult and a child risks being out-placed. When the family can maintain contact with the child, after the placement breaks down, they can still be main attachment figure. When the foster or adoptive parents cannot guarantee this continuity, they cannot be main attachment figure.

6.2.4.1 Come to a decision on guaranteed contact

The foster parents or adoptive parents need to make up their mind about their wishes or possibilities. Next the legal guardian and the foster care organization need to approve of the plan to maintain contact after the placement ends. Foster or adoptive parents and professionals do not always understand how important and crucial this can be to the child. They say that they cannot decide that now. They will see how things turn out or want to leave it up to the child. When contact is not guaranteed, the child will not risk deepening the attachment relationship. Imagine having a relationship with a partner who does not commit to the relationship and says he is unclear whether he wants to stay with you. You will keep your distance until your partner commits to the relationship. The Sleeping Dogs method can be used to explain to them that the child will not be able to engage in trauma treatment and that it is therefore important to make this commitment. Discussing and arranging this can be a timely matter. When the arrangements are made, the child needs to be informed of this.

6.2.4.2 Inform the child

The legal guardian and the foster or adoptive parents can inform the child. The foster or adoptive parents can explain that the child is a part of their life and family now. They can make a photo of the family and hang the photo in the living room or put it on their online profile. They can talk about the future and how they want to be part of the child's life. Children might reject this and say they do not care, out of fear of being rejected. The foster parents need to be persistent and say that they really hope they can be there.

6.2.5 Others can be attachment figure

Other caregivers can also be attachment figures (grandfather, grandmother, previous foster parents, neighbour or mother of a friend) on condition that the connection is potentially lifelong. Siblings can be attachment figure when they are adults. When they are children themselves, they cannot take care of another child. Children need another adult to make sure they are doing OK.

Nine-year-old Kevin had lived in several foster families and was now in a temporary foster placement. The child protection worker struggled to find him a permanent placement because his violent, defiant and sexualized behaviour was difficult to manage. He had no contact with his parents since he was taken into care, due to the severe sexual, physical and emotional abuse that the parents even continued during supervised contact. He was referred for trauma treatment to hopefully reduce his symptoms, but refused to discuss his memories.

Not having an attachment figure was identified as a barrier for Kevin. The child protection worker started searching for options. A year ago, Kevin had lived with a temporary foster family that really liked him. They understood his difficulties and managed his behaviour well. Unfortunately he could not stay, as they had planned to go travelling, but they continued having sporadic contact with him. After they returned, the previous foster family took in two other foster children because Kevin was in a permanent foster placement.

The child protection workers asked them whether they were willing to become his attachment figures, which they were. The child protection worker established bimonthly visits and regular phone calls. They explained to Kevin why he could not live with them, but that they were going to stay in his life, even though he could not live with them. They were present when psychoeducation was given to Kevin and they motivated Kevin for treatment. He agreed and they supported him during the sessions. Kevin's behaviour became less difficult, which enabled the child protection worker to find him a permanent placement.

6.2.6 Professionals cannot be attachment figure

When children grow up in a residential facility, the residential staff are the daily caregivers. They can however not be attachment figures, because the continuity of the relationship is not guaranteed by love, but by their contract with their employer. For the same reason, a therapist cannot be the only attachment figure. They can definitely have attachment relationships, but when there is no other long-term attachment figure, the professional risks that the child attaches to him. That can cause even more damage because the professional will make the child feel abandoned and rejected, simply because of the way their relationship is regulated.

Children need love, just like a plant needs water. When a plant is thirsty, they search for water with their roots. Children without love search for love, wherever they can find it.

6.2.7 Support person besides attachment figure

When the child has minimal contact with the attachment figure, the child may need more emotional support. Daily caregivers, family members or other adults, even professionals such as residential staff, can give this emotional support by creating an 'extended parenting environment' (Cohen, Mannarino, Kliethermes, & Murray, 2012). The parent remains the main attachment figure for the child, even though another people are providing emotional support. The support person can be a temporary person. He does not have to stay in the child's life, because the attachment figure is doing so.

6.2.7.1 Inform the child

This parent then needs to inform the child that he approves of the child being supported by the daily caregiver as a substitute. In a conversation with the attachment figure, the support person and the child, the attachment figure can give the child permission to confide in this support person. If this is not possible, the attachment figure can talk to the child on the phone, via a video message, a letter etc., when there is the long-term attachment figure that they can refer to: 'Let's tell mum about what you did today, she will be so proud. Did you ever do that with dad?'

6.2.8 Decisions by child protection services

When child protection services are involved, they are very important partners in overcoming the safety barriers. Their decisions can support the child's treatment greatly. They can find an attachment figure for the child, or locate parents or family members with whom contact is lost. They can allow therapists to have contact with parents in prison or a parent who lost contact with the child or never had contact. They can introduce the therapist to the family. They can support and arrange for the contact with foster parents to be guaranteed. They can change contact arrangements or initiate contact, when the child has lost contact with a parent. They can pressure parents or reward parents for their collaboration.

6.3 Barrier Id: No permission from outside

Children can fear consequences by people from outside the family when they would talk about their memories. The child can be afraid that disclosures will have legal consequences for their parent, the police will be informed and his parents or he himself will be convicted. Or the child fears that the child protection worker will change contact arrangements or reunification plans. Besides traumatic memories of incidents that were already disclosed or are known, the child may also have secrets or think they have secrets, which would be *new* disclosures. The child can be afraid the police will be informed about new disclosures, and his parents or he himself will go to prison. Children can refuse to talk because they want to go home and they are afraid the legal guardian will reduce contact arrangements, not reunify the child. This was the case with six-year-old Mandy and eight-year-old Myrtle.

> Their mother was a drug addict and worked as a prostitute, which was why the child protection services had decided to place the children in a foster family. The mother wanted the children back and started a lawsuit. She told the children during visits that she wanted them to come home. The children talked about sexual abuse by the maternal grandfather, who had also abused the mother. Their mother wanted the children to process their trauma, but the child protection worker strongly suspected that their mother's clients have also abused them. The children denied this and did not want to talk about the time when they were living with their mother. All they wanted was to go home and live with their mother. After the court decided they would permanently stay in the foster family, they disclosed the abuse actually did take place.

A child can also fear the opposite, that the legal guardian will intensify contact, make contact unsupervised or reunify him with his parents because his problems are solved. Reassurance needs to come from people outside the family. The possible consequences need to be clarified to the child, so the child can decide what to do based on this information.

6.4 Barrier 1e: No permission from parents

This forms a barrier when the child is worried that talking about his memories will damage the relationship with one of his parents or both. He is afraid of his parent's reaction. Parents may officially consent to treatment, which can be important from a legal perspective, but some children need to feel their parents' emotional consent. Children often do not know whether their parents approve of them talking about their memories, or the parents have told them not to. Parents may sometimes be pressured to take their children to therapy, even if they are not comfortable with it. Sometimes parents will literally tell their children not to say anything. More often the children will think of this themselves, out of loyalty. The child's parent can also not give emotional permission out of fear of repercussions from the police or child protection services.

To overcome this barrier, the child needs reassurance from his parent. Parents can also fear consequences from outside the family, which can be the reason for them telling the child not to talk. Reassurance from outside for the parents can also help to overcome this barrier. When the child does not really care about what his parents think, this does not have to form a barrier. Or when the child has one parent who gives him permission and he lives with this parent, and does not really care about the other parent not approving.

6.5 Interventions to get permission

When the consequences of talking are unclear to the child, they need to be clarified so the child can decide whether he wants to risk them or not.

6.5.1 Involving the abuser-parent to get permission

When 1e forms a barrier, the parent that the child needs permission from needs to be involved in treatment to provide the child with this information, even when this parent has abused the child unless, of course, this would jeopardize the child's safety. Even abuser-parents who are in prison can sometimes get permission to visit a therapist or the therapist can visit the parent in prison.

Professionals or the other parent can question this by arguing the parent does not have custody and therefore does not have to consent to treatment. However, the child is not interested in legal regulations. This is about emotional permission. The child does not want to be rejected by his parents or lose them. When a parent has custody and does not consent to treatment, involving the parent can actually lead to consent. An (alleged) abuser-parent who feels that his side of the story is also heard and is informed about treatment can be more willing to consent. Sometimes an abuser-parent can even have helpful suggestions about treatment, as he knows the child well.

6.5.2 Discuss permission with parent

It is explained to the child's parent that their child may be afraid to talk about his memories because he is unsure his parents approve of this. When the parent struggles with this, it can be important to listen to his story first. Ask the parent what he is worried about and what he wants for his child. Explain that child protection files can have information that is incorrect, and they are given the opportunity to give their views on what happened. The purpose of these conversations and the parents telling their story is to make them feel more comfortable and allow their child to tell his story, not to discover the truth. Psychoeducation can be used to explain the importance of processing traumatic memories for the child. They can actually help their child heal by giving this permission.

6.5.3 Discuss permission with others

Not having permission from foster parents, caregivers or a stepfather or grandparents, can also form a barrier. The same intervention can be used with them.

6.5.4 Memories are not facts

It can be explained to parents that the purpose of the child's therapy is to help the child overcome his trauma symptoms, not to investigate what happened in the past and to gather facts. When parents argue about facts, explain to them that the only thing that matters is the child's memories, not their version of reality. Children's memories can be influenced by time, other things that happen, things that they have been told, fantasy. Children can even be traumatized by a story, without witnessing the actual event. The child is now struggling with the memories they have constructed, not with the facts.

6.5.5 Inform the child about parent's permission

The parent is then asked to give their child permission to talk about all his memories in a subsequent session with the child. When direct contact is not possible, the parent can also do this via a video message, phone call, text message, a letter etc. Many children do not know that their parents give permission to talk. Therefore it is advised to make this a standard intervention for all children.

6.5.6 Secrets and new disclosures

When it is suspected that the child may struggle with a secret, parents or caregivers can explain to the child that there are good secrets, such as birthday presents and bad secrets that make you sad and afraid. That it is important to talk about the bad secrets, despite of what adults or other children may have said in the past, so your head gets clear. That 'drawing' what happened is not 'talking' about it. This conversation is prepared with the parent, caregiver or child protection worker before involving the child. When the parents have pressured the child into secrets in the past, this conversation can help the child to disclose the secret, despite of the parent's pressure.

6.5.7 Children in a high conflict divorce

Children in a high conflict divorce often have this barrier. Everything they say about one parent, can be used against the other. To overcome that barrier and help the child, the parents can both give the child permission to discuss his memories with the therapist in private, without the parents knowing the content of what is discussed. When they allow the child to have confidential sessions that may help the child to overcome this barrier. Obviously this confidentiality is limited, and new disclosures of unsafety or abuse may need to be reported.

6.5.8 Parent not giving permission

Some parents continue to refuse to give permission, even after investing in building a relationship with this parent. The child could overcome the barrier by getting explicit permission from the other parent, or from foster parents for example. They will need to guarantee to take care of the child and to protect the child from the parent's possible rejection.

6.5.9 Discuss external consequences with child protection services or police

When child protection services are involved, they are very important partners in overcoming the safety barriers. With the child protection worker can be discussed what the possible consequences are of the child's disclosures. They will need to make if … then … scenarios. Child protection workers can struggle to answer these questions. They, or their managers, may not see the importance of making these scenarios and do not want to provide clear answers. Some may argue they would rather not inform the child of the consequences, because they fear the child will then not disclose. Children have children's rights, just as humans have human rights, and it is in fact a child's right to know what is going to be done with the information they provide (Convention on the Rights of the Child, 1989). Child protection services need to act within these rights.

Again, decisions by child protection services can make a huge difference. The Sleeping Dogs method can be used to explain how withholding this information forms a barrier to treatment. Making these scenarios is not easy. The child protection worker can be assisted in defining the possible actions. There are three main issues that guide the plan: making sure the child is safe now or in the future, making sure other children are safe and punishment for actions in the past. The child protection worker can discuss the consequences of possible disclosures with the police if applicable. Child protection workers may be obliged to report to the police and the police are obliged to bring the child in for questioning. The child however is not obliged to answer any of those questions if he does not want to.

In many cases the plan is quite simple and the child's disclosures will not lead to any actions. Most information is already known by child protection services and action has already been taken. The parents have made a Safety Plan or the child has been removed, contact is supervised. In those cases, the child protection worker can tell the child and possibly parents which information is already known, such as domestic violence, sexual abuse or neglect. The child protection worker can assure the child that the child disclosing further details about this would not lead to a change in contact because they have already intervened.

Even if new disclosures may lead to contact being reduced or supervised or reunification being postponed or called off, it is important to inform the child about this and explain why that would be necessary. All those scenarios can be drawn on a flipchart with the child and possibly parents. By providing the child with this information, the child may choose to disclose and protect himself or siblings against unsafe parents, or not disclose and protect himself against parents blaming him for the rest of his life.

6.5.10 Inform the child and parent about external consequences

The child protection worker informs the child of situations in which their managers or the police will be notified. The child protection worker can give examples of information that would be new and lead to consequences, such as if the child would say his parents have made a bomb to destroy the child protection building. They can then explain to the child that the child has the right not to speak to the police. The child's therapist or caregiver can ask questions to further clarify such as:

> If Jake told me that his parents have hit him when he was living with them, would you change the weekly visits? No, that would stay the same. The most important thing is that Jake is safe. I am sure Jake's parents cannot hit him again because I am always there at contact to make sure Jake is safe.

> If Mimi told me that her parents used drugs and she saw their needles when she was living with them before, would she still be reunified? Yes, she is still going home because we have made sure in the Safety Plan that her mum and dad do not use drugs now. We were already worried they were using drugs. That is why, for example, they wrote in the Safety Plan that they will go to the doctor to test their blood and urine, so they can show me that they do not use drugs now.

David (3)

For David 1a and 1e were identified as barriers. David's father had custody over David. He did not want to be involved in the treatment and also refused to give permission for treatment. David was then placed under guardianship, and after a written summons the father finally agreed to the treatment. This meant that David's father could not force David to have contact or take him out of school and physical safety was provided. Even though legal permission was arranged, the lack of emotional permission for David was still a barrier. David's mother told David that she gave him permission. She explained to him that even though his father did not give him permission, it was still important for David to discuss his memories. She explained that she would never return to her ex-husband, because she was not in love with him anymore. In this way she was able to assure David that he would still be safe even if he rejected his father's behaviour and risked his father's anger for doing this.

Chapter 7

Interventions to overcome barrier 2

Daily life

The prince needs a fence around his training field to be able to concentrate on his practice and not be distracted by the threat of the dragon. This chapter describes all daily life barriers, with interventions to address the barriers and some background information that can be useful. Then a number of interventions are described that can be used to address multiple barriers.

Interventions are done with the child and his network depending on the child's age. Despite the numerous problems in daily life, for most children these rarely form a barrier. The older adolescents get, the more these problems can begin to form barriers. The Sleeping Dogs method tries to shorten treatment for these children, because trauma processing relieves symptoms. However sometimes children cannot start trauma processing because of, for example, waiting lists, lack of permission or other barriers that need to be removed first. When daily life is not identified as a barrier, this means it is not imperative to work on these issues before trauma processing. Even then these interventions can be used by, for example, residential staff or foster parents to improve the child's daily life functioning. In the integration phase these interventions can also be used.

7.1 Severe problems do not have to form a barrier

Many children have severe problems in daily life and often the caregivers and school struggle or have struggled a great deal. They say the child's situation is not stable enough for trauma processing, as they fear that they cannot deal with a temporary worsening of symptoms. However these behavioural difficulties continue to cause severe problems, without addressing the traumatic memories creating them. This often leads to a stuck situation: the child needs trauma processing to reduce his symptoms but his symptoms are too severe to start trauma processing. Rather than trying to improve the *child*'s functioning, which usually is not successful because of the unprocessed trauma, the Sleeping Dogs method tries to make the situation manageable by influencing the *circumstances*. Treatment focuses initially *only* on those issues that really form a barrier for trauma processing, not all the other problems, to make the daily life chaos manageable, just good enough to get through the trauma-processing phase. 'Good enough stability' as Kliethermes and Wamser (2012) call it. After trauma processing, in the integration phase, all the remaining problems become the focus of treatment, as these problems need to improve for the child to grow up safe and healthy.

7.2 Barrier 2a: Home

This barrier, having too many problems at home, or the child being afraid to be removed from home, consists of several different aspects. Children can have many problems at home that require attention, such as moving placement, moving school, having a court case coming up, being a refugee, being arrested, getting a new brother or sister, a dying family member. Some children are homeless. They live in temporary placements or on the streets. These children need their energy to fight for their survival. This can be a valid reason not to talk about traumatic memories, but it does not have to be. Some children, despite their unstable daily life, do have awake dogs and want to process them to get rid of their symptoms, which is fine. When a child does not have the headspace, interventions such as psychoeducation, prevent triggering, Within My Window, the Safe Deposit Box, the Here and Now, and the Safe Place, can make the problems in the child's daily life manageable enough so they have spare energy to dig up their old memories. The caregivers can make a plan to reduce the child's pressure.

The child's placement can be under pressure and when caregivers worry about child's difficult behaviour worsening, are fearful of waking up sleeping dogs, children can try and avoid that. However, trauma processing usually reduces externalizing symptoms and it reliefs the pressure relatively quickly. The children that seem to be easier to handle, with internalizing symptoms or dissociation, are more at risk of an increase in their difficult behaviour. Psychoeducation and parental support can assist the caregivers to reduce their stress level. Another problem arises when the child does not obey the caregiver and absconds constantly. Then the caregiver is unable to discuss things with the child, simply because he is not there. The Sleeping Dogs method reduces the child sessions to a minimum, but the child must at least be accessible to provide him with information and psychoeducation. Usually the absconding improves significantly after contact with an attachment figure is established.

The foster parents of fifteen-year-old Joey struggled with his violence and total lack of respect for them. 'He comes and goes as he pleases', they would say. Joey often stayed at his mother's house who was an alcoholic and pregnant with her sixth child. His stepfather had been a sadistic and dominating man, who physically abused Joey and his mother. The child protection worker suspected Joey had a negative self-image, but he had always refused to speak about the abuse. Whenever the child protection worker, the foster parents or other professionals tried to speak to Joey, he would not show up or take off. The mother was the only one with access to Joey.

The child protection worker discussed the risk of the placement breaking down with Joey's mother. She worried about Joey, but said she could not have him, with the baby coming. She wanted him to get well, so he could be a big brother and she offered to discuss treatment with Joey. The child protection worker kept visiting the mother until she finally spoke to Joey. Since his mother thought it was a good idea, Joey agreed under the condition that his mother would be involved.

When involving the attachment figure does not improve contact with the child, the child needs more boundaries. There are many programmes that can be used to address children's behavioural difficulties. Non-violent resistance (NVR) (Omer, 2004) is a systemic approach to support parents to work with their children violating the parent's boundaries. NVR's respectful ways and focus on connection fits very well with the Sleeping Dogs method. When that is not an option, children can be placed in a more restricted setting, after which treatment can start.

Fifteen-year-old Kate had been in many foster and residential placements, after being removed at five. She was in a residential placement; however she did not go to school or obey the caregivers. She would stay away for weeks, use drugs, break into houses and sold herself on the streets. She had been in juvenile prison several times. She did not like 'lockup', but her child protection worker thought she was doing much better there. Her child protection worker worried about her sexualized and violent behaviour, a consequence of abuse, and wanted her to do trauma treatment. She decided to wait until Kate was arrested again. She then asked the judge to sentence her for a longer period so she could do trauma treatment. After two weeks in lock-up Kate agreed and processed part of her memories, which made her calmer and more confident.

7.2.1 Compensation plan to manage trauma symptoms

Rather than trying to change the child's or the caregiver's behaviour, which is often very difficult, a compensation plan provides the caregiver with extra support from his network to compensate for what the caregiver is unable to do. This plan is made with the caregiver and his network. The child can for example temporarily stay with grandparents, go to respite, or an uncle can come over and help the mother. The network can take care of the other children on the day of the child's therapy, or cook or do the washing, so the parent has time for the child. The caregiver can plan stress-decreasing activities around the sessions, such as heavy physical exercise or activities that make the child feel connected and distracted, such as movie night or eating your favourite dinner together. When this is not possible, temporary residential or foster care placement may provide a space where the child can go through the trauma-processing phase, after which the child can return home.

When this plan is made, the caregivers can explain to the child that they understand that the child is going to do difficult work, and that they will support the child. That they can manage some more anger or more nightmares if that would happen and want to make a plan on how to do that with the child. When the placement is not under pressure, but this is only the child's fear, the caregivers can explain to the child how they are going to manage his behaviour.

7.2.2 Metaphor of car in the water

When the caregiver struggles with this suggestion, or professionals insist on working with the caregiver on his behaviour the following metaphor can be used.

Have you ever seen a movie where a car gets into the water and sinks? The water level in the car rises. You try and get out of the car but your seatbelt is keeping you stuck. You are trying to breath but there is less and less air in the car, until your neck is stretched to the roof to try and breath the last bit of air. That is how life with your child is at the moment. You are trying to breath and struggling to survive. Rather than trying to improve your breathing techniques (caregiver changing his behaviour) we can lower the water level (compensation plan) first, so you have space and air to work on trauma treatment for your child.

7.2.3 Background information on problems at home

7.2.3.1 Eating problems

Traumatized children can develop eating problems such as anorexia, binge eating or bulimia. Overweight in adults is actually determined to be one of the long-term consequences of childhood trauma (Felitti et al., 1998). Eating problems may be a struggle in daily life, but they rarely present an actual obstruction to trauma processing. Only children with anorexia, who will not survive a possible temporary worsening of the anorexia or risk becoming severely injured, need to gain some kilos before they can start trauma processing.

Some eating tips may nevertheless come in handy. Traumatized children sometimes have trouble feeling the hunger signal, or the signal for being full, which causes them to eat too much or too little. When they have been neglected, flashbacks of being hungry can cause them to overeat. They risk being punished time and again for their 'disruptive' behaviour, whereas they do not understand themselves why they do it. When the eating problems are directly related to traumatic memories, there is not much point in trying to change it before the memories are processed. They then need to be limited in the quantities they eat.

Eating may be a way to regulate emotions. The child can view eating as a reward or punishment, and eating too little as a way to sedate himself. He may also eat as consolation, or as a compensation for loneliness. For those children, the emotion regulation interventions from Chapter 9 can improve their eating. Eating unhealthily or too much can also be an acquired habit. Van Mil and Struik (2017) describe a systemic multi-factorial approach to reduce overweight in children, which includes trauma treatment.

7.2.3.2 Lack of self-care

Traumatized children may be untidy and chaotic. In no time their room will look like it has exploded, just like their hair and their clothes. They forget appointments, their homework assignments, their therapy notebook and so on. Some children are unable to structure their life or focus their attention because of their chaotic inner world. The child may also feel undeserving of care, or he may not take care of himself because neglect is a familiar feeling. This may change by itself after trauma processing, and it is pointless to blame the child for his untidiness or lack of interest. On the contrary, he needs acknowledgement and explanations about the background of his behaviour, and help with organizing.

> Because you have been through a lot, there are still many open drawers in your filing cabinet. That is why it is not so tidy in your brain. This makes it hard for you to tidy up your room, for instance, and also to remember things. But it is nice for your brain when everything is tidy around you, it makes things calmer. That is why I will help you tidy up, we'll do it together.
>
> Because you think you are no good, you don't care what you look like. You don't enjoy taking care of yourself, because you don't love yourself. But in fact you are a beautiful person and someone who deserves to be loved, who deserves to be taken care of, even if you think that you are not. That is why I think you should wash properly, and put on clean clothes. This will help you to love yourself, and be proud of yourself again.

7.3 Barrier 2b: School

Having too many problems at school, or/and the child being afraid to get expelled from school, can form a barrier when the child is barely managing at school and refuses to talk about memories, because he does not have the headspace to also dig up old memories. Or the child does not want to talk about his memories because he is afraid he will get more difficult to handle and the school will be unable to manage that and he will get expelled, or the child needs to pass exams. The child may have been expelled several times and been given a last chance, and this can even be discussed with the child. They rather keep 'a lid on it' than risk this.

Children can struggle in school. When they are studying hard for an exam and they do not want to talk about their memories because they want to pass, they should be rewarded for doing so. Getting an education and going to school is a very important developmental task and, if the child manages to do that, that comes first. The sessions can, for example, be planned on Fridays or during school holidays, or after the exams. The Safe Deposit Box, or other interventions, can increase the child's control and ability to study.

School staff can struggle to manage the child's trauma symptoms. Traumatized children can have trouble dealing with authority: this may give them a feeling of impotence, which frightens them. Flashbacks may also be triggered by a loud voice, a facial expression, a word, a feeling of failure, of being dependent, of losing control. The child may then lose control over himself and become aggressive, or flee, or freeze up and become completely passive. Traumatized children often have trouble concentrating at school. They are exhausted, or they worry all the time, which prevents them from doing their schoolwork. If they fail to complete their assignments, children may have an overall sense of failure. They may feel that it does not matter whether they are there or not. They lose their feeling of self-worth and their thoughts may wonder off to bad memories of having the same feeling.

Their behaviour at school may cause so many problems that they risk being expelled. Trauma processing could reduce these symptoms in the long term, but initially they could also get worse. This could result in children being expelled from school. They will then think twice before continuing trauma processing. They need space for a temporary deterioration in their behaviour.

David (4)

David has trouble dealing with authority figures and he gets angry easily. When the teacher says 'David, get to work', this can be enough for him to start throwing chairs. The teacher understands his behaviour, but it frightens other children. He thinks David needs to be disciplined strictly to discourage this type of behaviour. He has even been suspended, because he kicked the teacher. David is afraid he will be expelled from school.

'Having to obey' the teacher is one of David's triggers. The feeling of impotence reminds him of traumatic experiences with his father, and this enrages him. Trauma processing could probably help David deal with his anger, but this would require him to dig up the old memories. He does not want that, because he is afraid it makes him more angry and irritated.

He would then risk being expelled and that would only add to his problems instead of making things better. Despite the problems, school would not have been a barrier, if David had not cared about being expelled. Then trying to improve David's school circumstances would not have been necessary. It would have been better to focus on the other identified barriers, instead of losing time and energy on school.

7.3.1 School support and compensation plan

Teachers may sympathize with these children and be reluctant to demand more of them. A teacher may suggest that the child comes to school for half days only. This would relieve the child, but it is not good for his stability. Children need the rhythm of schooldays and the distraction. They prefer to be normal and go to school like other children. This gives them a sense of self-worth. That is why it is important for their stability to go to school for full days, even if they do not learn very much.

Ideally the school would adopt a trauma-sensitive approach to these children. The psychoeducation interventions can be used to increase the school's understanding. When the child is present at this explanation, talking *with* the child instead of *about* the child can increase the mutual understanding. If the child feels seen and understood, this may just be enough to keep him within his Window of Tolerance.

With the Window of Tolerance child and teacher can make a plan on how to manage triggers and survival behaviour. They can agree on a sign for the teacher when he sees that the child is having a hard time. Teacher and child may determine together what the child can do when he is angry, such as taking a break, taking a walk, going to the toilet or working in the hall. The teacher can also help the child come out of a flashback. If the child is given some responsibility (such as watering the plants, copying, taking care of an animal or helping in toddler class), he may feel important. Adjustments can be made in the curriculum, or other ways can be found to help the child concentrate. The child may work with headphones on, or in a concentration cubicle, so he doesn't hear noises from the class. A place at the back of the class may be safer for a frightened child, so he will feel calmer. A place in front of the class near the teacher can also make the child feel protected.

Regrettably, in some cases it is impossible to make a plan for the child because the teacher or school won't cooperate. One alternative would be to move the trauma-processing phase to the school holidays.

7.4 Barrier 2c: Daily routine

Some children do not have a daily routine and the child or network are afraid the child does not have enough distraction because the child does not have a daily routine. They do not go to school, have no job or lie in bed all day and go out at night. Some sit behind the computer or play videogames all day. Obviously this is not good for a healthy development. However it does not have to form a barrier for trauma processing, unless the child or caregivers are worried the child will have too much time to think about all the bad memories and is not distracted enough. In that case a distraction plan with activities can be made around the trauma-processing session. The child does not have to return to school first or have a job to be able to engage in trauma processing.

7.4.1 Distraction plan

The distraction plan is constructed with the child and his caregivers. When the child has reduced school hours, the child can for example study at home, do puzzles or other challenging activities. They can engage in household chores, cooking, shopping with the caregivers, do volunteer work at the animal shelter, walk the neighbour's dogs, ride the bike every day. Activities should include contact with others, so the child does not feel so lonely. Days when there is no school may be very long for the child. It may help to also introduce routine items here, such as: on Saturday we do the shopping, on Wednesday we have macaroni for dinner, on Sunday I help with the cooking or we play a game of cards. On stressful days or when the child is having a hard time, it is wise to stick to the routine as much as possible.

Stress levels in the brain decrease when the world is predictable. Order, repetition and rhythm make the world predictable for traumatized children like this. The daily routine for these children should contain as much routine as possible. Before or after a therapy session, it is best that children keep their daily routine and go to school or music lessons as usual. Make a planning board describing the day's routine, if possible with illustrations or pictures. A diary or calendar may help the child to better remember the routine.

7.4.2 Physical exercise

Recent studies have shown that intensive physical activities can support trauma processing (Bongaerts, Van minnen, & De Jongh, 2017). Traumatized children may be physically exhausted by the constant stress they are under. They can feel tired and irritable, and be in bad physical shape. Sometimes these children may not look exhausted at all, and just rage on like a tornado, not to feel their exhaustion. They may feel negative and helpless, and have the idea that nothing will help.

By improving their physical condition and getting fit again, these children create chances to improve their mood as well. A mood cannot change from one moment to the next, but a physical state can change – for example, by standing up or running – and the physical change can then facilitate a change of mood. Moreover, strengthening the muscles and improving the condition is measurable. This gives a sense of control over the body. During exertion, the body produces endorphins, which produces a good feeling. That is why it is good for traumatized children to train their body.

It is important to make a structured plan with the right balance between rest and training, in which the training is built up slowly. Children may run more and more laps (running therapy), ride their bike, do inline skating or push-ups, and make a graph to indicate how much stronger they have become. Their muscles also need rest to recuperate. In moments of rest, children may lie on their bed, take a bath, listen to music, rub themselves with massage oil or body lotion, or lie in a hammock. Enough sleep and healthy nourishment are important as well. Doing these activities with others can help the child feel supported and connected.

7.5 Barrier 2d: Flashbacks and sleep

Flashbacks and sleeping problems only form a barrier when the child or network are afraid they are unable to handle an increase in flashbacks and/or sleeping problems. For example, when the child already has so many flashbacks and sleeping problems that it can barely function. Or the child's caregivers are exhausted, and they fear that talking about memories would cause more flash-backs and sleeping problems and they would not be able to handle that. They can fear not being able to take care of the other children, losing their job or failing at work. This was also the case for seven-year-old Eline.

Eline and her brothers were neglected and abused by their parents in every possible way. Eline was six years old when the child protection services removed all the children from their home. She was placed in a foster family with young children, including a baby. Eline only falls asleep when her foster mother sits with her and holds her hand. This may take an hour sometimes. During the night Eline has nightmares and wakes up screaming, which wakes up the baby who then starts crying as well. The foster parents often end up letting both Eline and the baby sleep in their bed, just to quiet things down. The father has a demanding job, and the fatigue is starting to take its toll. His superior has warned him that his work is falling behind. Eline's foster parents are desperate and referred her for trauma processing. Trauma processing should solve the sleeping problems quickly so Eline can stay with the family. However Eline refuses to talk about her memories. She notices the tension in them and is afraid her nightmares will get worse (2c) and they will send her away (2a).

For Eline, trauma processing might temporarily increase her fear and her nightmares, which jeopardizes her placement in the foster family. The foster parents would like to keep her, but just cannot take it anymore. Eline will avoid everything that might worsen her symptoms. Trauma processing is just too big a risk for her. There is too much pressure on her, when there should be as little pressure as possible for her to be able to process the trauma. Too much pressure reduces her Window of Tolerance. First Eline and her foster parents must learn to deal with the nightmares and make the situation manageable. This will stabilize the situation and create more space for Eline to start processing the trauma, without having to be afraid of temporarily increasing her nightmares.

Eline's foster parents made a sleep-management plan. They moved the baby to another room and bought earplugs and they took turns in staying up at night. When the foster father had an important meeting, the foster mother's sister would sleep over and help out. Every night Eline put her nightmares away in the Safe Deposit Box. She had a nightlight, mosquito net around her bed with Mega Mindy and Spiderman posters on the inside to protect her. The bed routine was the same every night. After that the foster mother would do ironing outside Eline's door, and peek around the door every five minutes until Eline fell asleep. She slept with her foster mother's T-shirt on and has a strong tasting lolly beside her bed to take when she would wake up. The foster parents explained to her the Volcano and told her that they could manage her sleeping problems now, but that these problems would get less if she would get rid of her bad memories. Eline agreed and processed her memories.

The child and caregivers may fear that processing traumatic memories increases the flashbacks and sleeping problems, where they actually reduce significantly in most cases. This can be explained with the Filing Cabinets.

7.6 Barrier 2e: Drugs and alcohol

Children may turn to drug or alcohol abuse as a form of self-medication, in an attempt to numb their emotions or reduce stress. They may also use drugs or alcohol as a form of self-harm. They feel so bad about themselves that they try to destroy their body or punish themselves. In the trauma-processing phase, these negative feelings may temporarily increase, and the drug and alcohol abuse may increase as well. Trauma processing will eventually diminish these strong emotions, and after their memories are resolved, many children can reduce their drug and alcohol abuse.

The child does not have to stop using, but their use of drugs and alcohol needs to be manageable. Drug or alcohol abuse only forms a barrier when the child or his network fear that the child cannot come to the sessions sober, and when they fear that that talking about memories would increase the child's need to numb bad feelings with alcohol or drugs and this would lead to an overdose, serious injuries or death. This could be the case for seventeen-year-old Tamara.

Tamara was abused between the ages of five and twelve by her grandfather. It happened when she was staying with granny and granddad. Granddad would take her to buy groceries and abuse her in his car. He would say to her: 'You're so beautiful, you're asking for it. You must want this yourself too, why else did you come along with me?' Tamara was so scared that she did not dare to disagree, or to tell her mother or grandmother about it. Tamara has gradually started to believe herself that she was asking for it. She has started to hate herself and her body, and she started to drink when she was thirteen. This has become worse and worse, and now she sometimes drinks an entire bottle of spirits. She has been hospitalized repeatedly for alcohol poisoning. Tamara's therapist was worried she would show up drunk or overdose after a session and possibly die.

Tamara would have to come sober to the sessions, which might be difficult for her. In the sessions Tamara will be confronted with her feelings of inferiority, her guilt and her sense of 'being bad'. She seems to run the risk of actually drinking herself to death or damaging her body. Children may have good reason for their alcohol or drug abuse and may even depend on it to keep them going. For them, it is not a question of 'simply quitting'. The first step is for therapists to acknowledge this. Subsequently a plan can be made to make the drug and alcohol use manageable.

Tamara said she was able to make it to the sessions sober unless they were planned after 1 p.m., when she usually started drinking or on Fridays because on Thursdays she would go out late. They agreed to schedule them on Tuesday mornings. She was a little bit worried that she might want to numb her bad feelings with too much alcohol, but thought of a plan. The next session her best friend came with her and they discussed how her best friend would pick her up after the sessions. They would go to the movies, where alcohol was not allowed, and Tamara would give her wallet to her friend so she could not buy any alcohol. Her friend would stay at her house and in the morning take her to school. Tamara processed her memories in four sessions and reduced her drinking significantly.

This example was used to illustrate only this barrier. The other barriers that Tamara also struggled with are not described.

When the child uses drugs and alcohol to regulate overwhelming negative feelings, the child's emotion regulation (4b) needs to be discussed. When the child cannot use his normal ways to deal with emotions, he may need additional skills. If the adolescent is not prepared to try to limit his alcohol and drug abuse, trauma processing cannot commence.

7.7 Interventions

The following paragraphs describe interventions that can be used to make the child's daily life more stable when a barrier is identified. Depending on the child's age, the caregivers have a more prominent part in these interventions. It is important to practise these interventions regularly to increase the positive effect. Because the brain learns new ways the best when practised in a pattern, it is best to practise these at the same time every day.

7.7.1 The Safe Deposit Box

This exercise is a standard exercise taught to nearly all children. With this exercise, the child imagines or makes a place to store away his traumatic memories, to increase the child's sense of control over flashbacks or nightmares. The child is asked to imagine something to put his bad memories in, such as a container, a hole in the ground, a cave, a rubbish bin or a safe deposit box. Or he can imagine that his memories are DVDs, which he can put in a cupboard, or files, which he puts in folders on his computer. The child can put all the bad pictures in his mind in there, and then make this into an imaginary store-away ritual. Greenwald (2005), Gomez (2013) and Waters (2016) describe similar exercises. The following text can be used.

> We are going to do an exercise to store away all the bad things in your head. Where would you want to put them so they cannot bug you anymore? Aha, that is a good idea. Can you draw that? Ok, now you can put all your bad memories in there. Have you got everything? Have a last good look. All those bad pictures from your head have to go into the safe deposit box. Then we lock the safe deposit box with a big padlock. Is that enough? Or does it need another lock? Then we add another chain, and another, and one more lock, number four … and then the biggest one of all, number ten. Now where shall we store the safe deposit box? On the moon, at the bottom of the sea or in my office? OK! You lower the safe deposit box to the bottom of the sea until it is hidden in the deep. Now all those bad pictures that were in your head are lying at the bottom of the sea and they cannot bug you anymore when you are in school or playing. And they have to stay there until you take them out, because only you have the key. If you have any new bad pictures in your head this week, you can also store them with the rest. This exercise works best when you practise it every day before you go to sleep or before you go to school. The more you practise the better it works.

The child can make a drawing of their Safe Deposit Box (see worksheet 'Daily Life 1 – The Safe Deposit Box'), construct a more concrete Safe Deposit Box with wood or matchboxes, or they can buy an actual safe with a real key. The concrete version normally works better. When the child worries that it is not accessible from a distance, it can be explained that they can use magic to put their memories in there from a distance. The child does not have to discuss what is in the Safe Deposit Box, just put it in there. When it would be discussed, the child's memories would get activated without being able to process them. That can potentially be traumatizing again. The child then has to practise this exercise daily.

Some children say they do not have any bad memories. They still need to learn the exercise because when we are waking up sleeping dogs, the bad memories might appear. When they do, they already know how to handle them. This exercise can also be used for daily life things that are not in the past, such as difficult things from school, or bad feelings, a dead hamster, an annoying therapist. Just be mindful that these daily life things cannot be resolved by trauma-processing therapy.

When children complain this exercise does not work, they can be reminded that they are right. This is only a temporarily solution to make it manageable. Trauma processing will cure the problem for good. The Filing Cabinets explanation can be repeated to explain that the brain keeps having flashbacks until the wise lesson is learned.

7.7.2 Prevent triggering

The child and caregivers need to learn to recognize triggers and avoid them if possible. Triggers can be things such as knives, blood, hospitals, yoghurt (because it looks like semen) or alcohol, actions such as a loud voice, hard noise, sudden movement, touch, situations such as the dark, showering, going to bed. Feelings can also trigger the child, such as authority, or loss of control. Together with the child a list can be made of triggers that take him outside his Window of Tolerance (see worksheet 'Daily Life 3 – Within My Window').

> Tim's mother decided not to drink any more alcohol when Tim was around. Alcohol was a major trigger for him, and in this way she avoided a situation in which he could panic. She decided not to drink alcohol until the trauma-processing phase was over.

Certain foods (colour, consistency, smell, feeling when swallowing) may trigger a flashback of traumatic experiences in the child (e.g. of oral sex, semen). This was the case for Gerard.

> Eight-year-old Gerard has been living with a foster family. The foster mother had prepared a meal with mushrooms and Gerard had a severe panic attack when she told him he definitely had to eat them. He absolutely refused. Fortunately the foster parent stayed calm and tried to find out why Gerard felt such a revulsion against eating mushrooms, instead of

forcing him to eat them. She told him that he had eaten mushrooms the week before and that he hadn't protested then. Together they tried to find out why. The mushrooms of the week before had been sliced and so they looked different. That turned out to be the problem. When he still lived with his mother, she had once forced him to eat his own vomit, and it had looked exactly like the dish with mushrooms. This had turned mushrooms into a trigger for him.

For Gerard it is important that his foster mother avoids preparing whole mushrooms again. The child can gradually be exposed to triggers again in the trauma-processing phase. After trauma processing, the problem will in most cases disappear (partially). Sometimes the child will have to get used to the particular food again.

However some triggers cannot be avoided. Children need to shower, they have to listen to their teacher and they cannot always be in control. For those situations a plan can be made on how to manage the triggering. If the child is able to recognize the situation and the adult in the vicinity is too, it may be easier to stay within the Window of Tolerance. The adult may say: 'Right, this is something, which upsets you. I can see that you are almost outside your window.'

Suzan was triggered by 'having to do certain household tasks' and every day there would be fights about her not putting her plate in the dishwasher, her dirty clothes piled up in her room etc. The residential staff used the Volcano to discuss with Suzan whether her 'allergy' for doing chores could be related to the past. They asked her whether the powerless feeling caused her volcano to erupt, because it triggered her memories of her mother calling her a house slave and controlling her. Suzan recognised this and together they came up with a plan. Whenever the residential staff would ask her to do a certain task, they would put on a silly apron and approach Suzan. Only the sight of the apron already made her laugh and relax and she knew what was coming. Then they would say: 'Suzan, I need to ask you something difficult. Can you remember you are seventeen and you live her with us now? Ok? Yes? Ok, can you please clean up your dirty clothes while I make a cup of tea for us?'

This creative solution reduced Suzan's outbursts significantly. She could still get angry on occasions, but she calmed down easier. She now has language to discuss what was going on inside her. The plan they made together made Suzan feel competent and connected.

Showering triggered Jody and she had not washed herself for months. Jody suggested putting her favourite music on loudly while she was in the shower. The music had recently come out and reminded her of the present. She bought shampoo with a strong nice scent and a nice towel, which reminded her of her independence. When she was really triggered, she showered in her bikini. She gradually overcame her fear.

7.7.3 Within My Window

Besides avoiding triggers, the child also needs to learn to calm himself when he has been triggered. With this exercise a plan is made on how the child can get back into his Window of Tolerance (see worksheet 'Daily Life 3 – Within My Window'). The Window of Tolerance explanation can also be combined with techniques that such as the Thermometer, the Traffic Light, or integrated into a crisis intervention plan, or a de-escalation plan.

7.7.4 The Back of the Head Scale

When children have a flashback or nightmare, they can dissociate or even switch to another part of the personality. The child can learn Jim Knipe's Back of the Head Scale (Knipe, 2018) to learn to communicate about their inner world, which is important because connection to others is the antidote for dissociation. The child indicates with his finger, where on an imaginary line running from 30 centimetres in front of their head to the back of their head, he feels he presently is. The back of the head is completely dissociated and 30 centimetres in front of the head is completely present, or somewhere in between. The Here and Now exercise can bring the child further back to the present.

7.7.5 The Here and Now

The child needs to learn to orient himself out of dissociation to the here and now. Depending on the child's age, the caregivers have a more prominent part in this plan. The Here and Now exercise is an exercise to bring the child back to the present. It can be combined with the Back of the Head Scale. By making the plan and practising this daily, the child gets more control over his flashbacks and nightmares. There are several things that can bring a child back to the here and now. When making this plan, the child and caregiver can experiment with different things to develop a plan that works best.

When the child is outside his Window of Tolerance, the human brain is temporarily shut down, and the child operates from his mammalian or reptilian brain. To take a child out of a state of dissociation or conversion, the human brain has to be re-activated. This can be achieved by making children do something for which they need to think (Wesselmann, 2007). Parents say to their children: 'count to ten' first, because counting activates the human brain. The caregiver can, for instance, ask the child to count back from ten to zero, or to do sums. He can change the subject, ask the child for his birthdate or do a puzzle together.

Another way to change the child's focus from inside to outside, is by scanning the environment. The child is asked to name three blue objects, or how many power points or lights are in the room. With young children this can be a game without them being aware of the purpose of this. They can be asked to look outside and count the trees, watch the sun and the clouds or a nice bird.

Differentiating the past from the present makes clear that what the child experiences is not happening now. The child can be instructed to try to think of things, which 'prove' that he is in the present and not in the past: things the child can see now, that weren't there in the past. For instance, a calendar with the current year on it, a poster which the child bought recently, a recent photo, a nice new sweater. If a child is disoriented or is having a flashback, the child can be instructed look around the room and name what he sees. For instance, the therapist can say: 'You are here with me in the room. It is Monday, a quarter to three and it is raining. Look at me, who am I, where are we? It is safe now, you are safe, it's over.' It may also help to point out to the child that he is not so small anymore as he feels in his flashback or nightmare.

A soft and calm surrounding diminishes the feeling of being threatened. Speaking in a low voice makes the child listen attentively, or ask to repeat what was said. Soothing words, a big smile, humming, singing and distraction ('look, a beautiful bird') can also help the brain to calm down. Slowing down movements and announcing movements: 'I'm now going to get up and walk to the window.'

Strong sensory stimuli shift focus from inside to the body. The child can hold a cold washcloth to his face, squeeze his toe very hard, smell a scented candle, or eat a sweet with a strong flavour, or a lemon, ice cream, ice cubes, a warm shower touching the child or speaking loudly. Strong smells have the fastest access to the brain

Using the body by clapping hands, stamping feet, star jumps or running can bring the child back to the here and now, as well as activating the reflexes. Throwing a ball, pillow, tissue rolled up to a ball unexpectedly, makes the child catch it, and this will 'bring round' the child.

7.7.6 Sleep management plan

Traumatized children may have sleeping problems, such as not wanting to go to bed or getting out of bed, wanting to sleep in their parents' room or bed, waking up too early or often. They may be afraid of being alone and are often scared of being abandoned. They have experienced insufficient safety in their life to be able to depend on not being abandoned. They constantly get out of bed, asking the caregiver to reassure them. The child should learn to reassure himself, so that he will become less dependent on others and more self-confident. The lack of a sense of safety makes this difficult. Children may be frightened of the transition from waking to sleeping, because they have to release control over their body. Falling asleep may feel like dissociating. Relaxing may feel like falling, and this may be frightening.

Traumatized children may wet their beds. This can be related to general stress or it can be a symptom of sexual abuse and they can have difficulty feeling bodily sensations in their genitals. When there is no physical cause for the bed-wetting, it is better not to address this before trauma processing. The bed-wetting may temporarily increase during this phase, but most of the time the problem disappears after trauma processing. Children can feel embarrassed about it and explaining the potential relationship between traumatic memories and bed-wetting may increase their motivation and release the pressure from caregivers.

The following elements can be included in the sleep management plan.

7.7.6.1 The bedroom

All possible triggers should be removed from the room. A nightlight can be bought, a nice poster or photos can remind the child of the present time. Sometimes a suggestive idea may help, such as a 'dreamcatcher'. A dreamcatcher is a kind of small net used by Indians to catch bad dreams. It can be hung next to the bed and bad dreams get caught in it. In this way, dreams cannot reach the sleeping child. A mosquito net around the child's bed can make children feel protected. On the inside, they can put photos of their protectors or heroes. The weight of heavy blankets can make children feel safer. A notebook in which the child can draw or write down his nightmares also helps to gain control over them.

7.7.6.2 Transitional object

An object symbolizing the attachment figure for the child, such as a cuddly toy, a picture or a nightshirt, which belongs to this person and holds his or her smell can be found. The child can be taught to talk to this object when he feels scared and to find support and reassurance in it. If the child knows the object is important to the attachment figure, this may also give a secure feeling, because the child knows he will want to have it back, and therefore will come to see the child again.

7.7.6.3 Bed routine

Learnt behaviour may also play a part. Because the parents feel sorry for the child or have trouble leaving him alone, they may unconsciously reinforce the child's behaviour. The child experiences insufficient authority and will continue to get out of bed. A fixed and calm routine of undressing, washing, laying out clothes for the next day, reading (from the same book) and a relaxing piece of music or song (the same one each time), together with a regular bedtime will help these children.

7.7.6.4 Boundaries

To help children to learn to reassure themselves, it is important that they stay in their room. A rule can be established that the child is only allowed get out of bed once to use the toilet. If possible the bedroom door should be (nearly) closed, so the child does not stay focused on the sounds from outside. The child will be anxious at first, but eventually will become more self-confident when he manages to sleep alone. When the child does get out of bed, he should be taken by the hand and brought back directly, without making eye contact or talking. Caregivers should be directive and repeat this any number of times if necessary.

7.7.7 Relaxation exercises

Traumatized children are often disconnected from their body, and are constantly tense from being alert. Relaxation exercises may help them to loosen their muscles. This may be frightening because they have to let go of their survival strategy. Children with a dissociative disorder sometimes have no feeling in their body parts, because the feeling has been dissociated to other parts. Starting in a playful manner, children may first practise tightening their muscles and relaxing them alternately, and do breathing exercises. This will allow them later to surrender to relaxation. In the CBT (cognitive behavioural therapy) programme 'Friends for life', Barrett, Turner and Webster-Lowry (2001) describe some very good relaxation exercises that can be used for children.

7.7.8 The Safe Place

The exercise 'the Safe Place' can also be used to help children to relax. The origin of this exercise is difficult to trace. Shapiro (2006) described it in an EMDR protocol, but it was part of psychodynamic imaginative psychotherapy and trauma therapy long before that. It was probably also described by others. Boon, Steele and Van der Hart (2010) describe the Safe Place exercise elaborately in their skills training for adults with a dissociative disorder (pp. 84–86), Gomez (2013) for children in preparation of EMDR therapy and Waters (2016) for children with dissociation.

The child is asked to choose a place where they feel good and completely safe and to imagine they are there. They are asked to describe what they see, hear, smell, feel and think. Next they are instructed to imagine they feel good and completely safe. Then they draw the safe place on worksheet 'Daily Life 2 – The Safe Place'.

For severely traumatized children, using an imaginary private island may be a better option than asking them to choose a real place. These children never feel really safe in daily life. They have trouble describing a real safe place. The idea is to create an island for them full of positive sensations and associations and to ask them to expand on that (which often works because these children are so susceptible to suggestion). They can fly to their imaginary island and they can decide who is allowed there and who isn't. The description of the island should include elements and sensations, which are the opposite of what children usually remember from traumatic experiences (cold, thirst, lonely). There can be animals, a safe person, a feeling of being strong together, feeling good/safe, feeling free, having control, feeling warm (children are often punished with cold), having good food, a full stomach (children have often been malnourished), a good smell (as opposed to the bad smell of semen, alcohol, sweat), being allowed to drink (as opposed to the thirst one gets from stress). Children with a dissociative disorder have parts that feel very frightened and/or alone. They can be assured that all the parts are allowed to go to the island. The following text can be used:

> Now we are going to do an exercise, which will make you feel good. Imagine, Inge, that you can fly. You go up in the air, above the trees, to the clouds, ever higher and higher. And you leave your backpack with bad things behind on the ground. The sun is shining and it is nice and warm and you fly on and on. You fly over the sea and then you see an island. It is your island. On that island there are beautiful trees and there are lots of good things to eat and drink, as much as you want. Your stomach is full and you are not thirsty anymore. It is nice and warm and you feel the sun on your skin. You smell lovely flowers and you hear the sea and the waves. This is your island and nobody is allowed to come there, only when you say so. You feel completely safe there. And scared Inge, who feels very small, feels safe. And the Inge who was so sad when she was five years old, does not have to be sad anymore because it is over. You don't have to be afraid anymore, because it can never happen again. You are not one year old, and not three years old, but seven years old. And foster mum will make sure that it never happens again.

A recording can be made of the text, spoken by the caregiver or other person that will give the child a safe feeling. The child can then practise at home with headphones on. At first the child should only try this when he feels relaxed and not frightened. After practising for a week or so, the child may proceed to play the recording at night, when he is actually scared.

Chapter 8

Interventions to overcome barrier 3

Attachment

The child needs support when he gets scared or the memories are too painful: supporters who encourage him to see it through, who tell him that he must listen carefully to the coach, that the coach is teaching him useful techniques. He also has to stay in contact with the coach during the fight and to act on his instructions. This chapter first describes how to overcome the barriers so the child feels enough emotional support *to process his memories*. Minimal work is done, only to overcome the barriers. The attachment figure does not have to be emotionally supportive in daily life and the child does not have to have a safe attachment. Background information on intergenerational traumatization, traumatized parents and interventions to improve trauma-sensitive parenting in daily life is described. This information can be useful to understand how to overcome the barriers.

8.1 Use the interventions to improve the child's development

When attachment is not identified as a barrier, this means it is not imperative to work on these issues before trauma processing. All chronically traumatized children have difficulties in their attachment relationships but in most cases it is not necessary to address these first, unless attachment forms a barrier to trauma processing. Many chronically traumatized children also have chronically traumatized parents. Some live with their parents, some live in foster or residential care. Working with traumatized parents can complicate the child's treatment or child protection services' decisions. The Sleeping Dogs method tries to shorten treatment for these children, because trauma processing relieves symptoms. Sometimes children cannot start trauma processing because of, for example, waiting lists, lack of permission, other barriers that need to be removed first. The interventions in this chapter can be used by, for example, residential staff or foster parents to improve the child's attachment relationships. In the integration phase the described interventions can be used to further improve the attachment relationships and the child and parent's functioning.

8.2 Barrier 3a: Attachment figure no calm brain

When the child is afraid that the child's attachment figure cannot keep a calm brain because of the traumatic memories, this can form a barrier. The child fears that the attachment figure will become triggered and upset when he would talk about his memories, and he does not have enough emotional support. He takes care of his parent by not talking about his memories

To overcome this barrier, the child's attachment figure has to remain calm when the child wants to discuss traumatic memories. Strictly speaking, the attachment figure does *not* have to remain calm in daily life when managing the child's behaviour to overcome this barrier. The barrier is about dealing with the past, not the present. Obviously the child does need a calm adult in daily life as well, in order to grow up healthy and safe. In the integration phase this can be worked on.

8.2.1 Improve the parent's self-regulation

The interventions from Chapter 7 Daily Life can also be used to improve the parent's self-regulation. The Safe Deposit Box, Safe Place, Here and Now, managing triggers, getting inside the Window of Tolerance, and relaxation exercises can be explained to the child, in the parent's presence. The parent can be encouraged to use the exercise as well to make the child feel more connected to the parent and motivate the child.

8.2.2 Compensation plan to keep a calm brain

Parents can be very reluctant to allow their child to talk about trauma. They can struggle so much in daily life and worry about the child starting to ask questions about the past, or telling them about their memories. When the child starts to process his trauma, he may afterwards want to talk about his experiences, about new memories that have surfaced or details of the trauma, which were not discussed before. This can be difficult for the attachment figure to hear. Children may sense this and consequently spare the attachment figure.

These are legitimate worries and the first step is to acknowledge that and explain to the parent that he is not going to be pressured into doing it anyway. The child will not want to risk his parent falling apart. By providing the parent with psychoeducation, most parents shift to a position where they want to support their child, but they do not know how.

The next step is to go through all the possible problems that could arise and make a plan to deal with these situations and discuss this plan with the child. By involving the child, the child can gradually become more confident that his parent can deal with it. The parent can for example buy a notebook for the child's questions. They can agree to write down the child's questions so the parent can think about the answer carefully. The parent can discuss the answers with a professional or child and parent can discuss the questions in a session. When a parent is very fearful of these questions, answers to the five worst questions can be already prepared. When the parent is really struggling, they can agree that the questions will be discussed in three years' time. Knowing what to do or say can reduce the fear of these situations significantly. The following example illustrates how the parent does not have to have a calm brain in daily life to overcome this barrier.

Sixteen-year-old Ellen was sexually abused by a maternal uncle when she was fourteen. She had severe posttraumatic stress, but refused to discuss her memories. When her barriers were analysed, the child protection worker said Ellen's father was very violent. He was ex-military and working as a kickboxing trainer. With his biker friends he got into bar fights regularly and occasionally he spent a night in jail. He loved Ellen dearly and would never harm her and he was very upset by her being sexually abused. The child protection worker said he had become violent whenever his daughter's trauma was discussed. She was afraid of him and said he did not have a short fuse, but no fuse at all. Ellen may be protecting her father by not wanting to discuss her trauma (3a).

Ellen's parents were invited and the dilemma of needing to make a plan and not wanting the father to get violent was discussed. He suggested that when he would get angry, he would smoke a cigarette to calm down, and return to the meeting. The possible barrier for Ellen was discussed with

Ellen's parents and her father got very upset but was persistent to find a solutions. After smoking nine cigarettes they had drafted a plan. Ellen would go to therapy with her mother. After the sessions, they would go for a walk so Ellen could talk to her mother. When they would come home, Ellen's father would then take her to his studio to do some kickboxing and let Ellen release her anger. He said he really wanted to help her, but Ellen could not discuss the trauma or therapy with her father. The next session this plan was discussed in further detail and the parents presented the plan to Ellen. Ellen's father smoked four cigarettes. Ellen liked the plan and was impressed with her father's effort to help her. She then agreed to process trauma and participated in EMDR therapy.

Ellen's father did not have a calm brain at all, but with this plan her parents managed her father's feelings so Ellen could stop taking care of him. When a compensation plan is still not enough for the child, the child needs another support person.

8.3 Barrier 3b: No support person

When the parent cannot manage to discuss the memories with the child at all, the child may need someone else to talk to. When the child does not want to talk because he does not have that person or is not sure it is OK to talk to this person, this forms a barrier. In cooperation with the attachment figure, a support person who is close to the child, like a grandmother or an aunt, needs to be found to temporarily take over this role. For children in out of home care, foster parents or residential staff can be this support person. This person can for example meet the child regularly, or take the child to therapy sessions and stay for the rest of the day with the family. It is then agreed that the child will not discuss his memories with the parent. This is definitely not ideal, but the child would be alone anyway, with or without these memories. The parent needs to discuss this plan with the child or ask the therapist to explain it, so the child knows that the parent gives him permission to discuss his memories with someone else.

8.4 Barrier 3c: attachment system not activated

Even when the child has an attachment figure with a calm brain, some children can still not use the attachment figure to regulate themselves. This forms a barrier when the network, or child himself, fears that the child will dissociate or run away during the trauma-processing sessions. The caregivers or previous therapists are asked for their views and whether they think the child will stay in contact or not. However, even when they believe this forms a barrier, this should be checked in a session with the child.

The child's attachment system refers to the child's internal action system of attachment. For most children this does not form a barrier, even when they dissociate frequently in daily life, or have run out of therapy sessions. Children can feel very ashamed of their behaviour and they can run off or dissociate when their symptoms are discussed. It is more difficult to tolerate discussing their behaviour, which is their own responsibility and makes them ashamed. When it is unclear to them what the purpose of therapy is, like with non-directive therapies or an assessment, they can try to avoid discussing their traumatic memories by dissociating, running off or becoming opposi-tional. However, once the purpose is clearly explained and they have a prin-cess, they have an attachment figure who supports them and stays calm, they have permission to talk about their memories and, most of them are able to stay in contact.

When this is identified as a barrier, for example for children with a dissoci-ative disorder or conversion, who do not remember their trauma, the child needs to overcome his anxiety. His attachment system needs to become activated just enough to get through the trauma-processing sessions while staying in contact with the therapist when he is stressed and seek support and comfort instead of dissociating, blocking or running out of the session.

Working on improving attachment relationships is time consuming and it is important to consider if it leads to unnecessary delays in trauma processing. The following paragraphs describe some brief interventions to activate the attach-ment system. When extended work on attachment is needed, methods such as Interaction Guidance with the use of video, Circle of Security (Cooper, Hoffman, Powell, & Marvin, 2007), Sherborne Developmental Movement (Sherborne, 2001), Dyadic Developmental Psychotherapy (Hughes & Baylin, 2012) or Theraplay (Booth & Jernberg, 2010) can be used.

8.5 Interventions to activate the attachment system

Activating the child's attachment system is therapeutic work with the child and an attachment figure. This does not have to be the child's main attachment figure, but the child must be certain that this relationship is continued. These exercises are done in a therapy setting, after which the attachment figure can practise them at home. The therapeutic contribution of the attachment figure can vary from minimal, in which case it is mainly the therapist who works with the child, to a maximum contribution, when it is mainly the attachment figure who works with the child, while the therapist only keeps the process on track. The attachment figure can play a more significant role if traumatization took place outside the present family and if the attachment figure has not been traumatized himself. A therapist or residential worker should not do these exercises with the child.

8.5.1 With younger children

The attachment system is sensitive to sensory and non-verbal stimuli, such as eye contact, cuddling, touching and stroking, mimicking the interaction between a mother and her baby by using a gentle voice, whispering, slow movements, rocking and facial expressions. A rocking chair or a hammock, in which the attachment figure can lie with the child, provides a nurtured feeling; just lying comfortably and rocking to and fro, or (with a little more distance) reading aloud, playing music or singing nursery songs. Make sure that the child is nice and warm and has had something to drink. Thirst that has just been quenched is the opposite feeling to the dry mouth that usually accompanies fear. Sucking on a lollypop or drinking from a nursing bottle also gives the sensation of being cherished. Rituals calm the brain such as reading the same story or playing the same game over and over.

Another calming exercise is listening to the heartbeat of the attachment figure. A baby calms down when it feels and hears its mother's quiet heartbeat. Its heartbeat is synchronized with that of its mother. The child can listen to the heartbeat, with a stethoscope or just putting his ear to the attachment figure's chest.

These exercises can be very scary for the child at first and they may therefore avoid physical contact. A child must never be forced. They can participate in other forms of contact, such as writing a letter on the child's back, combing his hair, rubbing hands, feet or the whole body with body lotion, giving a massage, horse play and tickling. If that is still too scary, the child can begin by touching himself and getting used to that. The attachment figure can feel and massage his own hands, feet, arms or legs, together with the child. If the child is still too scared for all this, looking after a doll together provides safety and more distance. When the child sees the adult in interaction with the doll, he may start to feel a little of that loving care himself. The attachment figure can then affirm that the doll deserves this loving care and that the child should have been given such care too. That the child had a right to it and it is all right to catch up on this.

8.5.2 Baby and toddler games

Another way for attachment figures to stimulate the child is to pretend that the child is younger. In baby games the attachment figures emphasize the fact that it is all 'make-believe', it is a game. By playing such games the child can catch up on the care he missed. The 'make-believe' age of the child in the game depends on the age at which the child stagnated. The attachment figure can have the child pretend that he is a baby: give the child a bottle to nurse from and treat him like a baby, rocking, carrying, washing, dressing him and so on. This is followed up by toddler games: reading to him, doing things together or using this game as an excuse to play what would, ordinarily speaking, be childish games, For example, games such as feeding the child, peeling an apple and giving him some pieces to eat.

Some children can be almost limitless in this game and want to go on being a baby all day. That does not contribute to a safe attachment relationship, but would promote regression. Safe attachment can grow out of a combination of love and limits. The attachment figure needs to give the child clear boundaries on when this game is played and for how long. A fixed time and duration can support the child to grow from these games, instead of regress. When the child is playing the game, the child can behave as a younger child. At other times the child can be expected to behave age appropriately. Generally the child's desire to be treated as a younger child will get less over time, as the child moves on to the next stage in his development. This exercise is not suitable for adolescents, since these games evoke too much regression.

8.5.3 With adolescents

Stimulating attachment in adolescents is more complicated because they (have to) focus more on contact with their peer group than on contact with attachment figures. Just as in children, the adolescent's reptilian brain is sensitive to sensory stimuli. The attachment figure can still make contact by doing things such as combing the child's hair, hugging him, sitting close to him or giving a backrub, doing the child's make-up or nails, using face paint. The attachment figure can speak in a low voice and try to make eye contact.

Sharing activities has a stimulating effect on adolescents. Activities can include helping with homework, shopping together, walking the dog or a mother-and-daughter outing. If adolescents say they don't feel like doing these things, attachment figures can exert some pressure in a light-hearted way. The attachment figure can explain that he likes spending time together and what he likes about it. Rituals can also strengthen the feeling of togetherness – for example, we always wash the car together on Saturdays. Adolescents are very good at breaking rules. It is important to set the rules even if the child does not obey them. For the child the fact that attachment figures set limits is, subconsciously, a sign that they actually care for him.

In conversations, the attachment figure can ask the child for his opinion, or how he feels about things, and if the child does not want to talk, the attachment figure can tell him about his own experiences – not only his own success stories but his experience of failure or embarrassment as well. The attachment figure can tell the child how proud he is of the child, how he sees the future and/or what he is afraid of. The attachment figure can talk about the adolescent's childhood and look at baby photo books, emphasizing how happy he is to have this child.

8.5.4 Eye contact

It is also important to make eye contact, but this too can be very scary for these children. The brain is programmed to be wary of eye contact in dangerous situations. In the animal world making eye contact with a predator can provoke an attack. So obviously this should be avoided when danger threatens. Caregivers or residential staff can do this intervention. Caregivers can play peek-a-boo games with these children: who can look the other person in the eyes longest without blinking, or games involving signalling with one's eyes. When the child can maintain extended eye contact, the caregiver can look the child in the eye and say 'I would love to be your (foster) mother or (foster) father and to look after you and protect you.' The best thing would be if the child could maintain extended eye contact.

8.5.5 Naming the child's actions

Another exercise consists of observing and describing the child's behaviour. Caregivers or residential staff can do this intervention. Mirroring the behaviour of the child, what he does, makes the child feel that he has been noticed, and makes him aware of himself and his body. The caregiver describes what the child is doing, without any interpretation, just the actual actions.

> I see that you are picking up your marker pens. You look at them one by one. You stop at the red marker pen. You take the red marker pen with your right hand and take off the cap. You put the cap on the table. You put the red marker to the paper, your tongue is sticking out of your mouth. You colour Father Christmas's hat red with the marker pen. You are sitting very still on your chair and not saying anything.

This is a good exercise for caregivers to learn to look at the child without interpretation or judgement. This can help the child to realize what he is doing and it can contribute to the child's feeling of being seen. For the child, noticing that by his behaviour he can make his caregivers say things, that he can direct them, brings a sensation of being cherished.

If this exercise works, the child will start to enjoy directing the caregiver, and this can be the start of interaction with the caregivers. Stimulating activities and activities in which the child directs the caregiver encourage the production of endorphins (which make us feel good) in the child's brain (Wieland, 2007), so these are good activities to practise. It is important that the child is explicitly the leader, with the caregiver following. The caregiver follows the instructions of the child (within limits of course), or asks for instructions, so that the child can feel that he has influence on the caregiver.

8.6 Life-story work

8.6.1 Relay stick of attachment

Attachment can be seen as a relay race with attachment figures passing the 'stick' of attachment to each other. When the child is born, the child attaches to

Figure 8.2

his biological father and mother. When the child moves to a foster family, the relay stick of attachment is passed on to this foster family and the child attaches to them. When the child moves again, the relay stick is passed on again and so on, until the traumatic memories of abandonment are so painful, that the child gives up and drops the relay stick. The child can be moved again, and superficially attach to the new caregivers, but he has given up trying to form deep attachment relationships. Those children stay attached and loyal to caregivers from the past.

When a child has been placed in a foster family, it seems logical that the foster parents eventually should become the main attachment figures. However conflicting loyalties in the child, conflict between parents and foster parents, and uncertainty about reunification can discourage a child from forming an attachment relationship with the foster parents. For those children their biological parents still are their main attachment figures. When the foster placement is permanent, it is important that the foster parents also become attachment figures. Otherwise the child does not have enough emotional support in daily life, which can unintentionally lead to emotional neglect. These children grow up alone because they do not have the attachment figure with them to regulate stress for them and to comfort them when they are stressed. They do not form an attachment relationship with their daily caregivers and they do not see their parents enough.

Not having or breaking off contact with biological parents can make it extra difficult for a child to form an attachment relationship with the current care-givers. There is a serious risk that the child will fail to integrate the first part of his life and dissociates or denies it. At first sight the child may then seem to be functioning well, but the attachment relationship cannot deepen. When the relay stick of attachment is still with the biological parents, working with the biological parents can bring the stick back to the present caregivers. Specifi-cally in the case of foster children with serious behavioural problems involv-ing the biological parents in the interventions for this barrier is well worth the effort.

Children can only become attached to new attachment figures when attach-ment relationships and experiences can be integrated into their life now. New foster parents must actively help the child to go back to where the stick was left or fell down, integrate those experiences with the child and then continue the race. Many foster or adoptive parents make the mistake of only looking to the future. Then the child will not really become attached to them. They can be afraid that contact with former foster parents or biological parents jeopardizes their relationship with the child. The outcome however is the contrary. By sup-porting the child in doing this, their relationship normally improves, on the con-dition that the child also processes his traumatic memories. The child needs to work through the past pain and happiness with them. Having no contact with biological parents complicates this process. It may seem to be in the best interest of the child because those contact visits are really disturbing, but it makes it more difficult for the child to deepen the attachment relationship with his foster or adoptive parents. Tom's example illustrates that.

Six-year-old Tom has been placed in two foster families in the past year. They were temporary placements, because he would possibly return to his mother, whom he saw once every two weeks. When it became clear at the end of this year that Tom was not going to return to his mother, a family was found where he could stay permanently. During the preliminary phase of establishing contact, Tom stayed in a residential unit awaiting place-ment. At this stage he had said goodbye to his second foster family, to which he had become attached, while the attachment to the new family had not yet developed. It was still uncertain whether this placement would be definitive, which depended on the matching.

In this phase it was believed that Tom should see his biological mother less often, so as not to hinder attachment to the new family. But this deci-sion failed to take account of what this meant to Tom, who now had to emotionally distance himself from his previous foster family and his mother, without having the safety of a new attachment figure. A seven-year-old without a 'hand that feeds' will panic. What Tom needed was in fact a more intensive contact with his mother to be able to let go of the old foster family and bridge the transition to a new attachment. Tom became depressed and was often in an angry mood. He became homesick for his previous family and begged his mother for more intensive contact.

Instead of understanding Tom's distress coming from thirst (he needed love), the staff believed Tom was not detached enough from his foster family and he had not yet distanced himself enough from his mother. But how could he, since there was no replacement?

The preliminary contact phase with the new family ended in failure after six weeks because Tom exhibited strongly defiant behaviour; the foster placement was aborted. It was concluded that he had not been able to detach himself from his former foster family and that had prevented him from forming a new attachment relationship. A new family was looked for, but in the meantime Tom had to live in a residential facility where he could stay for a longer period. There it was decided that he first needed a cooling down period without any contact with this mother, just when his mother was the one he needed most to regulate all these rejections and the lack of safety.

Of course the development of attachment relationships is way more complicated than this simplified metaphor and much is still unknown. However, by using this metaphor, the importance of involving biological parents and contacting former caregivers can be explained to the child's current caregivers, foster care organizations and child protection organizations.

8.6.2 Bringing the relay stick back

To improve the current attachment relationships of those children and lower their anxiety, the relay stick needs to be located and brought to the current family. By providing the child with a narrative and explanation of why the former relationships have ended, the child can understand that this was not his fault and he is lovable. With information about why he was removed from his parents and why former placements have ended the child can also estimate chances of the current caregivers ending the placement. For example: 'Mum and dad did not want me to leave, I had to leave because this was a temporary placement and because this is a permanent placement I will most likely stay.' Then the child can integrate those experiences and learn wise lessons.

8.6.3 Life-story book

Children who have been traumatized in early childhood very often have no overview of the events in their lives. Their memories are fragmented and chaotic. They do not feel in control and they cannot anticipate anything, because they do not understand what has happened in the past and why. That means that at any moment something bad can happen. Besides, some children have been in so many foster families and homes that nobody really knows what actually happened. For children it is of great importance to know their own life history.

Making a life-story book with or for the child can help the child to get a grip on his life. It is important to indicate in the book who the present attachment figure is and with whom the child belongs – for example, with photographs of the child and his family/the important people. The child can be asked to add drawings of the people he loves and belongs with now. Besides making a life-story book, the child could visit all his former placements, schools and houses, with the current caregiver and interview his caregivers, or search on Google maps. Golding and Hughes (2012) do fantastic life-story work with traumatized children.

In a foster care organization in the Netherlands, all children entering care receive a suitcase with a stuffed animal, a life-story book and a camera to be able to take photos at their next placement and insert these.

8.6.4 Results of activating the attachment system

When the attachment system is activated, the child may start to behave like a younger child and become more affectionate, and the child appears to go back in time (regression). That is a good sign of the attachment process picking up where it stranded. The child usually catches up rapidly.

8.7 Background information on attachment

8.7.1 Intergenerational trauma

Chronically traumatized children often grow up in families suffering from intergenerational trauma. Their parents grew up in the same circumstances with violence, neglect and (sexual) abuse and it can be very hard for these parents to break this cycle of intergenerational abuse and trauma. Child protection services have been involved, children have been removed and their sense of failure as parents triggers feelings of worthlessness or guilt. Often, they themselves have been removed from their parents, and suffer from unresolved trauma. In some families, child protection services have placed the children with those same grandparents, who have eventually managed to create safety in their family. Parents can have mixed feelings of gratitude towards the grandparents but also feel angry that their parents were unable to care for them, but are now caring for their children. Grandparents can feel these grandchildren are their second chance and can be determined to make amends for their mistakes. However the grandchildren can trigger their own unresolved childhood trauma, which led them to abuse drugs and alcohol in the past. Intergenerational trauma can create complicated family dynamics and relational trauma, with the child caught in the middle.

8.7.2 Traumatized parent

Traumatized parents can experience the same difficulties as their traumatized children. They can have problems in regulating their emotions and limited impulse control. They have a chaotic brain, a limited capacity for mentalizing and negative cognitions about themselves and others. They can be mistrusting and defensive, hypervigilant, feel rejected or threatened, have emotional outbursts or they can be too trusting, submissive and anxious and not show any emotions. This means that, just like their child, they are at the mercy of their sensations, bodily reactions and emotions. Their Window of Tolerance is small and they have limited ability to use their human brain. This causes problems in relationships with others and makes parenting difficult. These parents can find it difficult to show and share their feelings, to attach, to show love and to set appropriate limits. It is difficult for this parent to empathize with the child, because the parent still needs a lot of empathy himself. The parent tries to suppress his own needs so he can be empathic to his children.

8.7.3 Child triggers parent's trauma

However, the child's behaviour can trigger the parent's traumatic memories taking the parent outside his Window of Tolerance. When these subconscious, old feelings are activated, the empathy that the parent has consciously produced is insufficient. The parent becomes unable to focus on the inner world of the child. Triggered by the child, the parent may then unintentionally burden the child with his own old feelings that do not belong to the child, such as violent (old, unprocessed) rage or guilt, rejection and anxiety. On the other hand the parent does not limit the child's survival behaviour, or behaviour in which the trauma is re-enacted sufficiently. To a lesser or greater degree this may lead to unintentional emotional neglect or psychological abuse.

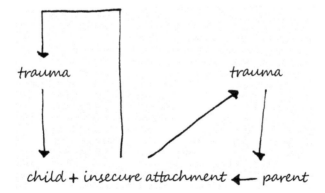

Figure 8.3
Source: Struik (2009).

One can imagine how hard it is for these adults to be an emotional available good parent. And when these parents also have to bring up a traumatized child, a child that makes much higher demands on parenting, it is clear that they are stretched to the limit. These parents often do not realize that traumatization is repeated by their own interaction with the child. The child triggers their pain and they reject the child as being the cause of their pain. The parent's rejection activates the child's defence action system and reinforces the child's fear of attachment. The result is that the traumatization of parent and child becomes interwoven (see Figure 8.3).

8.8 Trauma-sensitive parenting

8.8.1 Reduce the pressure

The first step is to reduce the pressure on the relationship by increasing support for the parent. Psychoeducation, respite care or sometimes (temporary) placement outside the family combined with treatment can bring enough relief for a positive attitude to return. Creating physical distance can calm both foster parent and the child, because the attachment system is not as strongly activated.

8.8.2 Ideal parenting to heal a traumatized child

To be able to heal, ideally the child needs a parent with a calm brain in order to organize his own chaotic brain and learn to regulate stress. A parent who can control his own emotions and focus on the inner world of the child without being emotionally dysregulated; and who is calm and predictable and calms the child's brain. The parent needs to be a safe attachment figure who can activate the child's attachment system and mirrors the right intentions of the child, such as surviving instead of tormenting his parent. The parent should be able to take responsibility and acknowledge what he did wrong if he is one of the abusers.

8.8.3 Good enough parenting

This description of an ideal situation for these children is far from the reality these children grow up in. As described, most of the caregivers do not always have a calm brain. However, this does not mean that these caregivers cannot raise the child, or that the child would be better off in another family. The fact is that the description of the ideal situation does not take into account how important and valuable it is for the child to be allowed to grow up with his own parents. In spite of any shortcomings, this still offers the best perspective for mental health. If the child can understand the caregiver's shortcomings and they can make a plan on how to compensate for those shortcomings, the parenting becomes good enough (Kliewer, Murrelle, Mejia, Torres de, & Angold, 2001).

8.8.4 Parenting not good enough

A decision to remove the child from his family needs to be considered only when the caregiver's parenting is too damaging to the child. The caregiver's stress continues to frighten the child and in return the child's anxiety triggers the caregiver and provokes negative reactions, which in return frightens the child etc. When during this cycle neither the child nor the caregiver can calm their brain sufficiently to de-escalate the situation, the caregiver's parenting is not good enough (Wieland, 2007). The child and caregiver's trauma is too interwoven. These children have to focus their attention on the unsafe external world to such a degree that it becomes impossible to focus on their own inner world and develop.

Making an assessment of whether the caregiver can profit from parental support and how harmful the parenting situation is at a particular moment is difficult. Will it be better for the child's development if he is removed from his family? Will the child be placed in a foster family, be adopted or will he grow up in a residential facility? The above description of the ideal situation can be helpful in analysing the existing problems and the factors contributing to them. Analysis and evaluation should ideally be done together with the caregiver. In this way the caregiver gains an understanding of what is going wrong between him and his child, what is needed to change this, and whether this is possible. After this, a plan can be drawn up concerning the factors that need work, the order in which this should take place and which factors need (temporary) compensation. Even when the caregiver's parenting is not good enough for a healthy development, this still does not have to form a barrier for trauma processing for the child.

8.9 Coaching traumatized parents

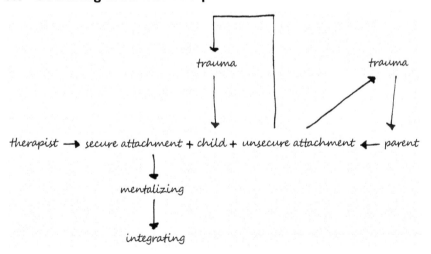

Figure 8.4
Source: Struik (2009).

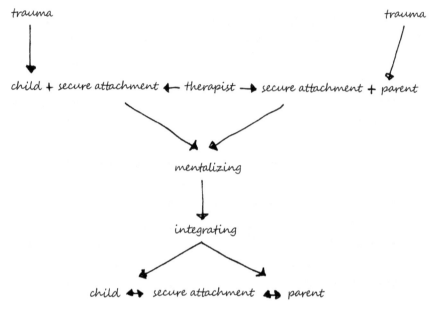

Figure 8.5
Source: Struik (2009).

Treatment for the child without involving the child's parent is only effective when the child and parent's trauma is not interwoven. Otherwise the relationship with the parent creates ongoing new traumatization (see Figure 8.4). Parents can integrate their own traumas so they can enter into a safer attachment relationship with the child (see Figure 8.5).

Silberg (2013), Wieland (2015) and Wesselmann et al. (2014) have done a great deal of work on the child and parent dyad and especially those including difficult parents. The following suggestions are inspired by their work.

8.9.1 Accepting and supporting attitude towards the parent

The parent's functioning can improve by having an important role in the child's therapy. The person supporting the parent needs to develop an empathic and understanding relationship with the parent, so the parent can then use this experience in the relationship with his child. This person can be the child's therapist, a family therapist, foster care worker, a child protection worker and residential staff, as long as this person is able to reflect on the relationship and to offer corrective emotional experiences without repeating old patterns.

Parents may find it hard to put themselves in the child's position or have difficulty feeling empathy for the child. This may at times be a challenge, because these parents' rejection of their child understandably arouses irritation, criticism and disapproval. However, a critical and disapproving attitude repeats the parent's own childhood trauma and touches painful areas. The professional becomes the critical parent. It is hard for a person to give something to another person if he has never had this experience himself. If the professional manages to maintain a supportive, accepting attitude, this will make it easier for the parent to do the same for the child.

8.9.2 Do not give advice

The best way of avoiding a critical attitude is by asking questions instead of advising or giving an opinion. Many of these parents have participated in a parenting programme where they were given advice, without success. Giving advice and trying to convince the parent makes him feel dependent and incompetent. Confidence in the parent reinforces the parent's faith in himself. And the parent's faith in himself reinforces his faith in the child. And this reinforces the child's faith in himself. Focusing on small changes gives the parent a feeling of being in control and the hope of improvement.

8.9.3 Parental support

Initially the professional supports the parent by placing himself in the parent's situation, asking the parent what it is like living with this child, and how it feels. The parent is given support when choices have to be made or when they encounter problems in their lives (legal matters, work, finances, relationships with others and so on).

Parents who are under too much stress, or who are themselves traumatized, can attribute the wrong intentions to their child. The stress that the (foster) parent experiences depends for a large part on how the parent perceives his situation. The behaviour of a child with attachment anxiety can hurt parents deeply and make them feel that they are a bad parents, that they are powerless and unsafe for the child, and that the situation is hopeless. It can be even harder for parents who have experienced 'being let down' and who have had the feeling that 'no one loves me'.

8.9.4 Psychoeducation

Children with attachment problems actually do long for intimacy. They really do want contact, but they have learnt that it is the person who cuddles them that usually hurts them most. They yearn for it, but they are also extremely scared of it, because intimacy makes them vulnerable and dependent. This inner struggle can lead to unpredictable behaviour, such as attracting and then rejecting, or simultaneously approaching and rejecting. In children with structural dissociation, this erratic behaviour is due to the way the various parts of the personality express themselves. For many children the only way to solve these conflicting needs is by having a fight. A fight with their parent is still a form of contact and proximity; however, it keeps the parent at a distance emotionally (see section 2.4.2.2).

This can leads to misperceptions about the child. Wesselmann (1998) describes fourteen common parental misperceptions, such as 'my child has no real feelings' or 'my child doesn't love me enough', which are very useful in working with parents. This list of misperceptions (mounted on a board and laminated) can be presented to the parent. Their ideas about the child's inner world are then explored by asking whether they recognize any of these thoughts. The fact that such a list exists and is obviously used so often that it is laminated can make the parent feel less abnormal or guilty; they are not the only ones who think such thoughts.

Insight into the child and his inner world and hope that things can improve can rapidly change the parent's negative feelings. Psychoeducation interventions from Chapter 5 explaining how the brain works, what the effects are of traumatization, what children can think and feel, will help parents to understand their children better. Other explanations for the behaviour of the child can then be sought. These insights can help the parent to understand the child better, but they also provide the parent insight into himself.

8.9.5 Parent in therapy

If the (foster) parent's traumatization is interwoven with the child's to such an extent that it stands in the way of safe attachment, therapy for the (foster) parents themselves may seem helpful. Therapy can focus on the present by improving the parent's functioning and self-regulation. Sometimes personal factors such as the work environment or the partner relationship or the way a parent deals with problems can contribute to the strain. Interventions can focus on helping parents with these issues. Therapy can also focus on the parent's traumatization.

Jody's mother grew up with a mother who was an alcoholic. She has four sisters and she says that she had a good time as a child. When the therapist reflects on her story, she gradually realizes that she was emotionally neglected. She begins to see that this has had a great impact on her life and on her parenting. She actually repeated the neglect with her own children. Because the therapist does not reject her behaviour but rather validates it (says that it is understandable that she behaves in this way), she has the courage to talk about her inner world. She says that she is actually horrified by her children's dependence on her, but that she now sees this horror as the result of her own fear of dependence and her defence against this. After this Jody's mother is better able to tolerate the fact that her children depend on her, and she even begins to enjoy it. She begins to see her children's willingness to rely on her as proof that she is indeed a reliable mother.

However, referring the parent for therapy can also create even more problems for the child's treatment. Some of these therapies can be lengthy. The child triggering the parent can form a barrier for the parent's therapy. The parent's therapist can insist on the parent taking more time for himself. This would be great if the child could wait that long, but in most cases that is not possible. This is why many parents do not want to go into therapy. They cannot afford to focus on their inner world, as they need all their energy to survive in daily life. Other parents do not have access to therapy or therapy has not improved their functioning. That does not have to be a problem.

All of these interventions focus on making the parent more trauma sensitive and managing the child's trauma symptoms. This is great, but getting rid of these trauma symptoms or reducing them with trauma processing is a far more durable solution.

8.10 Relationship with the professional

8.10.1 The professional as a bridge between child and attachment figure

Professionals, such as therapists, child protection workers, residential staff, cannot offer continuity of attachment. Therefore they cannot function as long-term attachment figures for the child. Nevertheless the relationship they have with the child is in fact very important in the development of new attachment behaviour. It is a one-sided relationship, because the professional does not expect anything from the child in return. This makes it easier for the child to find the courage to approach them and try out new behaviour. The relationship may be very important to them, but it is not their most important relationship. They can therefore permit themselves to make 'mistakes' – there is less at stake. In the relationship with a professional, it may be easier for them to try out new attachment behaviour. By doing this, and so finding out how it feels, the child is subsequently able to adopt the new attachment behaviour in the relationship with the long-term attachment figure. The professional acts as a bridge in this process. He helps the child to make this transition by stimulating the child to experiment with new behaviour. By discussing this with the child and the long-term attachment figure and doing exercises with them, he becomes the child's bridge. These are some examples:

It's nice, isn't it, working together like this? Do you ever have that feeling with your mum? I know you'll miss me while I'm on holiday, that's how it is if you like a person. But you can feel just as good with your mum as you do with me. We're going to work on that, because later when you're back home again I won't see you anymore. And we want you to feel just as good with mum.

Have you ever talked to mum about how guilty you feel about your bad behaviour? Do you think she is still angry with you? Maybe she isn't angry anymore, maybe she understands why you acted like that. I think it's a good idea to talk to her about this. If that makes you nervous we can do it together. I think you actually explain it very well. I'm sure you can explain it to mum. It's just the stress that makes it hard for you to find the words. I'll help you with that.

I think mum got so angry with you because she didn't really know how to help you. I think that actually she wants to make you happy so much, and if that doesn't work out, she gets angry at you without really wanting to.

If the child's behaviour in the relationship with the professional continues to be different from that in the relationship with parents, there is likely to be some sort of blockage, which makes the latter feel unsafe. Thirteen-year-old Eliza explained the following.

My parents so badly want me to talk to them about my feelings. In a way I want that too, and I would like them to know my thoughts, but when I want to tell them I just feel blocked. I can see them looking at me and I know what they expect of me and that they are disappointed because there I am, not saying anything, just sitting there. But that sort of paralyses me, all those expectations. And afterwards I hate myself even more, because I haven't said anything again. And they are angry with me because they think I'm not trying. They think I don't care.

It is then important to discuss this with the parents without blaming them or implying they do something wrong. By articulating how the parents feel, their emotions are acknowledged.

During therapy sessions Eliza actually does talk about her feelings quite a lot. She also says that it worries her that you're angry with her. That must be hard for you to hear, given that she says so little at home. I can imagine that it makes you angry, when I tell you this. How do you feel about it? Why do you think she acts like this, what is your explanation? There must be a big difference and we have to find out why this is. There is something that makes it very hard for Eliza to talk about her emotions at home. She is just as upset about this as you are.

8.10.2 Pitfalls in dealing with the triangle professional–child–parent

A possible pitfall for the professional is trying to convince the parents of the good intentions and progress of the child (which they cannot see) by saying something like this: 'Eliza is really working hard. During therapy sessions she actually talks about her feelings a lot. You should be proud of her.' This can make the parents even angrier, because in their eyes Eliza is quite able to talk but simply refuses to do so. If there is something blocking change, there must be a good reason for the child to behave like this. The important thing is to find out what that reason is. Eliza was clear about this: it was the high expectations of her parents that blocked her.

When trying to strengthen the relationship of the child with the attachment figure, it is of the utmost importance for the professional to have a good relationship with this attachment figure. If the professional views the attachment figure as being not good for the child, then the professional will become the critical parent to the attachment figure. This will disturb the relationship and, in addition, the child is given a mixed message. He is told to take risks in his relationship with the attachment figure while the professional actually thinks that this attachment figure is not safe. Disapproval and being judgemental will confuse the child, and this does not even have to be explicit for the child to feel it. For children with attachment problems this is often a breaking point. The therapist or residential staff try to protect the child and defend it against the (generally disapproving) parent. That is actually not helping the child but makes things worse, because the message is that this attachment figure is not safe, but the professional expects the child to attach to this person and does nothing to stop this, which makes the child feel abandoned.

8.10.3 Re-enactment of relational trauma

The trauma therapy can trigger all sorts of emotions resulting from the child's mistaken evaluation of the situation. For example: aggression, panic or submission, because the child thinks that the therapist is going to abuse him; sexual arousal, because the child thinks the therapist is going to have sex with him; extreme dependence and ambivalent attachment, because the child interacts with his 'old ways' in this new relationship and expects the new relationship to become the same.

It is very important to discuss this. By describing this interaction the child is given words to experiences from the past and these are corrected by reality. Seven-year-old Maggie used to close and lock the door of the therapy room. She would then look at me defiantly as if to say: 'When are you going to start?' Such cases can be discussed in the following way.

You're locking the door now, just like your father did. Maybe you think that I am going to have sex with you, just like he did. I will not hurt you. I know you have learned that other people can just have sex with you any time, but that is not how it should be. Nobody should have sex with a child. I am your therapist and I am supposed to look after you. I will not hurt you.

Foster or adoptive parents and residential staff can encounter similar (counter) transference phenomena. The child may, for example, act in a sexually provocative manner towards the foster parents and flirt with them. It is important that the therapist brings this up at an early stage, because the caregiver might be too embarrassed to talk about the subject themselves, whereas it can be a real source of tension between the foster father and mother if the foster mother notices that the child is trying to seduce her husband. Residential staff are vulnerable to claims of inappropriate behaviour. This behaviour can make them insecure. The explanation given in the intervention above can also be used.

8.10.4 Attachment to the therapist

In the treatment of very young children, a therapist is more like a mediator between parent and child (the main relationship). The relationship between a child and a therapist becomes more important the older a child gets. This relationship then forms the key to improving the child's attachment, and it is essential for the therapist to be aware of his position with regard to the child. This partly depends on the role the parents or attachment figures play. If the child's relationship with the professional does play a central role in strengthening attachment, the professional will be faced with more transference and countertransference phenomena. If this is the case, it is preferable that the person treating the child is an experienced psychotherapist, trained to make use of the relationship between him and the child as an instrument of change, and consequently to handle (counter) transference.

Chapter 9

Interventions to overcome barrier 4

Emotion regulation

The prince has to train and learn fighting techniques. The dragon may breathe fire during the fight, or corner the child. Even then the child must be brave and not run away. This chapter describes light and more intensive interventions to improve emotion regulation so that it is just good enough to process the traumatic memories. The exercises described are mainly exercises for younger children, because there are not many emotion regulation programmes for children, whereas these are readily available for adolescents. For the purpose of this book, differences in meaning between these terms are not relevant and therefore the term 'feelings' is used throughout this chapter.

9.1 Use the interventions to improve the child's development

Most children have sufficient emotion regulation. They can stay in contact with the therapist and continue until all traumas are processed, without losing control and harming themselves or anyone else when the session is over. Even when they cannot regulate their emotions in daily life, this rarely forms a barrier and they do not have to learn any emotion regulation skills. When emotion regulation is not identified as a barrier, this means it is not imperative to work on these issues before trauma processing. However, residential staff or foster parents can also use these interventions when the child cannot start trauma processing because of waiting lists, lack of permission or other barriers that need to be removed first. In the integration phase these interventions can also be used. The terms 'emotion', 'affect' and 'feeling' are often used interchangeably.

9.2 Barrier 4: Emotion regulation

When this barrier is identified, the child or caregivers fear that the child will dissociate, lose control or run off during the trauma-processing sessions or harm himself or others during or after the sessions.

Some children have trouble feeling bodily sensations. Sometimes they do feel the bodily sensation, but they ignore it. This is a consequence of caregivers ignoring the child's bodily feelings or hurting the child. In this way, a child learns not to pay attention to his own bodily sensations. After a while, the child will not feel them anymore. Children with medical trauma can numb their feelings to survive pain. The caregivers have to ignore the child's bodily sensations for the child's wellbeing, but the result can be the same. Caregivers can also over-regulate a child, to the extent that he has not learnt to feel his own bodily sensations. Such caregivers' actions are not synchronized to the child's inner world, for whatever reason. This often begins at a very young age, as one mother explained:

> When my child didn't like the cake, I always urged her to eat it anyway. 'Cakes are good', I would say. Even when she had finished her plate, I would say: 'Go on, have some more, finish them.' Now my child is always hungry, she doesn't seem to feel it when she is full.

Now this is a relatively innocent example, but one can imagine that an abused or neglected child has had many experiences of his bodily sensations (such as pain) not being taken seriously.

When the child cannot tolerate the feelings that come up when traumatic memories are processed barrier 4b is identified. It is feared that the traumatic memories overwhelm the child with anger, sadness or fear and the child will dissociate or run off. Children or caregivers can be afraid they will become violent and harm someone or themselves, or self-harm or be suicidal. Only 4b can be a barrier, or both, 4a and 4b. The child makes a plan to control his feelings temporarily, so he can get through the trauma-processing phase, after which these feelings often reduce. For most children light work on this is enough. Many times this barrier even disappears by the time the child has found an attachment figure who can support him and has permission from his parents to discuss traumatic memories. Children with a dissociative disorder and adolescents may need more intensive emotion regulation work.

9.3 Light interventions to improve emotion regulation

Psychoeducation about feelings can decrease the child's avoidance. The following explanations can be used.

9.3.1 Feelings are reaction patterns

Feelings can be viewed as fixed emotional reaction patterns consisting of different parts. When something happens that creates strong emotions, the pattern starts with a perceived trigger (for instance class mates laughing). This trigger is quickly and unconsciously assessed by the amygdala. Then the child feels a bodily sensation (for instance, the heart rate increases) and a basic emotion (for instance, anger). Then the child tries to find an explanation for what is happening (thought: they are bullying me) which is followed by behaviour (hitting them).

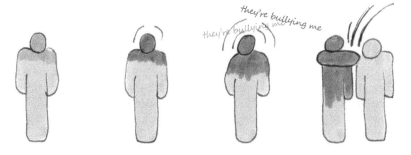

bodily sensation   basic emotion anger   thought   behaviour

Figure 9.2

9.3.2 Feelings are road signs

Children need to understand why feelings are important. The following explanation can be given.

> Feelings are like the road signs. They help you navigate by telling us what we like and do not like. We try and do more of what makes us feel good. We try and avoid things that make us scared or sad. Feelings protect us from danger. The sensations in our body, such as our heartbeat and breathing, help us to recognize our feelings. They also tell us when we are ill or hurt ourselves.

9.3.3 Normal and old feelings (adaptive and overwhelming feelings)

Van der Hart and colleagues (2006) explain that there is a difference between adaptive and overwhelming feelings. Adaptive feelings are appropriate for the given situation. They are normal feelings connected to daily life situations. They may be intense, but the child is able to talk about what he is experiencing and why. The perception of reality is usually accurate, and the child is able to control his reactions. When the child has unprocessed traumatic memories, these memories are filed in a temporary filing cabinet with strong emotions from the past, the old feelings. When these old feelings are triggered, they overwhelm the child. The child cannot regulate them, they go outside their Window of Tolerance and their perception of reality is disturbed.

9.3.4 Not having road signs

The Volcano (section 5.2.1) can be used to explain how having a normal feeling can trigger old feelings, which then overwhelm the child. Working on the traumatic memories can reduce the old feelings, so the child can use his normal feelings as road signs again.

Not feeling can be a great way to deal with too many old feelings. Unfortunately the downside is that means navigating through life without road signs, not being able to sense danger. These children, and adults, get involved with the wrong people and get into abusive relationships again and again. They have difficulty protecting their children because they do not pick up signs of their children being abused or become overprotective, scared of everyone. This explanation can also be useful for traumatized parents.

9.3.5 Manage feelings

Then they need to understand how to manage feelings.

Feelings are expressed through body language and by things you say or do. When you express your feelings, you can use them to communicate and achieve your goal. When you are angry about something and you tell the other person, they may give you what you want. When you are scared and you tell someone, they may help you and protect you. When you are sad and you tell someone, they can support you. When you keep feelings inside, you cannot communicate and it is more difficult to reach you goals.

Dorrepaal, Thomaes and Draijer (2008) use a useful metaphor in their book *Vroeger en Verder* (The past and beyond) for feelings that I find useful in working with children. It can be explained in the following way:

Feelings are like waves of the sea. Waves coming towards you become bigger and stronger and scarier. Then the wave breaks and roles out to the beach until the wave is gone. Feelings are the same. First they become very strong, but when you surf on the wave it will carry you to the safe beach, and become smaller and disappear. Feelings flow upwards from below and from inside your body to outside. However, when you block your feelings, you jump off the surfboard in the middle of the wave. The wave then catches you and makes you tumble and tumble and it feels like you are drowning. The feelings become overwhelming and you just want to not feel anything.

Figure 9.3

Figure 9.4

Children need to tolerate the old feelings during trauma processing. When they are unable to do so, they need to practise with normal feelings first. When they master that, they can deal with the old feelings. This is often done wrongly, and children are asked to do exercises with old, overwhelming feelings, which obviously fail and scare the child even more.

9.3.6 Managing feelings during the session and after

The next step is to explore which feelings the child cannot tolerate such as anger, fear or sadness. Then a plan is made on how to deal with those feelings during the trauma-processing sessions. Children can be afraid they will get so angry that they will punch the therapist or smash the windows. The sessions can then for example be done in a gym where boxing pillows are available and they can agree on a signal for the child to indicate anger needs to be released. Children can be afraid to get very scared. They can think of ways to reduce their fear during the session, for example bringing their stuffed animals, a photo, wear dad's T-shirt or a superman suit. Their attachment figure can sit outside the room, close by, or they can bring their dog. Children can be afraid they will become overwhelmed with sadness. For them it is important to elaborate on the solution for this sadness in the present, to differentiate the old sadness from the present feelings. When the child processes traumatic memories about the death of a parent, grief can be triggered as well. Prior to starting this, it is then important the child does have an attachment figure now to support him.

9.3.7 Self-harming, depression and suicide

Traumatized adolescents often feel sad or lonely or even experience pain. They can try and push these feelings away by substance abuse, binge eating or self-harming. Self-harm is often seen as a contra-indication for trauma treatment. However, most children cannot stop self-harming because they need it to regulate themselves. They can try, but usually they end up having even more problems. In his review Klonsky (2007) describes the seven main reasons why children engage in non-suicidal self-injury (NSSI) which are:

*   create physical sign of distress
*   anti-dissociation
*   emotion regulation (reduce bad feelings)
*   self-punishment or self-directed anger (50 per cent)
*   anti-suicide
*   seek help from others
*   influence others
*   sensation-seeking.

Many of these reasons are related to traumatization. Self-harm is part of a psychological defence mechanism to help the child to manage the guilt and shame. Similar to self-harm, suicidal thoughts or actions can seem a way out of the child's unbearable guilt and shame, intolerable feelings and hopelessness.

9.3.8 Managing self-harm, suicidal thoughts or actions

Similar to drug and alcohol abuse, the child needs to be able to tolerate these feelings without getting severely injured or die. Most children are unable to stop self-harming because it increases their guilt and shame to intolerable levels. Extensive stabilization does not improve things as their self-harming and suicidal actions are driven by traumatic memories. Waiting or postponing trauma work can actually make them lose hope and perspective.

Instead of stopping completely, the child and caregivers can make a plan on how to reduce and manage self-injury and suicidal thoughts during the trauma-processing phase. The interventions to increase acknowledgement of the child's innocence as described in Chapter 10, often reduce self-harm and suicidal thoughts and actions significantly. The child needs to be prepared to postpone suicidal actions until after that is done.

Processing traumatic memories can provide an immense relief for these children. They realize that they were not responsible, but their parents were. This can decrease the feelings of guilt and shame, reduce bad feelings and the need to dissociate. Then the child does not need to self-harm anymore or commit suicide.

9.4 More intensive emotion regulation work

When this light work is not enough, the child need extensive work on emotion regulation. The following paragraphs describe interventions that can be used to improve the child's emotion regulation. Depending on the child's age, the caregivers have a more prominent part in these interventions. It is important to practise these interventions regularly to increase the positive effect. Because the brain learns new ways the best when practised in a pattern, it is advised to practise these at the same time every day. Other therapies focusing on bodywork or emotion regulation can also be used to overcome these barriers.

9.4.1 Learning to feel the body

The most basic bodily sensations are hunger, thirst, warmth, cold, pain and sleep. Caregivers and the child can try to investigate how the child deals with these sensations. For instance, does the child notice that he is hungry or sleepy? To develop his perception of bodily sensations the caregiver can do exercises with the child. A worksheet can be used for that (see worksheet 'Emotion Regulation 1 – Bodily Sensations').

9.4.2 Feeling games

Caregivers can play feeling games with their child. Whilst wearing a blindfold, they can ask the child to feel different material, such as a wall, the fabric of the couch, skin, hard, soft, velvet or sandpaper. They can do tasting and smelling games with all kinds of food. They can ask the child to feel hot and cold water under the tap, or with ice and use a thermometer so the child can explore the difference between warm and cold. The child can pick clothes and find out what feels warm and what doesn't. Let the child step into the snow in his swimming trunks, just to try.

9.4.3 Observation games

Other bodily sensations can be practised by standing in an elevator and feeling the strange sensation in one's stomach, or going on a fairground ride, or sitting in a car when it takes a bend or brakes and so on. The child can feel his heartbeat in his body and then again after doing ten push-ups. He can feel his own temperature, when he is sweating and so on.

The child can be taught to feel sensations such as sleep, hunger and thirst. A caregiver can talk about how this feels around meal times and at bedtime. The caregiver can indicate what he feels himself and ask the child about his feelings. Preferably, the child can then try out when the feeling of hunger or sleep develops by itself. The child can try not going to bed until he is tired, or not eating until he is hungry. It is best to practise this in the holidays.

9.4.4 Relaxation exercises

The relaxation exercises from section 7.7.7 also fit with this barrier.

9.4.5 Feeling physical boundaries

Children can be taught to feel and indicate their boundaries by doing an exercise in which the child stands against the wall. The therapist then alternately approaches the child and walks away from the child. The child can say 'stop' when he stops feeling comfortable. Or both take turns walking towards and away from a rope or a scarf placed on the floor. This way, the child learns to experience distance and proximity in his body.

9.4.6 Imaginary protection for the body

Some children are very sensitive and may be disturbed by the feelings of others. Their feelings are strongly influenced by another's feelings. These children can be taught to shield themselves. They can imagine being in a cocoon, a glass pyramid or behind a *Star Wars* shield, or whatever protects them. The protection wall is translucent, and everything they choose to feel and experience is able to pass; everything they do not want to feel or experience stays outside.

The child could also imagine that he is pouring a can of paint over himself in a beautiful colour. The paint drips over his head and along his entire body until it is completely covered. This beautiful paint is impenetrable, and only things can pass which the child himself wants to let through.

> Imagine you are lying in your bed with a beautiful cocoon around you. Things can only pass through the cocoon when you want them to. Anything you want to hear, see, smell or feel can pass through, but nothing can pass that you do not want to hear, see, smell or feel. What does this cocoon look like? Of what material is it made? How thick is it? Is it smooth or rough?
>
> Now we practise pulling up the cocoon around us and dropping. Try it. Now try again really fast. Right, so you can do it really fast. How do you want to control the cocoon, by a remote control, a snap of your fingers, a secret sign? Now practise pulling up and letting down the cocoon this way. Practise negative energy coming at you, and shielding yourself with the cocoon.

Boon et al. (2010, pp. 171–172) describe the Store Exercise for adults, but it can easily be modified for children. The child can pick out a protective cape or suit in an imaginary store. The suit is impenetrable to fear or anger, or to anything else the child wants to shield himself from. So if he wants to shield himself, he just puts on his imaginary cape or suit.

The following exercise may also help.

> You push your hands out in front of you while breathing out and thinking of the thing or person you want to push away. Repeat this a couple of times.

If children practise these visualization exercises daily, they will become more and more skilled. They can then use their protection when they are disturbed by other people's feelings.

9.4.7 The four basic feelings

Smileys can be used to explain the four basic emotions: angry, happy, sad and scared (see the worksheets 'Emotion Regulation 2A and 2B – Smileys'). The facial expressions accompanying the emotions can be studied in the mirror. Body postures and behaviour can be tried out in role play. The child receives an assignment to describe one situation every day and colour in the smiley with the feeling he had. The child will not be able to at first, and the caregiver will have to indicate situations in which he got the impression that the child felt one or the other. The caregiver may indicate what he saw when looking at the child (body posture, facial expression, things he said, behaviour) and ask the child whether he actually had this feeling. Situations at home can be discussed with caregivers and the child, and both the caregiver and the child can investigate what feelings they had in the situation. Then a connection with other situations can be made by asking when they had similar feelings, and what helps when they feel this way. Traumatized children may have trouble expressing happiness. Happiness is not worked on in this chapter because this is not necessary for trauma processing.

9.4.8 More complex feelings

After this, more complex feelings such as shame, pride, confusion, jealousy, hate, anxiety, excitement and joy can be discussed. All kinds of feelings can be explored using the worksheet 'Emotion Regulation 3 – More Feelings', with accompanying smileys and colours. Wieland (2015) describes great work on emotion regulation. Children make separate cards for the different sensations which go with these feelings such as: soft, hard, shaking, sweating, palpitations, quick or slow breathing, dry mouth, stiff muscles, a numb feeling, scanning the room with your eyes, heavy, light, floating, butterflies, itch, warm, cold, damp, uneasy, enjoying, love, irritable, tingling, cold or hot flushes, being stuck, stone in your stomach and insensibility. The child can then match the accompanying bodily sensations to the feeling. When this is done with both caregiver and child, the development of the caregiver's feeling and experiences can also be part of treatment.

9.4.9 Mirroring feelings

Section 8.5.5 describes how caregivers can mirror the child's behaviour to make the child feel noticed and activate the attachment system. In this chapter, the next step is taken by mirroring the child's feeling, his inner world, to improve emotion regulation. Children who are just starting to develop their emotion regulation often say they do not know what they feel or think. For them a curious attitude works best.

> It is possible that this makes you angry or sad. What do you feel in your body, and where? What kind of feeling could that be? I would feel sad because it would make me feel alone. But it could just as well make you angry. Interesting.

When this is explored together, one's own feelings can also be articulated or the feeling one would have in that situation. It is important to emphasize that people can have different feelings in the same situation, which is normal. The next step is to ask the child about his feelings.

> Your eyebrows are frowning and you are stamping your feet on the floor, I think you are angry, am I right?
> You were startled, I can tell. I think I scared you by doing something you did not like or which made you think of something bad, right?
> We have talked about your mother and now I notice you are saying very little. You seem deep in thought. Could it be that talking about your mother has made you sad?

9.4.10 Normal feelings management plans

Once a child can recognize the bodily sensations and feelings, he has to learn to let his feelings flow. In Chapter 7 Daily Life the child has made a plan to regulate old, overwhelming feelings and calm himself when he is outside his window. In this chapter, the child can make a plan on how to express and regulate normal, adaptive feelings. This can prepare the child to deal with the overwhelming feelings.

9.4.11 Anger management plan

When a child needs work on anger management, the child is asked the following questions. What do you do to regulate yourself when you are angry? Can you calm down on your own when you are angry? (See Worksheet 'Emotion Regulation 4A – Angry'.) The child may make an anger management plan. Things that help to express anger are:

- hitting a boxing ball or a pillow
- stamping your feet on the stairs
- being alone for a while
- playing loud music in your room
- singing loudly
- cursing alone in your room
- ripping up old telephone books or old clothes
- clay modelling
- running or riding your bike
- playing the drums
- chopping or sawing wood
- kicking against a big tree
- throwing a pillow
- pillow fight
- arm wrestling
- horse play
- hitting a pillow which your mother is holding
- kicking a football against the wall, and with each kick you swear at the thing you are angry about.

It is important that these are things which let the anger flow: not 'sitting on your bed and thinking happy thoughts'. When the child is not angry at the caregivers, they can help him to express the anger. The child will feel supported and learn that anger is normal. Remember when practising to express anger, the child is initially practising with daily life normal anger, not the old anger connected to trauma.

9.4.12 The child is never angry

Some children hardly ever express anger, or cannot use the things on the list when they are angry. In such cases it may be useful to do these exercises at one or two set moments daily. This may be strange at first because the child is not angry. The child may say: 'Why do I have to practise feeling angry when I'm not?' By practising the behaviour, the anger may start to flow. Practising the bodily action without actually being angry is exactly what helps the brain get used to what to do when he is really angry. The brain will then be trained, so to speak, in what can be done with anger.

The child's anger may start to flow by doing the exercises, which is great. Because the child has practised the behaviour, he will be better able to handle anger. Sometimes a lot of anger may emerge when the child has started practising. This may frighten the child, but that is OK. A young child also has uncontrollable fits of rage, and doesn't know at first how to regulate his anger. These children never learned to regulate emotions so they are at the level of a young child. They need an adult to regulate them and to teach them gradually to do this themselves.

It is surprising how many families do not allow expressing anger. Caregivers can indicate quite clearly what the child may *not* do when he is angry, but when asked what the child *is* allowed to do, they do not know. Caregivers suppress their own anger and cannot tolerate the child expressing it.

9.4.13 Passive aggressive behaviour

Some children feel angry but do not express their anger openly. They are passive-aggressive and secretly hurt other children, torture animals, break things, steal or lie. They have learnt that openly expressing feelings of anger, hate and revenge is not allowed and bad, while they are filled with these feelings. This phenomenon is described in section 2.4.2.2. Exercises to express anger are strange for these children, for they never seem to be angry. But precisely for these children it is very beneficial to learn these exercises. If they learn that aggression is normal and that their aggressive behaviour is allowed, they can unlearn their passive-aggressive behaviour. When their feeling can flow, the need to cover it up will disappear.

9.4.14 Extreme anger and sadistic feelings

Children may harbour very aggressive or sadistic feelings. They enjoy hurting other children or torturing an animal. This behaviour is unacceptable of course. However having these feelings is not wrong and therefore it is important to validate these feelings. It is crucial to be explicit about the fact that the child enjoys behaving this way, and that enjoying this is not abnormal but a logical reaction. Of course the child must learn to stop those behaviours, but the first step towards that is to acknowledge and validate the feelings and accept them as an understandable reaction to traumatization. Only then the helpless feeling of being the victim and the powerful feeling of being the perpetrator can be integrated, and the behaviour will eventually diminish. The following is a possible approach.

Can you tell me how it feels? I can imagine that it feels really good and powerful to hurt others or kill the hamster. Some children really enjoy that because they had to put up with so much and couldn't defend themselves. They feel powerless, a terrible feeling. To make themselves feel better, they need to feel powerful and strong. Hurting others or hurting animals makes them feel good. They feel so bad that they cannot think about the other people's feelings. If that is how you feel, I would understand that. That you can feel so miserable that you need that powerful feeling to feel better. We can try and find things that make you feel powerful and strong without getting into trouble by hurting others.

Unfortunately, the child's behaviour is often condemned, making the child too ashamed to admit to it. Or the child is punished and shamed for their bad behaviour, without addressing the feelings underneath that drive the child to behave this way. That only increases the need for these feelings to stay passively expressed or dissociated.

9.4.15 Fantasizing is not actually doing something

The child can also fantasize, together with the therapist, about what he would like to do. However, lots of children do not know the difference between feeling and behaviour. When they feel angry, they are afraid of losing control. They are afraid of actually doing what they were thinking about. They think that when they fantasize about killing somebody, they are actually going to do it. This makes them afraid of feelings and fantasies about anger. The following example can be used to explain the difference between feeling something and actually doing.

Look at the sugar cube lying on the table. Close your eyes and imagine you are eating the sugar cube, think along with me. Oh, that tastes wonderful, delicious! What a wonderful thought. Did you really eat the sugar cube? No, it is still there. When you think about doing something that does not mean you are actually doing it. The same goes for anger. If you think you could kill someone that does not mean you have to do it.

They can practise fantasizing about anger and revenge, and then exaggerate it. Children can talk about their fantasies, or draw them, mimic them. They can make a comic strip about their fantasy. Then they can choose for themselves whether they will actually carry out the fantasy or not. This way, the child starts to recognize the difference between feeling and behaviour, and he will become less afraid of his behaviour.

9.4.16 Sadness management plan

Sadness can be an obstacle to trauma processing. Intense grief may emerge during trauma processing. Children may be afraid they cannot handle it, and they may try to avoid feeling sad. A plan for expressing sadness can be made to practise this (see worksheet 'Emotion Regulation 4B – Sad'). Remember when practising expressing sadness, the child is initially practising with daily life normal sadness, not the old sadness connected to trauma or loss.

9.4.16.1 Psychoeducation

First, the therapist explains that sadness can be a good feeling with a healing quality. Being sad and crying can be a relief and relaxes the diaphragm and it can make a person feel alive. The following is a way of explaining this to children.

> Feeling sad isn't much fun, but it is good for you, it can make you feel better. Every cloud has a silver lining. If you never feel anything, it is always cloudy, with rain in the air that won't fall. But the sun doesn't come out either. You are never really happy.

Children may be afraid they won't be able to stop once they start crying. They can be asked whether they know someone who could not stop crying. They may not be used to looking for comfort when they feel sad. They might be afraid of rejection or they just don't think of looking for comfort. They have never experienced that this is possible or that it helps.

Together with the child a sadness plan is drawn up, with things in it that can be done to let the sadness flow:

- telling your father, mother, friend or girlfriend what is going on
- writing down or drawing what makes you sad
- using dolls or playmobil to act out why you are sad
- crying
- listening to sad music
- watching a sad movie or pictures of sad-looking animals
- cuddling your pet
- cuddling with your father or mother or sitting on their lap
- warming yourself
- lying in your parent's bed with a hot water bottle.

After this, actions that can help to stop the sadness after a while are described:

- getting something hot to drink
- washing your face with cold water
- taking a bath or a shower
- seeking distraction
- reading a good book
- going to the gym
- shopping
- running
- baking something
- thinking of something nice
- rubbing yourself with body lotion, giving yourself a massage.

Grief can be paralysing. That is why it's good to be active – keep that in mind.

9.4.17 Fear management plan

The central question for this emotion is: can you comfort yourself when you are afraid? What do you do to help yourself when you are afraid? (See worksheet 'Emotion Regulation 4C – Afraid'.) Young children can ask to be comforted by their caregiver, that is normal. When children are a bit older, they start comforting themselves, and become less dependent on their caregivers. They learn to tolerate a little fear. The only way to become less afraid is to do the frightening things in small steps instead of avoiding them. Children can practise this in small steps. Remember when practising to tolerate fear, the child is initially practising with daily life normal fear, not the old fear connected to trauma.

Sandra (5)

The therapy sessions with Sandra herself started with emotion regulation. She reported not a single feeling or bodily sensation. That is why we started with relaxation exercises and muscle-building exercises. Sandra received a tape to practise at home. Four months later she said in the elevator: 'Ow, that's a strange feeling in my stomach when we go up!' This was a sign she was improving. The only feelings she knew were angry and happy. She was never sad or scared, she said. She started filling out the smileys and got a workbook to practise daily at home. Her foster parents mirrored her. Sandra started to report nightmares and flashbacks. She wanted to get rid of her anger and asked for EMDR therapy.

David (5)

David learnt to control his anger. He had sadistic thoughts of which he was very ashamed. He was afraid they would come out during EMDR therapy and that turned out to be an obstacle for treatment. When he understood that this was a normal reaction, his shame diminished.

Chapter 10

Interventions to overcome barrier 5

Cognitive shift

When the prince is afraid that his parents do not acknowledge that the dragon is real and scary, he might hesitate to start the fight. This chapter describes interventions to inform the child about his parent's opinion on the child's responsibility for the trauma. This information prepares children to make the cognitive shifts during trauma processing and wakes up their sleeping dogs. The interventions in this chapter are only relevant when a parent or someone the child will maintain close contact with has harmed the child. When someone or something else, outside the family, traumatized the child, this barrier is not applicable. In this chapter the terms abuser-parent and non-protecting parent are used for clarity purposes. Obviously every parent is more than just an abuser-parent or non-protecting parent. The pronoun 'he' can also be read as 'she'.

10.1 Barrier 5: Child cannot hold the parent responsible

Children can struggle to make this shift, when they are not sure their parent acknowledges their innocence or when a parent blames them. The child feels that it is better to hang on to his self-blame because making his parent respons-ible creates more problems or is dangerous.

When the child realizes he was not responsible, they also realize that their parents were. When the child is afraid that making this shift creates more prob-lems, this forms a barrier.

Children can use idealization, guilt and shame as a psychological defence to survive trauma as described in section 2.4. Some children are so convinced of their 'badness' and find it impossible to believe they are 'good'. They cannot risk being rejected by their parents, or they prefer to continue to blame them-selves and idealize their parents and are extremely loyal to them, instead of feeling how much they have hurt him. They are afraid to let go of that defence, because the realization that their parent is not ideal and has actually hurt them is too painful and difficult. These children need their parent to acknowledge that it was not their fault to reduce their shame and guilt and overcome this barrier.

When barrier 5a or 5b is identified, the child fears that his mother or father blames him for the abuse or neglect. The child is worried his mother or father will

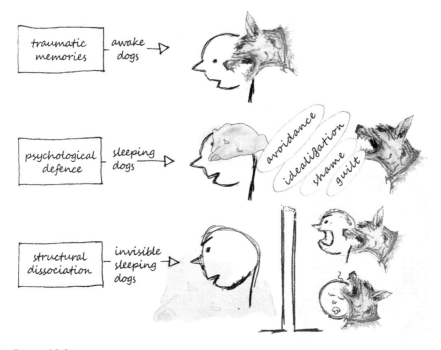

Figure 10.2

reject him if he believed he was innocent, and the child does not want to risk this. Barrier 5c is identified when there is another person who has harmed the child and the child will stay in close contact with that person, such as a sibling, a grandfather or a stepfather.

From a survival perspective the child can risk being rejected by one parent as long as the other parent can stay in his life. To overcome these barriers, the child needs to have at least one person who stays in his life and will take care of him to acknowledge his innocence. Then he can risk rejection from his other parent or both his parents.

10.1.1 Both parents blame the child

When the child's father and mother both blame the child, the child risks being rejected by both his parents. Then the child needs another attachment figure who will stay in his life. Barrier 5d is identified when the child does not have an alternative attachment figure who does not blame him and stays in his life, so he will not end up alone. However it rarely happens that both parents blame the child for the abuse.

> Jake is just a terrible kid. He never listened and terrorized me. He was always like that. Hitting him with the belt and locking him in the shed was the only way to make him behave. Our parents did the same and we turned out fine. He is evil. We have no trouble with his sweet sister.

When Jake would process his memories of the physical abuse, he would have to learn the wise lesson that he is not evil and he did not deserve to be hit. This could create even more trouble for Jake with his parents, because they do not agree and blame him. They might reject him even more and that could be dangerous, because he has no one else to take care of him. Jake can only make this cognitive shift if he would have another adult to acknowledge his innocence *and* that person would stay in his life and make sure he is OK when he would end up being rejected by his parents. Jake's aunt was that person.

> Jake, I know your mum and dad say you deserved it, but I do not agree. All children are born good, not evil. It is the parents' job to teach children to listen and behave. When children misbehave, the parents need to work harder or ask for help. They need to teach the child with words, not with hitting. Hitting can make children afraid and feel bad about themselves.

> They lose respect for their parents. I think your mum and dad did not know how to teach you with words, their mum and dad never showed them. Your mum and dad should not have done that but asked for help. I think you are a good boy.

This was good enough to overcome Jake's barrier. Jake's aunt had a close relationship with him, she was concerned for his wellbeing and she visited him often in his foster family. Prior to that conversation, Jake's teacher and the residential staff of the facility where he used to live had had numerous similar conversations with him without result. They were not going to stay in his life, so he could not risk it. Jake's foster family was also not option, because they could not guarantee to stay in his life either.

10.1.2 Not a barrier

Even when everyone blames the child, this still does not have to form a barrier. The child can have his own views and know he is not responsible. From a survival perspective that is quite unsafe, but children can do this. However this is a difficult position for the child. It can be worth trying to improve this anyway by using these interventions. Unlike young children, older children – able to 'feed themselves' – are sometimes able to make the cognitive shift without their abuser-parent acknowledging their innocence. This is a very brave step, because it leaves them 'alone in the world'. A relationship or group of friends may sometimes compensate for this. More often than not, adolescents or adults are unable to let go of the 'hand that feeds them' and stay loyal at the expense of their self-worth. If they don't succeed, their self-esteem will remain damaged, which can then only be fixed at a later age.

10.2 Exploring the child's possible views

Children tend to blame themselves or feel responsible for the traumatizing events in the past (negative core beliefs, section 3.3.5). Children blame themselves for not helping parents during fights and have thoughts like 'It was my fault dad broke mum's nose. It was my fault mum got hurt because I did not stop dad.' They feel they are responsible for their parent's depression or drug or alcohol abuse because they do not make the parent happy. They think they are worthless and therefore the parent neglects them. They are responsible for sexual abuse because they have taken presents in exchange for sex. When children lose a parent at an early age, they often feel responsible for their parent's death, whether it was a suicide, illness or accident. Young children cannot understand why things happen, so they make up their own reality. Since it is so obvious that the child is not responsible, this may escape attention. Children can have the strangest ideas, like eleven-year-old Thea.

Eleven-year-old Thea was referred for her depressed moods and negative self-image. Thea was three years old when she found her mother in the house. Mother had hanged herself. When Thea was asked why that had happened, Thea said that she thought her mother had hanged herself because she was such a nasty child. To her mind this was quite logical, because if she had been a nice little girl her mother would never have done that. Thea had never spoken about this and it was a complete surprise to her father. He told Thea that her mother had actually written a farewell letter. He had never shown that letter to Thea because she was young and he never thought she might be feeling guilty. Among other things, the letter said that she loved Thea very much and that Thea should never think that it was her fault. When Thea read the letter, a heavy load fell off her shoulders – unfortunately that was only after eight years. She had developed a negative dysfunctional cognition, 'It's my fault', about her traumatic memories of finding her mother.

Those negative cognitions around events in the past, add up and can eventually generalize and lead to the child forming a negative core belief, such as 'I am a bad person.' Thea's negative core belief was 'I am bad' and being bad and feeling guilty had made her depressed. Another example of how children can develop dysfunctional negative cognitions is nine-year-old Wendy.

Wendy had been sexually abused. After treatment her anxiety symptoms remained unchanged, however. She continued to be obsessed by death. Eventually it appeared that shortly after the sexual abuse had been discovered, her grandfather had suddenly died. She had had a strong bond with him, and it made her very sad. When Wendy was asked why she felt so bad, Wendy eventually said she had murdered her grandfather. She explained that the day before he died she had thought 'I think grandpa is going to die', and then it had happened. When asked how she could be so sure that she was to blame, she said that a week later she had been bullied by a boy at school. She had thought 'I wish you were in a lot of pain.' That same afternoon the boy had tripped and fallen on his head. Then she was quite sure that she had brought this about. It turned out that her symptoms were not caused by the abuse, but by her grandfather's death. Wendy believed it was her fault that her grandfather died and the boy hurt himself. She then started to believe she was a bad person, a murderer, which became her core belief.

10.2.1 Dysfunctional negative cognitions

There is a difference between dysfunctional and functional negative cognitions in relation to trauma. Children may struggle with a strong negative cognition that is actually correct, because it is a fact. It is impossible to change facts.

Nine-year-old Bas pushed his grandmother when he was very angry. She fell and broke her hip. Bas did not want to discuss what happened and became depressed. Grandmother recovered after nine months, but Bas still did not want to discuss what happened.

Bas has a strong negative cognition 'it is my fault' connected to the memory of his grandmother falling. However this is true, it was his fault. However, children can make mistakes. He did not intentionally harm her, which is why his grandmother forgave him. It is useless to try and shift Bas towards believing he is not responsible, because he was. The dysfunctional cognition here is 'I am a bad person' and to heal from this trauma Bas needs to shift to 'I am OK, even though I harmed my grandmother. I forgive myself.'

The child can be asked about his views on the responsibility for the trauma but most children with sleeping dogs do not want to talk about what they think or feel. It can be difficult to find out what negative cognitions the child may have. The child's parents, network and caregivers are asked how they think the child feels about himself. Child protection services' reports or reports from other former therapists, residential staff or school may describe things the child has said about himself or others to get an idea of what the child may think. The child's symptoms can indicate how the child may feel about himself. This information is used to form a hypothesis about the child's possible views. This hypothesis gives direction to what the child may need to hear. Whether that is going to be sufficient to wake up sleeping dogs and have the child open up about his memories, is only confirmed afterwards.

10.3 Determining the potential cognitive shift

To change the child's general core belief, the child needs to change the conclusions he has drawn in the past in regards to the traumatizing events. Trauma processing changes the negative cognitions the child has about himself in relation to the traumatic memories. The child needs to make a 'cognitive shift' (e.g. from 'it my fault dad broke mum's nose' to 'it is not my fault, I could not have stopped him'. Or 'I am bad child because I did not help mum' to 'I am not a bad child, I was only four, I forgive myself'). They need to learn a wise lesson and realize they were not responsible

Examples of a cognitive shift

I am bad	⟶	I am ok
It's my fault	⟶	It's not my fault
I am powerless	⟶	I am not powerless now
I cannot think about it	⟶	I can think about it now

To heal from trauma, the child needs to make these shifts in regards to all traumatic memories. Without this shift, the memory remains traumatic. When processing one memory, children often process a whole cluster of memories in the same category. They learn wise lessons for a whole cluster of memories, for example 'It was not my fault mum got hurt so much by dad when they were fighting.' This then changes their core belief: 'I am not a bad person.'

10.4 Key message

The professional then identifies a key message based on the child's negative cognitions or core beliefs about himself or others. For fourteen-year-old Sean his possible negative cognitions and core beliefs were discussed with his current and previous foster parents.

Sean's foster parents feel Sean does not want to connect with them and he avoids intimacy. They see he is distressed and lonely, but he does not allow them to comfort them. They mention Sean's aggressive behaviour increases for a few days when his parents do not show up for contact visits. They believe Sean might feel abandoned and unloved, even though he never talks about his feelings with them. The clinician rang one of Sean's previous foster families and they agreed with this hypothesis. They reported Sean had stated several times feeling unloved by his parents after being taken into care.

Sean's negative cognitions about the neglect and the day he was taken into care and his parents gave him to the child protection worker, could be: 'I am worthless.' For Sean an explanation of why he was taken into care, what his parents' views were on this decision and why they used drugs, would possibly make him able to talk about his memories and shift towards feeling more valuable and connected. His cognitive shift may then be: I am worthless → I am lovable (even though my parents did that when I was young).

Seventeen-year-old Maddy has lived with a foster family since she was six after severe domestic violence and drug abuse. She has been feeling depressed for years, but she does not know why. Her mother visits her occasionally and she has not seen her father in years. She does not know why. Her ten-year-old half-sister lives with her mother and stepfather. Her father and his new partner have three young children. Maddy says she does not remember living with her parents. She idealizes them.

Maddy is probably wondering why her mother and father have rejected her and are now taking care of their new children. There must be something wrong with her and she feels worthless. This is why she is feeling depressed. Her memories are pushed away (sleeping dogs). Her cognitive shifts about the domestic violence and neglect memories may be 'It's my fault → It is not my fault' or 'I'm unlovable → I am lovable'. These are still hypotheses and only the moment she processes these memories, will it become clear what she was really thinking. Hopefully the key message that was provided to her was good enough.

10.5 Discussing responsibility with the abuser-parent

The next step is to explore the parent's views on the child's responsibility. Any professional can have these conversations, such as a therapist, a family therapist, foster care worker or child protection worker. However, these conversations need to be done carefully, since the parent's inner world is discussed and his own sleeping dogs can be woken. It can be helpful to have some systemic knowledge, be experienced in using conversational techniques and having these conversations together with another professional.

10.5.1 Involving the abuser-parent

As explained in previous chapters, the child's biological parents need to be involved in the Sleeping Dogs treatment of the child, even when they have abused their child. The interventions described for this barrier with the biological parents can seem odd and inappropriate, depending on the context of the child protection system in your country. However the Sleeping Dogs method is used only for stuck cases. For traumatized children with severe symptoms who do not want to talk about anything and all other methods have failed. Involving the child's biological parents may help the child overcome their barriers. Chapter 6 on Safety describes how to involve the abuser-parent to give the child emotional permission to overcome barrier 1d. In this chapter the abuser-parent is involved to inform the child about the abuser-parent's views on the child's responsibility in the past. The interventions can be adapted to what is possible or appropriate in your country and system. Trying something new and out of the box may lead to surprising outcomes.

10.5.2 Absent abuser-parent

Information about the abuser-parent and what he does or does not acknowledge often comes from others, such as the other parent, the child himself or child protection workers. Never rely solely on these accounts, as the abuser-parent's own story is usually more complex than was suggested. For these interventions, attempts need to be made to locate absent parents. Homeless or wandering parents are located via family members or friends. Incarcerated parents can be visited or contacted via the child's child protection worker or a family member. When a parent is deceased or cannot be traced, family members are asked to formulate what they think the parent's views would have been so their views can be included in the information for the child. When the child is a foundling and the parents are unknown, there is not much that can be done. However, in most cases, where initially claimed that the biological father is unknown, the mother does know who the father is. Contacting him and including his story can be a very powerful intervention.

10.5.3 No contact between child and abuser-parent

The child does not have to have (regular) contact with the abuser-parent to be able to use the interventions in this chapter. When the child does not want to, or it is not possible to have contact, the information can be passed on to the child indirectly. These interventions do not have to lead to contact. However the intensive work with the abuser-parent and his role in healing of his child can lead to the child or parent wishing to start contact. Therapeutic work with the abuser-parent and child together can reconnect them and repair their relationship. The fear of this happening can make child protection services or foster parents reluctant to agree in this therapeutic work. They can be worried the parents may start a new court case or the child is drawn into a loyalty conflict between parents and foster parent. However 'not having contact' is not a solution to this problem. It is a temporary and superficial solution that in fact makes it more difficult for the child to attach to the new caregivers, when the relay stick of attachment lies with his parents. Another reason why it is important is that the child will have to deal with his parents in the future, when he is an adult. When he has not learned to deal with their ways, the child can struggle a lot. Parents can more easily manipulate or pressure the child when the child has not learned to be resistant to their pressure, for example

10.5.4 Explain the goal

Discussing their child's abuse can be very scary and painful for parents. They do not know what is going to be discussed. They are used to being blamed for what they have done wrong. They are used to being told they need to change. They question whether it is necessary and state their child does not need to know all of that. They tend to avoid by cancelling appointments or not showing up. Explaining the goal of the conversations can reduce their stress. Parents are asked to help professionals to help their child heal from the past, not to point a finger at who is wrong or blame the parent. Children value their parent's opinion way more than the professionals'. It is far more powerful when mum or dad says it was not their fault. The parents are not portrayed as the cause of harm, but the key towards healing.

> I have been asked to help your child because he is struggling with his anger and depression and I want to ask you for your help. You know your child way better than I do and your opinion is much more important to him than mine. I was hoping you are willing to help me help your child. Children tend to blame themselves or feel responsible when bad things have happened. Of course they can be afraid those things can happen again. Some children believe their parents do not love them and that is why they were taken into care. Or children think their parents do not understand how difficult things were for them. They may have started to believe bad things that were said about their parents and are not true.
>
> Now I am not sure what your child thinks. Therefore I want to make sure to say the right things about you, when he would ask or tell me things. I believe you do love your child very much and I would really like your child to know that and feel that and believe that. That is so important for children. Together I would like to make some kind of message for your child about what happened, to help him know that you love him. I hope that if your child feels guilty, this message can help him not feel guilty anymore because he was only so little and help him feel better about himself. This message is your gift to your child to help him heal. Would you be willing to help me?

Many parents want to help their child and are more than willing to participate once they understand they are not going to be blamed or criticized.

10.5.5 Blamed for the past or the present

Children can be blamed or blame themselves for traumatizing events in the past or for their present difficult behaviour. This barrier *only* refers to the past. Most parents can acknowledge their child's innocence for the past, even when they continue to blame the child for their behaviour now. Rather than trying to change the parent's view about the present, it is good to start with what they can acknowledge, the past. From there, the child's negative core belief starts to change and that could also change his symptoms. For the parent, openly acknowledging the child's innocence can improve their relationship and increase empathy.

10.5.6 Helping the abuser-parent understand the child's perspective

Conversations with the abuser-parent can be difficult and time consuming, but that investment can be rewarded with great outcomes for the child. The abuser-parent's views of what happened can help to form an idea of the child's position. Reflecting with the parents on their experiences can also help the parent in their own healing. His side of the story is important information, particularly his explanation for what happened. The conversation with the abuser-parent is also an opportunity to confront him with the consequences of his actions for the child. It happens that abuser-parents have never heard how the child experienced the abuse. They have no idea of what goes on in the child's mind, or of what one can and cannot expect of the child. Abuser-parents sometimes have the idea that their child never noticed anything or that their child didn't really mind.

Psychoeducation interventions from Chapter 5 can help the abuser-parent to understand the child's perspective. By asking the parent for his views, the extent to which he can acknowledge is explored.

10.5.7 Levels of acknowledgement

A parent can acknowledge the child's innocence at several levels. The first level is to acknowledge it was not the child's fault.

> Dad says the fighting between him and mum was not Tom's fault. They were fighting about adult things. No matter what Tom had done, or if he had been more compliant or a girl, they would have still been fighting.

Most parents can acknowledge to this level. They may blame the other parent or external circumstances. For the child it is not important who is to blame, as long as *he* is not.

At the next level the parent acknowledges the impact on the child and they can say it should not have happened.

> Dad says the fighting between him and mum was not Tom's fault. They were fighting about adult things. No matter what Tom had done, or if he had more compliant or a girl, they would have still been fighting. Dad says he feels bad about Tom seeing those fights. He understands that must have been difficult for Tom.

It can be painful for parents to acknowledge that their actions have impacted on their child. They can try and minimize the impact and stay at level I or alternate between acknowledging this and the next moment minimizing the impact. At level III the parent also acknowledges his own responsibility or even says he is sorry.

> Dad says the fighting between him and mum was not Tom's fault. They were fighting about adult things. No matter what Tom had done, or if he had more compliant or a girl, they would have still been fighting. Dad says he feels bad about Tom seeing those fights. He understands that must have been difficult for Tom. Dad says he is sorry for fighting with mum in front of Tom. He should not have done that.

The realization that they have made mistakes that have impacted their child is even more painful for parents. Traumatized parents often have negative core beliefs and carry guilt from their own childhood. They can start to feel over-whelmed with guilty and think negatively about themselves especially when they have felt responsible for their own childhood trauma.

> Sara's mother was very open about the domestic violence between her and her partner and her daughter's sexual abuse. She spoke about her own sexual abuse history and was very sorry for letting this happen to her daughter. After two hours the clinician left with a lot of useful informa-tion. Later on that evening Sara's mother attempted suicide and was admitted to a psychiatric ward.

Discussing their child's innocence can activate their own 'sleeping dogs'. For those parents it can be more helpful to direct them back to level II or I instead of discussing level III.

> I understand this is very difficult for you and you feel very guilty. You have made mistakes, but we are not here to look at the past and point a finger and look at what you did wrong. There is no point in blaming your-self for the past. You did not do this on purpose. We are here to make your child feel better by explaining that it was not his fault. You are very important and you can now help your child heal from this.

Levels of acknowledgement
  Level I   Not the child's fault.
  Level II   Not the child's fault and negative impact.
  Level III   Not the child's fault, negative impact and parents responsible.

10.5.8 The truth

Conversations with parents can end up in a discussion about the truth, espe-cially in a high conflict divorce, where both parents have a different story or when parents disagree with child protection services' decisions. The child does not have to be informed about the truth. As discussed in section 6.5.4, the child's *memories* are creating problems for him, not the facts. We do not want to create more problems by trying to correct the memories with facts. Those new facts may confuse the child even more. The adults do not have to agree, they need to provide their views. Based on those views, the child can determine his own view. To the child it is not important who is to blame, all that matters it that he is *not* to blame for whatever the child remembers that happened

10.6 The parent's intentions

10.6.1 Parent's intentions

The next question then arises: When it is not the child's fault, whose fault is it? Rather than blaming the parent, the clinician assists parents to formulate their (often good) intentions behind the decisions they made. Parents can use drugs or alcohol to numb bad feelings from the past. Parents can hit children because they are worried about them and want them to listen. Parents can neglect children because they are overwhelmed with their own feelings, or their brain cannot do too many things at once or is slow at learning new things. Parents can stay in a violent relationship because they want their children to have a mother and father together. Parents can yell and get too angry with their children, even though they do not mean to do that. They can get angry because they feel bad about adult things, and take it out on the child. Parents can regret doing things because they have learned how that hurt their child and that was never their intention.

Children can feel very relieved when they understand the parent's inten-tions, because it gives them a way out of the dilemma of choosing between 'I am bad' or 'my parent is bad'. The parent has done bad things, but can still be seen as a good person. They can then try to understand and, if they want, forgive and move on. Forgiveness can help to heal from emotional pain. Making forgiveness part of the treatment enables the child and parents to regain hope, reinforces a more positive self-image and reduces anger, fear, sadness and depression. Forgiveness is believed to contribute to expressing anger, building meaningful relationships and increasing self-acceptance (Baskin & Enright, 2004; Fitzgibbons, 1986; Legaree, Turner, & Lollis, 2007). When formulating intentions, it is important not to make excuses for the parent's behaviour.

Bill heard his mother explain that she has a borderline personality disorder and how that makes her violent and say bad things to Bill. She said she just could not help it. She was crying when she told him and said it made her feel very bad and guilty and she was hoping Bill would forgive her because she did not mean to. Afterwards he said to his foster father: 'I'm glad I know now why I cannot live with my mother, but I still feel so angry and I have nowhere to put it.'

The child needs to understand why the parent did things, but they must still be allowed to hold the parent responsible. Bill needed his mother to say that she understood how difficult this must be for him and that this was not his fault, and he did not deserve this.

10.6.2 Non-protecting parent

In cases of domestic violence or incest, it often happens that one parent is seen as the abuser and the other as a victim. However from the child's perspective both parents are responsible and should have protected him. This is a difficult message for the non-protecting parent since he often already feels guilty. Therapists tend to minimize this parent's guilt, or even to deny it. This is a crucial mistake. The parent is indeed responsible; he should have protected the child and did not do so. It is true that this was not intentional, but a child does not have to appreciate that. Children can create dysfunctional cognitions as a consequence of having a non-protection parent such as:

- My mother isn't strong enough to protect me. I have to take care of myself and protect my mother.
- My father is such a monster, nobody can protect me from him. So I am helpless, and at the mercy of others who hurt me.
- I am not worth being protected. I deserve this.

Without correcting these cognitions, the non-protecting parent continues to be unsafe for the child. These unprocessed memories undermine the parent's authority over the child. The child will either continue to feel responsible and take care of his parent, or not accept the parent's authority.

Ten-year-old Sebastian was abused by his father at an early age and witnessed his mother being physically abused. When he was five years old, his parents divorced. After this Sebastian saw his father regularly. His mother did not know that his father still physically abused Sebastian during those weekends. Sebastian told her that he did not want to go to his father's but his mother made him go. It was only after a year that he told his mother what exactly was happening there, after which his mother terminated the visits. Sebastian had anxiety symptoms and temper tantrums and he was protective towards his mother. After he had processed the traumatic memories with EMDR, the anxiety and rage were diminished. However, his relationship with his mother stayed the same.

His mother, who had been in therapy herself, was able to support him in processing his memories and his anger at his father. She felt very guilty that she had not kept him away from his father sooner, but continued to justify this by saying that she had not known. She did not take responsibility for what had happened to Sebastian. From Sebastian's perspective, she should have protected him. Therefore Sebastian was not able to feel anger for his mother (and he didn't), which, logically, he should have done. He kept saying that he understood. After processing, Sebastian was no longer troubled by anxiety or rage, but he continued to look after his mother – this was the maximum we could achieve in treatment.

That was not a good thing. A child does not have to worry about adult reasoning, and the child should not be placed in the position of having to understand these arguments. A child should be able to feel angry with a parent because this parent did not protect him. This usually is only for a short time, but if the child skips this anger in order to protect the parent, the child maintains the core belief: 'I must take care of myself and my mother because my mother cannot protect me.' The non-protection parent can say the following.

I was so scared of dad that I did not dare to protect you. I know now that I should have left him and taken you with me. I should have found help and I should have protected you. I know that now, back then I did not. I know you are very angry with dad, but you can also be angry with me. I am your mother and I should have protected you.

The same issues can also lead to oppositional behaviour. After sexual abuse, children can defy their non-protecting parent's authority. This may be a way of expressing their anger toward the parent for not protecting them. This can be extremely difficult for these parents, especially when they did not know. When the parent tries to justify not protecting the child by saying she did not know, she does not take responsibility. This only makes the child even angrier: the child does not feel acknowledged and on top of that he is supposed to understand and feel sorry for his parent. The child can only make the cognitive shift if the non-protective parent can explain why she did not protect him. For example:

I didn't know that dad was abusing you. I quite understand why you were afraid to tell me. You were scared that dad would hurt you and kill me. Still, I should have protected you. I am your mother and mothers should see to it that their child is safe. Dad said that he is responsible, because he should never have done this. He told me he is very sorry about it. But you live in my house and I am responsible too. It is OK to be angry with me.

10.7 Providing the child with information

After the key message is prepared with the parents, this needs to be discussed with the child. This can be done in a face-to-face session with the parent. When a direct confrontation with the abuser-parent is not be possible, the abuser-parent can then write a letter or send a video message. If that is not possible either, the child can be told what the abuser-parent said. Some parents find it difficult to formulate this key message or change their views every meeting. Parents with an intellectual disability may struggle to explain things. Some parents have very different and conflicting views. A parent can be absent or deceased, or other people's views need to be included, such as child protection services' views and parents disagree. In those cases it may be useful to write a Trauma Healing Story for the child with the parents.

10.8 Trauma Healing Story

The Trauma Healing Story intervention is developed in parallel to the Sleeping Dogs method by a group of clinicians, C. Dierkx, M. Pijpers, F. Jans and B. Ubachs and I, while working with these children. The intervention was first described in Dutch in the second edition of the Sleeping Dogs method (Struik, 2016), co-authored by C. Dierkx and M. Pijpers and described in an article (Struik, 2017b). A Trauma Healing Story is a short written story of eight to twelve pages that explains in simple language and drawings the traumatic events the child has experienced. The Trauma Healing Story describes the views and intentions of parents, child protection agencies and other important people like foster parents on the child's responsibility in relation to these events. The story provides the child with information about his or her past and describes his or her innocence about what has happened. A Trauma Healing Story does not require the child's active participation, which is great for children who refuse treatment.

10.8.1 Drafting the story

The clinician drafts the story with the parents, other important people and, if the child is in care, the legal guardians. In each Trauma Healing Story, both parents' views are described, however sometimes very briefly. When a parent cannot be located, someone who knows this parent describes in the story what they think the parent would say. The story is refined until the parents and legal guardians agree on the wording. Simple drawings illustrate the key messages of each page. The brain processes visual information in a different way from verbal or written information. Traumatized children are trained to scan their environment for danger. Drawings can deliver the message quicker and more powerfully. The drawings are symbolic so the child's traumatic memories are not activated or influenced. Photos are not to be included in a Trauma Healing Story because photos contain detail and can activate traumatic memories.

10.8.2 Views of other adults

When the parent's views do not provide the child with enough acknowledgement for his innocence, other people's views, preferably attachment figures, can be included in the story. For children in care, child protection services' views need to be included as well to explain why they are involved. When the parents deny or minimize part of the abuse, the child can understand why decisions have been made. The adults do not have to agree and the story can have different views, for example:

> The child protection worker says mum and dad were fighting and used drugs and the police came sometimes to stop the fighting. The police reports say Jeremia was crying when they came. Mum and dad say this is not true.

10.8.3 Denied abuse

Parents can deny abuse. They can blame a child for lying saying it is his fault that the police or child protection services are involved, or the children are removed. When abuse is denied, children can be removed or can continue to live at home. When abuse is disputed or denied, there is a risk of the abuse happening again. Safety should be guaranteed by making a Safety Plan, but that does not always happen. Resolutions is a safety-planning programme for children in families with disputed or denied abuse (see section 6.1.7). Resolutions reduces the risk of re-abuse and the child can be returned home without even knowing whether the abuse took place or having parents admit it. Resolutions is focused on safety only and it does not address the negative impact on the child's emotional development because he has to live with secrets. Children growing up in these families do not have the emotional support to correct their negative cognitions and wake up sleeping dogs. This can be very frustrating. Those children can be assisted to put away their possible memories with the Safe Deposit Box (section 7.7.1).

Children can also be placed in out of home care. This provides safety and if the child becomes attached to a foster family, he can risk the consequences of disclosing and being rejected by his parents. The child can then put the responsibility where it belongs: with his parents. Even though this is confronting, it is important to include these parents' views in the child's story. Informing children with disputed or denied abuse about other people's views such as the foster parents, child protection worker, family members or adult siblings, besides his parents' views, can help the child form his own opinion and views on what happened. Rather than feeling and knowing his parents blame him but not being able to defend himself, these different perspectives written down enable the child to formulate his own perspective.

The parent can also be asked to give his views on hypothetical situations, such as sexual abuse, physical abuse or drugs and alcohol abuse.

> I hear you when you say that you did not sexually abuse your child. It must be difficult for you that the child protection services believe you did. May I ask you about your views on sexual abuse? Do you believe it is OK that adults sexually abuse children? Do you think it hurts children when adults sexually abuse them? How do you think it makes them feel? Do you think children should tell others when they are being abused? Even when they have been told to keep it a secret? If your child were abused, would you want him to tell someone and get help? Is it OK if we discuss your views about this with your child as well?

Hearing the parent talk about this increases the chance of the child disclosing the abuse, even when the parent has also told the child prior to keep it a secret. Some parents acknowledge only one part of the traumatizing events, but deny the rest. It is still worth working with what the parent can acknowledge, better something than nothing.

10.8.4 Secrets

There can be secrets in the family such as an unknown father, dad not being the biological father, a child born out of rape, sexual abuse at a young age, a parent's detention or suicide. Parents can wonder whether their child needs to be informed about these secrets. Many of those secrets will one day come out, because other people know, children in school know, it has been in the paper, or their blood group or DNA does not match. It is best to inform the child as young as possible. Children only process what they can comprehend and the realization of what happened comes more gradual and is not a shock. A Trauma Healing Story can be a good way of explaining these secrets. When the story contains an important secret, it is best to discuss the page with the secret separately first, prior to reading the whole story.

10.8.5 Reading the story

The clinician reads the story to the child if possible in the presence of his parents. For children in care it is important to have their legal guardian present to justify the decisions that were made. Preferably the child's caregivers are present at the session as well, so they are informed about the child's life-story and can motivate the child for further trauma treatment afterwards. The child can invite other support persons if that is important to him. When a parent is incarcerated, the clinician can attempt to organize the meeting in prison, so an incarcerated parent can attend. Parents can also attend via Skype or a video recording can be made and sent to the parent. When a parent could not be located, this absent parent can still be included in the process by making this recording.

> ## Case study Cynthia
>
> *(Source: Struik, 2017b)*
>
> Fifteen-year-old Cynthia has expressed suicidal thoughts and has been depressed for a few years. She is insecure about herself and feels unloved. She was taken into care four years ago, when her mother was hospitalized after she overdosed on drugs. Cynthia is now in her eleventh foster family and does not go to school. She uses drugs and absconds regularly. Her mother has a posttraumatic stress disorder and is still using drugs. She cancels contact visits regularly. Her father left when Cynthia was five, after severe domestic violence. Cynthia does not want to participate in trauma-focused treatment.

It is likely that Cynthia feels guilty or not valuable because her mother tried to kill herself and is still using drugs even though she has a daughter. Children are supposed to make parents happy and be their pride and joy. In order to alleviate her self-blame, Cynthia needs an explanation from her mother about why she is not able to stop her mother from using drugs and trying to kill herself. She also needs an explanation from her father about why he left Cynthia with her mother being so unwell and did not save her.

> Cynthia's mother did not have any contact details for her father, but knew his sister still lived at the same address. Through the sister, Cynthia's father was located and contacted via phone. He stated to be willing to discuss the story. The clinician drafted the following words for Cynthia's story:
> *When Cynthia was five, dad and mum were still fighting a lot. Dad says he decided to leave because he thought the fighting was not good for Cynthia and it could not be fixed. Mum says that is true.*

Figure 10.3
Source: Struik (2017b).

At that time dad was very young and he felt he could not take care of Cynthia well enough, so he left her with mum. In hindsight, dad says he should not have done that. Dad says he did not realize how ill mum was and how difficult that was for Cynthia. Dad says he always thought about Cynthia and wondered how she was doing, but he was scared to contact her because he felt he was wrong. He was very happy to hear from her now.

Figure 10.4
Source: Struik (2017b).

Cynthia's father said up until now he had hesitated to contact her, not knowing what to say. He was relieved to have found the words to explain to Cynthia why he was not there for her.

Mum says she has a lot of bad memories from when she was a child. She tries not to think about them by using drugs. Mum says the memories make her feel depressed and bad about herself, so bad she tried to kill herself. She felt so bad that she could not think about Cynthia at all. Mum says Cynthia tried to make her happy, but it is not children's job to make mums happy, they cannot. Mums and dads have to make themselves happy or ask other adults to help them, not children. Now mum says she is happy she did not die, because she wants to be there for Cynthia. She has done therapy and does not think about killing herself anymore. She still uses drugs because it is very hard to stop that. Your body just wants to have more and more. Mum says that she wants to try to stop drugs too.

Figure 10.5
Source: Struik (2017b).

Cynthia's mother found it hard to discuss her suicide attempt, but was eventually very pleased with this description to explain to Cynthia why she did it. She said they never spoke about it and felt it was always between her and Cynthia. She felt that both of them would be able to move on from here. The story was read to Cynthia in the presence of her mother, the child protection worker and foster parents and a recording was made for her father. After hearing the story, Cynthia said she was happy her mother did not die, because she loved her very much. She said she really wanted her mother to stop using drugs and suggested trauma therapy for her mother. Cynthia's mother laughed and said she would consider it, if Cynthia would too. Cynthia's father, who started regular phone contact, also encouraged her and Cynthia eventually engaged in therapy. Cynthia's mother went into rehab, where she processed some of her childhood memories in trauma therapy. Cynthia's relationship with her foster parents improved and she stated that she actually felt she was better off staying with them. If her mother would stop using drugs, she would like to spend weekends with her, but not live with her anymore.

10.8.6 Waking up sleeping dogs

The story starts with a page on the pregnancy and the child's birth, describing the parents' good memories (if they are good). In the last page of the story everyone expresses their feelings towards the child and their wishes for the child's future. This reconnects the child to his network. The parents describe that they give the child permission to talk about his memories. Trauma treatment is discussed as an option to help the child overcome his difficulties and the child's network is asked to motivate him. Even resistant children tend to engage in this session, once they find out their parents made a story for them about their life and are coming to present the story to them. They can be encouraged to formulate important questions they have for their parents and ask them after the session. When a child refuses to attend the session, the booklet is handed to him and he can request a meeting at a later stage when he is ready.

10.8.7 Results

It is a time consuming effort, but making a Trauma Healing Story can tackle several barriers at once. The Trauma Healing Story prepares the child for the cognitive shift during trauma processing (barriers 5a–5d). The parents also give the child permission to talk about his memories (barrier 1d). The story also provides the child with an overview of his life (barrier 3c), and can facilitate reconnecting child and family (1c). The story can help a parent process his own trauma and calm his brain (3a). Conflicts in family, between family and foster family or child protection services can be resolved, and the narrative can help parents accept their child being placed in foster care and give him emotional permission to live there.

10.8.8 Difference between Trauma Healing Story and other stories

The Trauma Healing Story is similar to a 'Words and Pictures' story (Turnell & Essex, 2006). A Words and Pictures story is part of the safety planning process and focuses more on the worries in the family and the child's safety. Life-stories provide the child an overview of what happened in his life. The focus of a life-story is more on the facts, rather than the reasons why. The EMDR Story Telling Protocol (Lovett, 1999) contains as much details about the traumatic event as possible, including bodily sensations, and is used to activate traumatic memories during EMDR therapy. The Trauma Healing Story contains very little detail about traumatic events and its purpose is to prepare a shift on a cognitive level, not to activate traumatic memories.

10.9 Improving self-appreciation

The previous interventions focused on providing the child with information from his parents and network to enable the child to make the cognitive shift. When adolescents struggle with a very negative self-image, they can also work on improving their self-appreciation within themselves. The child can make a list of his positive and negative characteristics on the worksheet 'Cognitive Shift 1 – Positive and Negative Characteristics'.

Psychoeducation can be used when the child struggles with positive characteristics. It can be explained to the child that his value or worthiness is not determined by what has happened to him.

> Ask the child if he has a cuddly toy that he has had for a long time, or an old pair of jeans or a favourite sweater. Then ask the child how much that toy, or those jeans, or that sweater is worth to him. How would he feel if they were exchanged for new ones? The value they have for him, even when old and dirty, remains the same. This shows him that the value a thing has is defined by how you feel about it. Whatever may have happened to you and whatever you may have done, it does not make you any more or less valuable.

Some adolescents are convinced they deserve misery. They question whether they are even allowed to feel better. It can be explained to them that everything, even the most ugly thing, has the right to exist.

You can bring in a rock, an ugly grey piece of stone. Put it on the table and ask the child if this rock has a right to exist. Then ask him why this rock has a right to exist. It isn't pretty, it isn't worth anything, it isn't useful, it doesn't know any tricks. Nevertheless this rock has a right to exist, simply because it's there. The same goes for a child. No matter how ugly or dumb the child thinks he is, everybody has a right to exist.

The child can work on improving his self-appreciation by giving himself a compliment every day. These can be written down on the worksheet 'Cognitive Shift 2 – Compliments'.

Chapter 11

The Motivation and Nutshell Checks

When the prince feels he is ready for the fight with the dragon, the coach organizes a test fight as a final check. The Motivation and Nutshell Checks assess whether the child's sleeping dogs are awake and he is ready for trauma processing. These checks can be done at the start of treatment, when it is not clear whether the child has awake or sleeping dogs or after working on the child's barriers to make sure the child is ready. The Nutshell Check is not appropriate when using a less structured and indirect method for processing trauma and can be skipped.

11.1 Motivation Check

Children need to consent to trauma treatment before being able to start. The child is *explicitly* asked whether he wants to talk about his bad memories to try and make them less bad. This check is preferably done with the child's attachment figure, caregiver or parent to support the child. To pass this check, the child's answer should be 'yes'. They can be reluctant or find it difficult, just like going to the dentist, but they must be sure they want to do it. Then the child is asked for his princess, to remind him of the reason he is going to do this. The princess can be discussed to strengthen the child's motivation.

> We have talked about your bad memories and how they bothered you before. Now I heard that you decided you want to get rid of those bad memories, is that right? Now can you tell me why you want to do that? What would be different for you if that would change? That sounds good. Now did I explain to you how we can do that? Let me explain.

Summarize briefly how many sessions the child needs to come to, and how that is going to be done. The following is an example how to explain EMDR therapy briefly:

> We are going to make a short summary of all your memories. Then we pick one and we put the other ones in the Safe Deposit Box. I will ask you to tell me the story and draw the worst picture. Then I will ask you some questions to make the memory come to your mind. Then I will ask you to think about the memory while I distract you with my fingers. I will ask you a few times what you notice. We continue until you still remember the memory but it does not make you sad or angry or afraid anymore. Then we will pick the next memory.

> Ok do you have any questions? Do you want to do that?

When the answer is no, the child has sleeping dogs and is not ready for trauma processing. There must be more barriers that need to be addressed. The Barriers Form is reviewed to make a new plan. The child's willingness to discuss traumatic memories is regularly checked to prevent unnecessary stabilization.

11.2 Nutshell Check

Chronically traumatized children have many traumatic memories, a whole minefield. To keep the stress levels manageable, the mines must be detonated in small clusters and not all at once. The Nutshell Check assesses whether the child is able to select one memory to work on, while storing the other memories away. This is assessed by asking the child to make an overview of all his memories.

Figure 11.2

Discussing these memories is difficult for the child. It can be easier when the child knows that the therapist already knows most of what happened. Before starting, the therapist has read all detailed information about the possible trauma-tizing events the child has experienced, such as child protection files, reports from other therapists, police reports. The therapist has spoken to the caregivers or parents to gather information. If the child feels more comfortable to do this in the presence of his caregiver or parent, they can attend the session. However dis-cussing traumatic content can trigger caregivers or parents and the child can withhold information to protect the parent or out of shame.

Making an overview of the traumatic memories with the child can activate trauma. It is important only 'authorized personnel' handles this hazardous material to prevent re-traumatization. The therapist who is going to process the trauma with the child preferably does this check, so he can build the relationship with the child, but a professional who is preparing the child for trauma therapy can also do the Nutshell Check.

11.2.1 Make an overview of traumatic memories

The therapist checks whether the child has created a Safe Deposit Box to store his memories in. If not, this intervention is done first (see section 7.7.1). The child is asked to name the bad memories or pictures he has in his head or mind that he wants to get rid of. The child does not have to tell the whole story, just

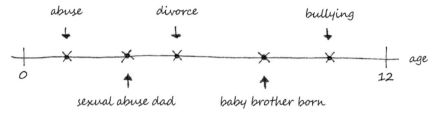

Figure 11.3

briefly, 'in a nutshell'. The therapist writes these memories down (worksheet 'The Nutshell'). The goal of this intervention is to make an overview. The child is discouraged to tell the details of these memories because talking too much about it might make him too upset. The child only names the topics, such as 'mum and dad fighting', 'granddad touching me', 'mum calling me names' and does not have to go into detail yet. For one child this nutshell may be a peanut shell (a brief summary) and for another a coconut shell (an extensive description). Together they make an overview of the child's memories or memory clusters. When there is a dispute over what really happened, remember that facts are not important. What matters is what the child currently remembers. The Nutshell Check checks whether the child can do this, without going outside his Window of Tolerance. When the child is able to do this, the child is ready for trauma processing, 'stable enough'. There are several ways to make this overview:

11.2.2 The timeline

The therapist draws a timeline and asks the child to mark the important events (the birth of brothers and/or sisters, divorce, death, changing schools, moving house, etc.) on the timeline. Then the therapist asks the child to name the traumatic memories and try and place them on this timeline, making sure that pleasant events alternate with unpleasant events. Together, they give each memory a short name (see Figure 11.3).

11.2.3 Clustering

Clustering is used when children have many memories in one category or several categories. Making clusters or groups of memories can help to children with too many pictures and who do not know where to begin. Clustering makes it easier to sort out the pictures and to organize the chaos inside their head. For example, a cluster 'mum and dad fighting' contains the memories of the time that 'mum broke her nose', the time that 'the table smashed', the time that 'dad was arrested'. The cluster 'sex things' for example contains the memories of 'sexual abuse by grandmother and father' of 'sexual abuse by sister's boyfriend' and 'rape in the woods'. Children can cluster memories around topic, person, time period, location or

dad hitting me   locking me up   stepdad's willy

mum angry   stealing from shop   don't want to talk
about it

Figure 11.4

whatever gives the best overview. The therapist draws a number of squares and asks the child to list his traumatic memories: 'Just name the pictures that you have in your head.' Every box gets a label. The child does not draw the memory in the squares, because this will activate the memory too much. This is continued until the child states not having any more memories (see Figure 11.4).

11.2.4 Memories I do not want to talk about

Children can be ashamed to mention a memory or they can barely look at the pictures in their heads. They may find it very difficult to talk about their pictures. Children may also say that they don't remember. In most cases they actually do remember, but they don't want to talk about it. Before starting to process, it is important to know if there are other memories. The therapist needs to tread with more caution and make a plan with the child on what to do when those memories are activated. When the child says there are no more memories, the following can be asked.

> You say there are no more memories. Now I know that children sometimes say that there aren't any more pictures, when in fact there are. They just don't want to tell anyone about them, or they're afraid or ashamed of them. So are there no more memories or do you not want to talk about them? You do not have to tell me the memory. It's just good to know that there are more that you do not want to talk about.

When the child has pictures he does not want to talk about, they are not discussed but marked with a question mark or named: 'I do not want to talk about' and the child's boundaries are respected. At least the location of these mines is identified and the therapist knows they are there. By continuing to talk quite naturally about 'don't want to talk about it', this memory gradually becomes easier to handle. The therapist provides the child with the words for an experience, which was formerly too overwhelming to comprehend. Most children eventually disclose the content of this memory during trauma processing.

Children can also get new memories or decide to tell about memories at a later stage. One box is therefore always left empty with the following explanation.

> At this moment you can't think of any more pictures but later you may remember another one. When that would happen you could tell me. I won't think it's strange if you add another one later.

11.2.5 I don't know if that really happened

Children can worry that they cannot really remember what happened or that what they remember is true or not. It can be explained to them that it does not really matter whether it really happened that way or not. It is the *perception of the event* that makes it a traumatizing event, not the actual event in itself. Children can have scary memories about a movie or a bad dream. That also did not really happen, but they can still cause problems to the child. So all memories that are bothering the child now are summarized.

11.2.6 Ranking the memories

After making the overview, the child ranks the memories by giving them a number on a scale of zero (not bad at all) to ten (the most bad it can be). The memories that the child does not want to talk about are also ranked. The child is asked: 'Which one is more difficult to look at, "mum and dad fighting" or "don't want to talk about it"?' The therapist could continue to explore this memory as follows:

> Can I ask you something about 'don't want to talk about it'? You know the rule, don't you, if you don't want to answer, you don't have to. Right, here it comes: Don't you want to talk about it because you are ashamed? Or is it hard for you to talk about, like there's a lump in your throat? Would you like me to ask you questions, to make it easier for you? All right? Are you scared that I'll think you are strange or dirty? Do you think I'll tell your

parents and that they'll be angry with you? Is it a secret and you don't want anyone to know? Are you afraid of what will happen when you tell the secret? What could happen? Do you want me to stop pestering you?

The worksheet with the overview of the memories stays with the therapist. The child is not allowed to take this worksheet home, as the child should not be exposed to traumatic memories outside the therapeutic environment.

11.2.7 End the check

After the child has ranked all of his memories the child can start processing. The child's memories are activated to a certain extent and the longer they need to wait, the more they can start to avoid again. If possible, this is done in the same session. One memory is selected to work on, while the other memories are stored away in the Safe Deposit Box. If this is not possible, the trauma processing should be done as soon as possible. All memories are then stored away and the child is reminded to practise the Safe Deposit Box every day.

11.2.8 Pass the check

This check is not a guarantee that the child is stable enough. Professionals need to use their own clinical judgement when making this decision. This check can guide them in that. The child passes this check if he was able to make this overview and rank the memories while staying in his Window of Tolerance. There are children who pass this check, but are *not* ready for trauma processing. Children sometimes seem to be able to list all the pictures and talk about them quite easily, where much more stress was expected. They do not demonstrate any tension or emotion because they cannot make contact with their feelings, or because they are partially dissociated. This occurs frequently in children who have been traumatized in war zones. If it is suspected that this is the case, any other indications of dissociation should be investigated before starting trauma processing.

11.2.9 Not pass the check

When the child becomes too overwhelmed or does not want to do this check, interventions to increase control can be taught to see if the child can pass the check subsequently. If not, there are still barriers that need more work. The barriers could have been analysed for certain traumatic memories, but there is another undiscovered landmine and the child has a secret, such as sexual abuse.

11.3 Interventions to increase control

This adapted version of the Remote Control exercise (Shapiro, 2001) can give children more control during trauma processing. By practising they can become more confident that they are able to do it.

I want to show you this trick because it can help you to feel more in control and less scared when you are working with your bad memories later. Can you think of a nice video clip? Now imagine that you play this on your TV. You pick up the remote control and hold it in your hand. You control the video, you decide whether you watch it or not. Now start the video. Can you do that? Now hit the pause button and look at the picture for a moment. Watch a little bit more of the video. Can you manage that? Now hit fast forward. You can see the video but it's very fast. Now you play it at normal speed again.

Next you lower the volume more and more, until the sound is switched off, while you continue to watch the video. You still see what happens, but it is much less lively, can you see that? Now switch the sound back on again. Good. Now can you change the colours to black and white? Use the button on the remote that makes all the colours disappear. How does that feel? Not as lively, is it? As if it's a long time ago, like a really old movie. Now switch back to normal. You're in charge of the video, because you have the remote control. You can practise adapting the video that you are watching.

Now you are watching the video and you imagine that you move your chair farther and farther back. The image gets smaller and smaller. You can still see the video, but it is not as intrusive. Then imagine that you go outside and look in through the window at the video. You can see the video but there is a thick glass window between you and it. Now go back inside and imagine that you are watching the video with someone you trust. You are watching it together. You see, you can decide how you watch the video, and from where. You are in charge of the distance between the TV and you.

Once you feel comfortable with the remote, you can play a video of something a bit scary or yucky. Can you think of something? Not one of your real bad memories, but a normal scary one. Now let's practise the same with this video. Well done! Now can you imagine putting the scary video in your Safe Deposit Box? You are the only one who can play these videos and only when you want to.

Chapter 12

Trauma processing and integration

The prince has to slay the dragon, which can be very scary. The prince needs to keep in mind the reason why he is doing that – his princess (the motivation) – and he needs his network to support him. This chapter describes interventions to support children and caregivers during trauma processing and the integration phase.

12.1 Trauma processing

The Sleeping Dogs method is *always* combined with a treatment to process traumatic memories, preferrably an evidence-based treatment for children with PTSD such as EMDR therapy or TF-CBT. These structured methods have a clear-cut phase to process traumatic memories. The trauma processing phase is relatively short in comparison to the stabilization phase. Sessions can be planned weekly, or even twice a week.

12.1.1 Selecting a memory

The child has made an overview of his memories with the Nutshell Check. An initial target is chosen, preferably the picture, which is the most distressing for the child at this time. The child will then process the maximum amount and the effect will be most evident, which will motivate the child to go on. If it is suspected that the child is not ready for this, or if the child wants to start with a less distressing picture, the most distressing picture that the child can tolerate is chosen to start with. However, do not give in to this temptation too easily, because children are always nervous about dealing with the most distressing picture of all, and they may also be relieved if this is tackled immediately.

12.1.2 Plateaus of processing a traumatic memory

During processing the child needs to learn a wise lesson in order to throw away the details and emotions and store the memory in the filing cabinet. Learning this wise lesson can be a gradual process in which the child moves through three plateaus (Shapiro, 2001). When processing the traumatic memory, first the child needs to realize that he was not responsible for what happened. When the child believes he is responsible, the danger comes from within himself. The child presents with complete terror and dismay. By attributing the responsibility to the perpetrator, the child can externalize the danger outside himself. The child then reaches the next plateau of fear. To go to the next plateau the child needs to realize that the trauma happened in the past and he is actually safe now. Then the child reaches the plateau of feelings such as anger or disgust, as it is now safe to express those feelings. By allowing and expressing these feelings, the child can reach the last plateau of healing and feeling calm. The child realizes he can make new or different choices now and in the future.

12.1.3 Preverbal trauma

Children who have traumatic experiences in the preverbal phase frequently have few, or no, conscious memories. Nevertheless the stress is stored in their bodies and their symptoms are likely to be connected to this experience. This is often the case in adopted children or children who have been given into care. Preverbal trauma can be processed with bodily focused therapies or EMDR therapy. EMDR therapy uses the Story Telling Protocol (Lovett, 1999) to activate the child's memories. The story for this method needs to be written carefully to prevent implanting false memories or traumatizing the child with new information. The parent or caregiver tells the trauma story with the child on his lap, while the EMDR therapist applies bilateral stimulation. This method can also be used to activate preverbal memories in an older child, if this child has no conscious memories.

Since it is unclear what the child's traumatization consists of, treatment is guided by the caregiver's close observation of the child's change in symptoms and behaviour. Various changes can be observed following this intervention. ADHD-like symptoms (hypervigilance and/or poor concentration) may decrease, anger and temper tantrums may diminish. Children can become livelier, show more emotions and be happier. A child can start to eat better or with more self-control. A child can exhibit less separation anxiety, sleep better and become more independent. Sometimes there is a temporary increase in affectionate behaviour and separation anxiety, where the child has formerly been distant. This is a sign that the attachment system has been activated and therefore a positive development.

Parents do not always report this of their own accord because they do not realize these changes may be related to treatment. The parent's reaction to these changes can support building the attachment relationship. Marianne Went (2014, 2018) developed the Parent–Child–Trauma–Therapy (Ouder–kind–trauma–therapie, OKTT), a brief trauma-focused therapy for infants in which she combines EMDR therapy with parent–child interaction therapy sessions to improve the attachment relationships. Even though there is insufficient research evidence for the effect of these therapies, clinical experience shows that children's symptoms can significantly reduce after these therapies.

12.1.4 Preverbal memories and verbal memories

When the child has preverbal memories and awake dogs in the same cluster, such as domestic violence from birth, treatment preferably focuses on the child's own memories, the awake dogs. Memories in the same cluster are usually processed all together and it is not necessary to address the preverbal memories separately. Treatment of preverbal trauma is experimental and it is advised to use these methods only when the child has severe symptoms, it is likely that these symptoms are based on preverbal trauma and all other evidence-based methods fail.

12.2 Support during trauma processing

Feeling connected is important for the child to be able to do this difficult work. Just like family and friends encourage athletes running a marathon alongside, attachment figures or support persons can encourage the child. They can come with the child to the sessions. They can send a text message or postcard to wish them luck or can ring afterwards to express their admiration. They can make a video message that the child can watch before every session. They can burn a candle while the child is having the session and send the child a picture of that. When it is difficult for them to take the initiative, the therapist or caregiver can facilitate this.

Jackson's mother loved him very much, but was unreliable. She rarely showed up for contact, made promises that were never kept. When she would visit, she could 'flip' and start yelling and screaming and take off. However, she always answered her phone, because she prostituted herself to maintain her drug use. Jackson's weekend foster parents were his attachment figures. They took him to therapy, but his mother was also a very important attachment figure for Jackson. The therapist had met his mother and she was supportive of him doing therapy (1d). The therapist rang her regularly to inform her superficially about his progress. His mother knowing and approving made Jackson feel safe. When he started with trauma processing the therapist rang his mother at the end of each session to tell her how well he had done. The therapist then gave the phone to Jackson so she could tell him herself how proud she was. The phone call was quickly ended before she could start to promise things that were never going to happen.

Jackson processed all his memories in five sessions.

12.2.1 Experimenting with new behaviour

In the trauma-processing phase the caregiver's attitude needs to shift from avoiding difficult and scary things to seeking challenges. The child should practise new behaviour, even though that makes him scared to break the avoidance habit. Children can become more emotional, without having the skills to manage these feelings. The child needs to be able to experiment with new behaviour. It is important for the child to sense that it is a good thing to have these feelings, that they do not upset the caregiver. That it is all right for him to have a tantrum or to be crying, and that they can help him to stay in control. With this attitude, the caregivers support trauma processing. An avoidant or controlling attitude, however, can hinder or block processing.

12.2.2 Supporting the parent

For children in out of home care, there can be a discrepancy between their behaviour with their parents, who traumatized them, and with others such as foster parents or residential staff. That can be difficult for the parents. If a parent is himself traumatized, the child can trigger the parent's own traumatic memories. Or a child can have more behaviour problems at home than in the residential facility. The child starts to practise new attachment behaviour at home and this causes tension. This may take parents outside their Window of Tolerance and they can become angry with the child. The therapist can explain to the parents how they can help their child to strengthen the attachment bond, for instance as follows.

Delia's trust in adults has been damaged by what she experienced with her father. She finds it difficult to form attachment relationships. Being attached to someone evokes anxiety in her. Now that she is working on trauma processing, she is going to try anyway. It is like being afraid of water and having to learn to swim. The group home is like a paddling pool. There she can practise becoming attached to the residential staff because the water is not so deep. That is much easier for her. She does this well, she behaves well in the group and she has the courage to trust the residential staff.

At home it is much more difficult: there the water is deep. This is still very scary for Delia. When she jumps into the deep end she panics. Have you ever seen a person drowning? They splash in panic and do not listen to what their rescuers are saying, even if the rescuers are trying to save them. A drowning person is in a panic and cannot think straight. This is what Delia is like at home with you as parents. And you are her lifebuoy. You stand on the edge of the pool and hold on to the lifeline, so that she can feel that she won't drown. Then she will eventually calm down and get over her fear.

The only problem is that she splashes so wildly that she keeps pulling you into the water as well. Then you get angry with her because of her strange behaviour. But it doesn't help to tell a drowning person to calm down. It won't work. And it doesn't help to tell you either, because the moment you get angry like that you are flailing around in the water yourself, and both of you are drowning.

The only way for Delia to get over her fear is for you to stand firm, so that she cannot pull you in. So that you can tell her that she can flail around as much as she likes, but that she can't drown because you are holding on to the lifeline. When she feels this, she will eventually calm down and overcome her fear of the water. In a paddling pool she can't learn to swim. She will have to practise in deep water, which will make her panic. That is inevitable. In the group she cannot learn how to behave at home. This is only possible at home, with your help. So what do you need to stand firm at the edge of the pool without falling in? (To have a calm brain.)

12.2.3 Talking about traumatic memories outside therapy

Children can suddenly start talking about their traumatic memories. If the child initiates the conversation, let him talk. Telling the story over and over again can be good for processing, when the child stays within his Window of Tolerance. Caregivers can ask open-ended questions, such as: 'And then?' or 'What happened after that?' The focus on the good ending and the child being safe now can help the child regulate his stress. It is best to stay at a cognitive level and asking for details should be avoided. The most important thing is that the child starts thinking of new ways to explain what happened. Questions such as the following can be useful.

> Who do you think is responsible for what happened?
> Why do you think fathers or mothers do those things?

Because they have not learned the wise lesson, children's reasoning can be strange. Do not try to correct them, because the child will feel he is not being heard. Ask questions and try to see things from his perspective.

> When you explain it like that, I can see why you think you are a bad child.
> I suppose I would think so too, if I were you. I think I can understand that.

Try to create perspective by asking what the child would think and how he would react if it happened again now. Or if it were to happen to another child.

> You are older now, what would you do now if this would happen? What has changed now? Do you think it can happen again? Why not? If this had happened to your friend, what do you think she should have done? If that happened to your friend, would you think differently about him? Would he be worth less? What would you need to forgive yourself?

Another possible intervention is to ask the child if he wants to know what the caregiver thinks or what they know about other children in the same position.

> I've got a different idea. Do you want to know what I think? I think that mum was so scared of dad that she didn't dare to protect you. I think she felt very sorry for you, but she just wasn't brave enough to do anything about it. Still, I think she should have done something. She is your mother and mothers should protect their child. Perhaps she thinks so too now. Perhaps she is very sorry that she didn't do anything.
> I know children who have been through this, and who think their father doesn't love them because he did this. Is that what you think?

I know other boys who have been sexually abused and they think they are homosexual. Is that what you think too? You know, anybody can have homosexual feelings, but being sexually abused doesn't have to make you homosexual.
I know other girls who have been sexually abused and they think they can never get pregnant or enjoy sex anymore. Is that what you think too? If that is what you think, you could have a check-up to see if anything has been damaged internally. Basically, there is no reason why girls who have been sexually abused should have trouble enjoying sex and no reason why they can't get pregnant.

Talking about these things can make a child vulnerable and scared. Indicate in advance what the purpose of a conversation is, and who else will hear what the child may disclose. If the child shows signs of becoming overwhelmed, the conversation can be deferred to another time. Let the child know the reason for this. Explain that he can tell his story but that he may get upset if he does so now, and that is not good. Then help the child to put away the memories in the Safe Deposit Box.

12.3 Layers

Chronically traumatized children, especially when they are young, often process their memories in layers (see section 4.7.11). Like peeling an onion, different aspects of memories or new memories can be processed over time. Traumatic memories consist of memories related to behaviour, affect, sensation and knowledge (the BASK model, Braun, 1988). All of the elements of the experience need to be integrated. If any of these elements is missing, there is a risk that the child will not integrate the complete experience. This is not a problem; sometimes it is necessary to process an experience in layers. Therapists must be alert to the fact that an experience has not been completely processed and explain this to the child: 'You've cleared away part of the memory now, but the rest of it will have to be done some other time.' In a following series of trauma-processing sessions, possibly months later, other aspects of this same memory may come up. It may then seem that the traumatic memory came back and the trauma processing did not work, but it is actually a deeper layer of the same memory.

12.4 Integration interventions

After slaying the dragon and marrying the princess, the prince also wanted to protect his kingdom against any new dragons. Dragons follow each other's tracks so the prince has to erase these tracks and learn how to keep his kingdom safe.

Figure 12.2

12.4.1 New treatment plan

After the trauma processing has finished a new treatment plan is made with the Integration Action Plan (see Appendix 4), based on what is needed. With the caregivers the child's functioning is assessed.

> Since the trauma processing, Bastian has become less scared and sleeps better. He doesn't have temper tantrums anymore, which is great. But he is suddenly quite forward and rebellious, he talks back all the time! That's healthy, though. He was always so docile. I just have to get used to it, all of a sudden.

The remaining problems in the child's life, ignored in the stabilization phase, can be addressed. The child can, for example, work on improving attachment relationships, emotion regulation, changing ideas about themselves, others and the world without the unprocessed traumatic memories interfering and blocking this. It is important to continue treatment and increase the child's resilience to prevent future traumatization. The following themes are common:

- keeping safe
- improving social skills
- improving defence skills and assertiveness
- seeking support and asking for help
- activating and expanding support systems
- initiating and maintaining social contacts
- improving emotion regulation
- constructing a positive self-image
- strengthening the attachment bonds and acquiring positive experiences
- making decisions about contact with abuser-parent(s) in the future.

The aim of the integration phase is to teach the child how to minimize the chances of being traumatized again and make him more resilient. The child makes the transition from '*surviving life* to *living life*' (Van der Hart et al., 2006, p. 339). The child learns that he no longer has to keep the surrounding world under control; he is now able to control himself. The child can adapt to the circumstances when these do not adapt to him.

12.4.2 Grief

Through trauma processing the child realizes what actually happened to him. Once children realize this, they can begin to feel sad. It is only after the child has processed the traumatic experiences that he can experience sadness over what he has lost, or never had. Grieving starts in the integration phase. Children who cannot grow up with their biological parents may feel sad about this. They can feel sad about the attention and love they never got from their parents. This can be mistakenly seen as a fall-back in treatment.

12.4.3 Decrease activation of defences

When the child starts to realize that the traumatizing events are behind him, the feeling of safety grows. The child needs to gradually expose himself to triggers, so that he can learn to react adequately to them. This is the moment when the child can decrease the activity of his defence action system. This is because the child realizes that there is no longer any reason for defence. Often one can see that the attachment system is activated and children suddenly seek to approach and find comfort. The child may also be very tired because he is starting to feel how much energy it has been costing him to keep that defence system going. After this, an increase in energy can be seen, the energy which is now left over because there are no more conflicting goals to be pursued. This energy can now be used for the sub-action systems of exploration, play and humour. Children try out new things and take risks. The child may feel the need to go back to the old house where the abuse took place, or to his old school, or to a previous foster family. All this contributes to the integration.

12.4.4 Dealing with difficult circumstances

When a child struggles with difficult circumstances, such as being a foster child, having a father who died, not having contact with a parent or having parents who divorced, they need help to deal with grief, mixed and conflicting emotions and thoughts, and make a plan on how to manage these circumstances. This can be done in the integration phase where the child is stronger and more balanced.

12.4.5 Re-connecting to family

A child may also feel the need to renew broken contacts – for example, with the abuser-parent or non-protecting parent. This is a theme to raise during the integration phase. Under supervision the child can then try out how he feels about it. Caretakers may be concerned that the abuser will disappoint the child and this is certainly a possibility. But it is also important to have confidence in the child. After processing his traumas, the child may have a more balanced approach to the abuser. The experiences have been well integrated and the child evaluates the abuser's behaviour with new views and wise lessons in mind. The child won't easily idealize the abuser any more. Idealization means not integrating all the experiences with a person in order to retain a totally positive image of that person. The positive experiences are remembered and the negative experiences are 'forgotten'. Idealizing generally takes place before trauma processing and not usually in the integration phase, unless part of the responsibility still rests with the child. The confidence of the supporting adults will communicate itself to the child and help him to have confidence in himself. Because the attachment system is activated, the child will also be quicker to seek support when he encounters difficulties. The child can now be assisted to form his own opinion of the abuser. The child can then withstand disappointment and no longer needs protection.

Sandra (6)

Sandra had clustered the bad pictures in her head. There were pictures of sexual abuse by her brothers, of being locked up and being beaten. But that was only part of the traumatic experiences she had gone through. She did not mention pictures of her mother's rage, of her father's cruelty and sexual abuse, of the loneliness and distress she must have felt. During desensitization she described only concrete associations of what happened and said it was 'not nice and yucky'. She did not mention anger, anxiety or distress. Nor did she mention thoughts such as: 'they shouldn't have done that, it wasn't my fault'. It just happened, she seemed to think. Nor did she mention associations that indicated how she had experienced the events.

In six EMDR sessions Sandra worked very hard at processing her pictures. Then she said: 'I haven't got any more pictures but there must be more because I still feel so angry.' And she was right. There were more pictures, but they were not (yet) accessible to her. Sandra had indeed been ready to deal with part of the facts but the emotional impact of the events was still too painful for her, she could not remember. The traumatization at the hands of her parents was still too difficult for her.

The following barriers were analysed. Sandra's attachment to the foster parents was not strong enough for her to be able to feel the pain of those memories. Her attachment system was insufficiently activated (3c). That is why she could not acknowledge that her parents were wrong. She could not yet risk rejection by her parents (5a and b). Sandra first needed further stabilization. But there was some effect of trauma processing. She had fewer tantrums but they had not completely gone.

Sandra then started taking part in a TF-CBT/psychomotor therapy group for sexually abused children. This is a type of treatment that incorporates a number of different psychomotor therapy exercises. In Sandra's case, the timing proved to be wrong. In the group she avoided many of the exercises, as they were too confrontational for her and activated a part of her that was sexually active. At home she was found with other children, forcing them to perform sexual acts on her. Sandra's safety and that of the other children could no longer be guaranteed in the foster family. There were too many problems in daily life. Sandra was admitted for inpatient child psychiatric treatment.

Only after her admission did it become clear how high Sandra's levels of stress had been in the family. She became calmer and her foster parents could see a change in Sandra's interaction with them. Sandra became more affectionate with them when she was home at the weekends. She sought more contact with and comfort from her foster parents. The foster parents began to feel that Sandra was attached to them. She was better able to show this. Because Sandra was not constantly with the family, she now felt safer. Contact was regulated and her defence part was not so active. The closeness in the family had apparently evoked more anxiety than had been expected.

The foster parents continued to work on the exercises on attachment. In the inpatient unit, work on emotion regulation continued. Sandra made good progress. She was better able to name and express her feelings. She became more assertive. She compiled a 'life-story book', which also included her life before she came to the foster family. Her abuser brother sent her an apology letter. This provided an opening for Sandra to think about her past. In order to break the avoidance habit, contact with her biological parents was arranged. These confrontations with reality helped Sandra to get over her fear. Together with her foster mother, Sandra was able to mourn for the love she had never received from her parents. This provided a better basis for processing the next level of her traumas.

In the second trauma-processing phase, the pictures that were related to Sandra's feelings of anxiety and distress were processed, on a deeper level than in the first phase. During this trauma-processing phase, spontaneous integration took place. At the end Sandra said: 'I have been through a lot in my life. I wonder what else is still to come?'

Chapter 13

Children in out of home care

This chapter describes specific aspects of the use of the Sleeping Dogs method in out of home care. It is based on a chapter from Struik (2016), co-authored by Danny de Bakker and Paul van Rooij, psychologists from a residential and foster care organization, and Linda Coolen, residential staff.

13.1 Out of home care systems

Out of home care systems and regulations differ greatly over the world. Residential care can be very common or very rare, foster care can be widely used and accessible or it can be very difficult to find foster families. Contact with biological parents can differ greatly. Some out of home care organizations work only intensively with biological parents when reunification is planned. When the child is not returning home, the biological parents are no longer involved.

Child protection services have different processes and systems. In some organizations child protection staff and staff providing assessment and treatment for children in care are joint together, in others children have to be referred out to treatment facilities or private practices. This chapter provides some general aspects. Information needs to be adjusted to the context of where treatment is delivered.

13.2 Top five problematic children

Every out of home care organization has a top five of problematic children. They are very damaged, not doing well, but nobody knows what to do with them. They have had therapy without success and they can cost a lot of time and money on, for example, one-on-one caregivers, home schooling, damage, psychiatric and psychological assessments, hospitalization or medication. It can be difficult to find them a placement and when they have a placement, it frequently breaks down. The Sleeping Dogs method is for those children.

13.3 Finding trauma-focused treatment

Finding trauma treatment for children in out of home care can be challenging. The child's behaviour is too difficult or their situation is too chaotic for therapy. Regular behavioural or attachment-focused approaches in out of home care do not work because the underlying trauma is not addressed. The child's traumatic memories continue to make the child assess safe situations as dangerous. They need their survival behaviour to defend themselves. Relationships and intimacy trigger memories of being hurt and the child cannot trust new relationships to be not abusive. It is said they need to be stabilized first, but who is going to do that?

13.4 Stabilize these children yourself

Residential staff, foster care workers, foster parents, child protection and youth workers need to stabilize these children themselves, so they can participate in therapy. The Sleeping Dogs method provides the tools and interventions for that. Interventions from the Sleeping Dogs treatment are done outside the therapy room in day-to-day situations when the child's network get a chance to discuss things with the child. In the period 2010 until 2018 a number of child protection and out of home care organizations in different countries over the world have used or implemented the Sleeping Dogs method with children in foster or residential care with success. Aggression and behavioural problems and drop-out rates reduce. Caregivers understand the children better and work more trauma-sensitive, resistant children engage in therapy and heal from trauma.

Making an analysis of their situation often reveals the same barriers: they do not get enough love because there is no attachment figure to support them and to rely on. Or the collaboration between child protection services and the biological parents is stuck, leaving conflicts unresolved. Difficult decisions are postponed sometimes for years. Or contact with the attachment figure is too sporadic and the child is unintentionally emotionally neglected. Or the child is too unsafe and the parents do not give the child permission to talk. Resolving these barriers requires collaboration with and decisions from child protection services. Without this collaboration, trying to help them is a mission impossible.

13.5 Residential care

The role and position of inpatient or residential staff also differs greatly between countries. In some countries inpatient or residential units are only for adolescents, in some countries very young children (two years old) can be admitted to an inpatient or residential unit. In some countries it is common to treat traumatized children in an inpatient unit in a child psychiatric hospital and in some countries this is not common at all. Residential care units can vary from group homes with staff on rotating rosters to caregivers living in the group home, to customized group homes with only one or two children or sibling groups. The number of children varies greatly, between eight to ten in one group, two, three or four in another. Staff can work the shifts alone, in pairs or with three; the staff on nightshifts can be sleeping or awake; the staff can be highly skilled and trained in dealing with traumatized children, or un-educated and new to the field. The doors can be open, semi-open or locked. Children can stay for a limited period of time, such as three to six months or be semi-permanent. The residential placement can be part designed as a treatment facility where the residential staff conduct treatment, or more as a home where children live.

13.5.1 Trauma-sensitive care

Traumatized children need residential staff to provide trauma-sensitive care. That means the staff can recognise trauma symptoms and understand the child's behaviour from a trauma perspective. The description of the Sleeping Dogs method is written in practical language with many case examples and psychoeducation such as the window of tolerance, the Volcano, the Heater metaphor can be used to create understanding for the staff. Filling in the Case Conceptualization Form can provide caregivers with an understanding of how the child's symptoms are related to their trauma and make it easier for them to mentalize. Providing trauma-sensitive care can improve the relationship with the children and reduce their behavioural difficulties. By making the staff more trauma-sensitive they can manage the child's trauma symptoms better.

This is great, but getting rid of these trauma symptoms or reducing them with trauma processing is a far more durable solution. When using the Sleeping Dogs method residential staff not only deliver trauma-sensitive care they actually do the stabilization part of the trauma treatment.

13.5.2 Biological parents

The Sleeping Dogs method requires close collaboration with the child's network. The biological parents are the child's attachment figures and the collaboration makes the child feel more safe and protected. Depending on the care environment and contact with the biological parents, these children can suffer from unintentional emotional neglect. These children can grow up with uncertainty about where they are going to live. They can move from residential placement to placement. There they function quite well, since the residential facility does not activate the attachment system to the same degree as a family does. Their attachment anxiety is less strong, the brain does not panic as easily and the child does not have to put so much effort into keeping the anxiety under control as he did in the family. For those children, it is often believed that they are actually better off without an attachment figure. However children need love, like plants need water. Some plants become cactuses with very strong spikes, but even a cactus needs water to survive. Every child, without exception, needs love from an attachment figure. Their biological parents are the only option they have.

For those children permission and acknowledgement from their parents is more important. Biological parents mostly want the best for their children. Years of problems may have disappointed and discouraged them and hurt them so much that they withdrew. Even though they may not say so, most parents worry about their child, they want to know how he is doing, they want to help if they can. Biological parents may have been excluded from their child's life by services, especially the fathers. Often services do not even locate the child's father. When these parents are contacted, they very often do want to be involved.

Residential staff need to invest in these relationships by actively informing and contacting the biological parents. They can phone them weekly to let them know how their child is doing, they can take photos and send them to the child's parents. If possible they can ask the parents or other family members for advice when dealing with certain behaviour or problems. They can lobby for an increase in contact. They can invite the parents to the residential home. By valuing and respecting their input, the parents may become more involved.

13.5.3 Doing interventions

Depending on the residential setting, residential staff can do many of the described interventions with children and/or parents, such as psychoeducation, the daily life interventions, some of the attachment system activating interventions such as mirroring and making a life-story book, the feelings games and emotion regulation exercises. Residential staff can make a workbook with the worksheets. The psychoeducation metaphors, the Safe Deposit Box, the Safe Place, relaxation exercises, feeling games, smileys can even be practised with a group of children.

In a group home, the window of tolerance is explained to Kate, Shirley, Dick and John, between eight and fourteen years old. Dick says he thinks he is mostly a lion when he gets angry, but Kate corrects him. She says Dick sometimes hides like a rabbit when his father is angry with him. Shirley thinks she is mostly a deer. Then she says: 'When you explain it this way, I think my whole family has a small window.' The residential staff hang a drawing of the window of tolerance on the wall in the group home living area.

The safety, attachment and cognitive shift interventions require intense collaboration with the attachment figure. When that is possible, residential staff can do even these. They can become the child's support person besides the attachment figure, the extended parenting environment. Making a Trauma Healing Story for the child with his parents can have a great positive impact. Even when trauma-processing therapy is not available or is not a goal, the child can benefit greatly from the Sleeping Dogs interventions. They can stabilize the child, give him more understanding of himself and more control over his behaviour. It is however important these interventions are done as part of an integral treatment plan.

13.5.4 Conflicts within the residential team

Waking up sleeping dogs reveals the child's trauma and with that his inner feelings and thoughts. This makes the child more vulnerable and increases the intimacy in the relationship with the caregiver. The (counter) transference is stronger and different views on what is best for the child within the team can become more explicit. It is easier to set rules with a focus on behaviour than with a focus on the emotional inner world of the children. Teams need to make a transition to a new way of working where individual differences are tolerated with respect for each other's view. Team members' different opinions reflect the child's inner conflict and this inner conflict needs to be explored. This way of working requires self-reflection and a certain tolerance for uncertainty and ambivalence. When that does not fit the staff's personal affinity and qualities they may choose to change jobs. Regular supervision and non-case-related team meetings are important to guide and support residential teams in these processes.

13.6 Foster care

Foster care systems and regulations differ greatly over the world. After children are taken into care, in some countries parents are given a certain period of time, for example two to three years, to address child protection services' worries and demonstrate new safe parenting behaviour over time. When the parents fail to do this, the child is placed in permanent foster care or is adopted, and the parents have lost their chance. This system provides certainty to the child and family about the future in the foster family, which can contribute to the development of attachment relationships with the foster parents. However the reduced contact with the biological parents can complicate attachment and hinder development as well, especially when the child is very loyal to his parents.

In some countries, foster care placements become permanent, but the parents can still apply for an assessment to have their child returned. In other countries, foster placements remain temporary and the child can be returned to the parents at any time. This system leaves the child and family with uncertainty, which can hinder developing attachment relationships and it is more difficult for the foster parents to guarantee contact. Contact between child and biological parents is maintained. It can be very difficult to find a foster family, or only possible for young children, but fostering children can also be very common. In the following paragraphs the term 'adopted' can replace the term 'foster'.

Another difference is that in some countries foster parents are paid only expenses for fostering a child, or receive a small financial compensation. In other countries foster parents receive a large financial compensation and for some foster parents fostering children is a paid job. This can have a great impact on treatment. Dropout leads to an immediate reduction in income. Foster parents can tolerate behaviour too long to prevent dropout, or the child is replaced with a new child immediately after the placement breaks down.

13.6.1 Foster care environment is not enough

Growing up in a foster family does not guarantee a successful recovery (Jonkman et al., 2017). Providing them with a safe environment and attachment relationships is not enough to overcome the consequences of trauma. Chronically traumatized children need a great deal from their caregivers. They learned survival behaviour in the past, but continue to use that survival behaviour in the present, even when that is no longer needed because the trauma has stopped, or they live in a foster family. They continue to use that survival behaviour because their traumatic memories from the past keep being triggered. While they were abused or neglected, these children have survived by staying connected to the parent in a dysfunctional way, as described in section 2.4.2. These interaction patterns were useful to survive the abusive relationships, however when the abuse has stopped, these children continue to interact in this way. Trying to change these attachment patterns is difficult.

By addressing the traumatic memories of these abusive relationships, the child learns wise lessons and it becomes easier to adapt to new ways of connecting. Evidence-based trauma-focused treatment in addition to the foster placement may improve the child's functioning in the foster family (Jonkman et al., 2017). Until that is done, the foster parents need to tolerate being drawn into these interaction patterns, keep a calm enough brain to reflect and understand, and respond differently. That can be very challenging.

13.6.2 Trauma-sensitive care

Traumatized children need foster parents to provide trauma-sensitive care. That means they can recognize trauma symptoms and understand the child's behaviour from a trauma perspective. The description of the Sleeping Dogs method is written in practical language with many case examples and psychoeducation such as the window of tolerance, the Volcano, the Heater metaphor can be used to create understanding for the foster parents. Providing trauma-sensitive care can improve the relationship with the children and reduce their behavioural difficulties. By making the foster parents more trauma sensitive they can manage the child's trauma symptoms better. This is great, but getting rid of these trauma symptoms or reducing them with trauma processing is a far more durable solution.

13.6.3 Trigger foster parent's own trauma

Even though foster parents are screened before children are placed in their family, they can seriously struggle to provide empathy and trauma-sensitive care. That does not necessarily mean the screening was not done well. Traumatized children can destabilize a previously emotionally healthy family (Wesselmann, 1998). Their chaotic brain creates chaos in the (previously stable) brains of all the family members. The foster parents may have their own traumatic experiences (in childhood, or with previous adoptive or foster children), which makes it more difficult to meet the specific demands of these children. Possibly these foster parents had to wait a long time for the child, or they were not able to have children themselves. When the child's foster parents are relatives, they may have their own trauma history or relationship problems with the child's parents. Caring for the child may trigger these problems.

Suzy (59) was caring for her nine-year-old grandson Sam and ten-year-old granddaughter Tina, after they were removed. Their mother was an alcoholic and had physically abused and neglected them. When Suzy was younger, her children were removed because she had been an alcoholic herself. Her children had witnessed severe domestic violence between their parents. After ten years, Suzy divorced and stopped using alcohol and her children returned home, except for Suzy's daughter who had become an aggressive teenager blaming her mother for her misery. This triggered Suzy's guilt and it was so painful that Suzy started to blame her daughter. Suzy rejected her and they did not have contact for years. Suzy's daughter then repeated her own history with her children, and Tina became an aggressive child. Even after she was removed, she was still aggressive. Now Suzy struggles raising her granddaughter Tina, as Tina's anger reminded her of her own daughter. Even though she loved Tina very much, she was unable to cuddle with Tina and be kind to her. The Circle of Security programme gave her insight into the interaction with Tina and made her aware of what Tina needed. Unfortunately this insight only increased her guilt and shame, as she still remained unable to change her parenting. Her own trauma was blocking progress.

13.6.4 Knowing the child's history

In some countries foster parents do not have access to the child's history to protect the parent's privacy. This can complicate fostering a child greatly. To enable foster parents to understand the child and mentalize the child's actions, they need to understand how the child's dysfunctional interaction patterns evolved. They need to be able to refer to the past when reflecting on the here and now. Knowing the child's history is imperative to overcome and change these patterns. Doctors also need to have access to the child's medical files to assess and value the child's symptoms.

13.6.5 Misinterpreted the child's inner world

The foster or adoptive parent tries to understand the child, but since they have missed the first period in the child's life, it can be difficult for them to form ideas about the child's inner world. These ideas can be wrong and disrupt the relationship even more. For example, the child's indifferent behaviour can give the impression that he has not formed an attachment relationship and that adoptive or foster parents are interchangeable. Foster parents can see the child as having a bad, manipulative, controlling character. They may think that the child is insensitive and that the child provoked them on purpose

He always starts whining just when I sit down for a rest. When I've been looking after him all day and working hard. I'm exhausted and I just want to watch TV for a bit. And the moment I sit down he starts to provoke me. He starts crying and when I come upstairs and stand by his cot, he stops. Then he looks at me and starts to laugh at me, with this big grin all over his face. Well, then I could just throttle him.

Foster parents need assistance in mentalizing the child's actions and the child needs trauma-focused treatment to get rid of the memories driving these interaction patterns. Unfortunately it usually takes a long time before children in foster care are referred for trauma treatment. Skills training or attachment therapies have failed, by which time the relationship with the child may have been seriously disrupted by continuous fights. These may result in a smaller Window of Tolerance for the foster parent, making it harder for them to keep reacting empathically to the child and to prevent rejecting him. The first question is whether the relationship with the foster parents can still be restored.

13.6.6 Are foster parents attachment figures?

The interventions for barrier 1b and 1c are standard for children in foster care. What is the child's perspective? If the foster placement is temporary it is important to discuss the possibility of continuing the relationship between the foster parents and the child even after terminating the placement. Will there still be contact after a child returns home? How close will that be? Can the biological parents permit this? If adoptive or foster parents want to stay in the child's life, maintaining the relationship is the main priority, not maintaining the placement. Foster parents often wrongly assume the child knows their intentions. Having this conversation can have a surprisingly positive impact on the child's behaviour. When a foster placement has ended, this does not mean that the foster placement has failed. Foster parents can still be attachment figures and be part-time parents. The distance that is thus created may help to keep the attachment anxiety under control. The attachment relationships remain intact because contact is regulated for the child and that calms him down and makes him less afraid.

13.6.7 Terminated attachment relationship

However, when the foster parents reject the child and refuse to maintain contact, the terminated adoption or foster placement damages a child and *becomes* a failure. Foster parents do not always realize this because it seems as if the child does not care. These children pack their bags seemingly quite happy and say goodbye as though they couldn't care less. However on the inside the child relates the rejection to himself ('I am such a loser that nobody wants me') and this rejection reinforces the child's negative self-image. These children are trained to disguise their feelings and they do not show their pain and hurt, especially not to the foster parents who have rejected them! Nevertheless, after this fresh rejection the child's attachment anxiety increases making it more difficult to give a new attachment figure a chance.

13.6.8 Decisions around contact between foster and biological parents

It can be common for biological parents not to have any contact with their child's foster family and not even know where their child lives. When there is contact, the child is picked up from and returned to the foster family by the child protection worker. Some children are transported in a taxi to avoid both families meeting. Those children grow up in two worlds, which can promote dissociation and sleeping dogs to keep them apart. They have more trouble with integrating trauma, they rather avoid. In other countries it is common for the foster parents and biological parents to meet each other at contact, unless this is threatening or unsafe. The biological parents know where the child lives and sometimes they even visit the child in their new home or come to his birthday party. This promotes integration of past and present, but the child can also be drawn into conflicts between both worlds and struggle with loyalty. If possible, it is in the child's best interest that his foster parents and biological parents know each other and have contact with each other.

13.6.9 Decisions around parents not showing up for contact with the child

Parents can be unreliable and not show up for contact arrangements with the child or make promises that are not kept. Children can be upset and hurt, which can be difficult to tolerate for the caregivers. It may seem better to avoid the child's disappointment by ceasing contact, not informing the child in advance of an upcoming visit or making excuses for the parent. However this provides only short-term relief. In the long term the child does not form a realistic image of the parent, and the child may start to idealize the parent or demonize the parent. When the child has not learned to deal with his parent's behaviour and understand his intentions he is at risk of becoming even more disappointed later. Later in life, the child may become curious and initiate contact. The child then has to deal with the parent on his own, without the support of his caregivers. It is therefore better to confront the child with reality, however young he may be, so the child gradually develops a realistic view of the parent.

13.6.10 Involving the biological parents

Waking up sleeping dogs for foster children often requires intense collaboration with the biological parents. Foster parents can feel threatened by this. The legal context of the placement can contribute to their fear of losing the child or disrupting the finally stable balance. However when the child's barriers involve his biological parents, it is necessary to involve them in order to wake up sleeping dogs. Much time can be spent on motivating the foster parents and explaining why it is necessary to wake up sleeping dogs. They need to get the relay stick of attachment back (see section 8.6.2).

13.6.11 Doing interventions

Depending on the foster care organization, foster care workers or foster parents can do some of the described interventions with children and/or parents, such as psychoeducation, daily life interventions, some of the attachment interventions such as mirroring and making a life-story book, the feelings games and emotion regulation exercises. It is however important these interventions are done as part of an integral treatment plan. The foster care worker can make a workbook with the worksheets for the child. The foster parent can do interventions with the child, but the foster parent's role is mainly supporting the child, not doing treatment. Foster parents can support treatment by doing work for themselves on keeping a calm brain and supporting the child in doing exercises learned in therapy as homework. The foster care worker may be able to use the safety and cognitive shift interventions. Making a Trauma Healing Story for children in care with their parents can have an enormous positive impact. The child protection worker can have a large role in this.

> Waking up sleeping dogs is a choice for short-term struggle and conflict, but long-term healing and recovery.
>
> Trauma-sensitive care manages the child's trauma symptoms, trauma processing reduces trauma symptoms and is therefore a far more durable solution.

Chapter 14

Specific target groups

This chapter describes the specific aspects of the use of the Sleeping Dogs method with children with a dissociative disorder and conversion. Then adaptations for people with an intellectual disability and cultural aspects are discussed.

14.1 Specific aspects in the treatment of dissociative disorders

Children with a dissociative disorder usually need more interventions to overcome their barriers because they have made their sleeping dogs invisible. They have amnesia for their traumatic memories and it can be a long journey to break through this amnestic barrier. Silberg (2013), Waters (2016) and Wieland (2015) developed excellent treatment models for dissociative children, with comprehensive descriptions of theory, psychoeducation and interventions. The Sleeping Dogs framework can be used in addition to these models, to help the therapist to keep an overview of the treatment process. Working with these children can be challenging. The difficult behaviours and crises can make therapists can lose track of where treatment is heading. The longer therapists work with these children, the stronger the transference of feelings such as fear and pain, leading to avoidance and uncertainty.

Another challenge lies in the fact that these treatments are done in a therapy room by a therapist and therefore require the child to attend sessions. Many dissociative children do not want or cannot attend therapy sessions. The Sleeping Dogs method describes interventions that can be done outside the therapy room by residential staff or caregivers.

The following paragraphs describe the aspects of the Sleeping Dogs treatment of children with a dissociative disorder requiring attention.

14.1.1 Goal of treatment

As mentioned, traumatic memories and detachment are the two main aspects of a dissociative disorder. The amnesia for traumatic memories is resolved by improving the child's attachment relationships, activating his attachment system and improving emotion regulation. The child can start to remember, because he now has someone to support and regulate him. The child does not need to dissociate anymore. He has to overcome his phobias of the traumatic memories and keep his level of stress within the Window of Tolerance while looking at those memories. By processing the traumatic memories and integrating them, the child does not need structural dissociation anymore and can integrate. He will have to acknowledge that all the parts are one, that he himself has experienced the traumatic events and not someone else. After this he will realize that a flashback is a memory from the past and not something that is happening now.

14.1.2 Therapeutic relationship

After engaging these children in therapy, children with a dissociative disorder need a large amount of therapeutic sessions with a therapist. Providing treatment to these children requires not only knowledge of dissociation, but also skills in managing transference and counter transference processes (see section 15.10). In the relationship with the child, there needs to be an optimal balance between proximity and distance. This balance is dynamic, and the therapist should adapt to the child, the phase of the treatment and whatever action system has been activated (Van der Hart et al., 2006). The attachment relationship with the attachment figure is the main relationship, and the professional keeps an emotional distance. At the start, the attachment system will be activated. This increases the need for proximity, but also activates attachment anxiety and the defence action system. If there is an increase in internal conflicts, children can react in a number of different ways. The professional should be on the alert for this, because too much intimacy and familiarity could also mean an increase in the defences. The child can put the relationship with the professional to the test, to see whether he can be trusted.

In the trauma-processing phase, the parts that are stuck in one action system will be activated. In the relationship with the professional, the child will then re-enact the attachment relationship that he himself has experienced. Processing means finding solutions and conclusions that are different from those the child experienced before. The professional can be put in the position and role of the negligent parent, the sadistic abuser, the idealized saviour or the seducer (Courtois, 1999). In this phase, the child will also have to recognize certain cognitions concerning himself (bad, dirty, shameful), and his fear of being rejected or criticized by the professional will be intense. During trauma processing, his fear of the traumatic memories will also intensify his need to be saved by the professional. The child may cling to the professional, for fear of being overwhelmed by his emotions.

During the integration phase, the attachment need will increase and the attachment anxiety will decrease. Secure attachment to the professional helps the child to take more risks in daily life and to discover new relationships. Towards the end of the therapy, fear of abandonment may be activated. This will therefore have to be a gradual process.

14.1.3 Safety

It is highly unlikely that treatment of a dissociating child will be successful in the long term if, after treatment, the child returns to a parent who reacts to the child on the basis of his own unresolved traumas (Wieland, 2007). If the parent reacts to the child with different internal self-representations (the frightening other, the anxious other, the caring other), the child will have to also develop various internal self-representations (victim, perpetrator, caregiver) (Liotti, 1999). When the child has contact with the biological parents or lives with them, it is essential to work with the child and the biological parents.

14.1.4 Daily Life: the child is one person

Children with a dissociative disorder experience their world differently. Thus the child may be faced with the consequences of damaging the curtains even though he does not remember doing so. They believe that parts of their personality are actually other people or voices or ghosts. It is essential to interact with these children, in therapy, at home and in school based on the reality. They are one child and one personality. Even though they do not know or feel that yet. When they say they did not do or say something, they are not lying but they have amnesia. Even when it is another part of the personality that is active, the child is still held responsible for this behaviour.

Various parts of the child may have different opinions and remember different things. This is similar to the internal conflicts and opposing ideas in all human beings. In these children, however, the internal conflicts are carried to extremes and are not tolerated. Such experiences will strengthen his motivation to work on dissociation and his traumatic memories. Going along with the child's wish that there is more than one person, means going along with the phobic avoidance of reality, and this can worsen the structural dissociation.

14.1.5 Daily Life: controlling switching between parts

Children and their caregivers need to learn to recognize switching between parts so they can try and reduce the need to switch. They switch between parts when they feel threatened and the defence system is activated. There is always a trigger and a transition period, before the child switches between parts. Before switching their perception and consciousness become focused on danger. Recognizing this twilight state and learning to prevent the switch from actually taking place is the first thing these children must learn. This will allow them to experience control, which will make them more stable. They need to learn interventions to control flashbacks, because when they have flashbacks these increase the anxiety and the phobia of the trauma and the other parts even more and it strengthens the structural dissociation. A Safe Place or Safe Deposit Box can be created for the child, or several different ones for the different parts.

14.1.6 Daily Life: strengthening the 'normal' part of the personality

In order to prevent switching, the normal part of the personality that holds the daily life action system needs to become stronger. That part of the child must learn to solve problems in daily life so the child does not need to switch.

14.1.7 Daily Life: internal boardroom technique

The child can be taught how to use the internal boardroom technique (a dissociative table technique/conference room) where all the parts meet and discuss the decisions that have to be made (Fraser, 1991; Forgash, 2009). The boardroom can also be used during trauma processing. The child can decide which parts will be included. The other parts can go to a safe place.

14.1.8 Language that stimulates integration for children with a dissociative disorder

Wieland (2007) describes how caregivers can promote the child's integration by addressing the child as one child with various different states. This calms the child and makes him feel understood. Caregivers can be taught to practise this at home in the following manner.

> My love is for all the Sandras, angry Sandra, cheerful Sandra, sex-Sandra and frightened Sandra, because I love them all.
> Cheerful Sandra wants to go to bed now, but angry Sandra wants to watch TV and pick a fight. Cheerful Sandra can help angry Sandra to go to bed anyway.
> Cheerful Sandra can tell frightened Sandra that it is safe now and that she needn't be scared.

Caregivers can visualize this with a Matryoshka (Russian) doll (see section 5.5.1).

14.1.9 Improving attachment relationships

The next step in treatment is improving the attachment relationships. This usually requires a lot of time. The child must learn that adults can help them. That his emotions are OK, that they are allowed to be there, that emotions are helpers in life and they must learn how to regulate these emotions. To achieve this they will have to form a meaningful attachment relationship with someone and to overcome their fear of trusting people. In adolescents with a dissociative disorder, frightened child parts may emerge which have a great need of being reassured. This need in the adolescent was never satisfied when he was little.

For these adolescents, it is important that they learn how to reassure themselves and become less dependent, instead of needing reassurance from someone else such as the therapist. These adolescents can soothe themselves by letting their adolescent part (the part acting from the daily life action system) do exercises or read the text for the child parts (defence action system). By taking care of themselves, they can learn to control their fear and their need for care (expressed in child parts which are perceived as 'foreign').

14.1.10 Improving emotion regulation

Children with dissociative disorders usually have a part with seemingly no feelings, and parts with violent, overwhelming feelings. Those parts keep and express the old, trauma feelings. Those feelings are very strong and overwhelming and they make the child even more afraid of feelings. The different parts then become afraid of each other. They don't understand the behaviour and feelings of the other parts. The child judges the feelings and behaviour of other parts from his own perspective, that is, his own action system. Anger may be used for protection and defence by one part, for another part it is a disgusting feeling that causes trouble. Fear may be overwhelming panic for one part, caused by traumatic memories, but another part does not share these memories and sees fear as a weak and stupid. Whereas sexual feelings can be disgusting for one part, for the other it is a habit, or a way of getting attention. The easy solution is to pretend that those other feelings and forms of behaviour belong to another person.

To be able to process the traumatic memories, all parts of the personality have to be able to integrate. The child must be able to experience and accept all feelings and kinds of behaviour. Explaining the purpose of the different feelings is the first step. This helps the child to learn to better understand his own feelings and behaviour. The child can learn to re-label his own behaviour as something with a positive value. The child can, for instance, formulate sentences about himself, re-labelling his behaviour.

I cut myself because it numbs the emotional pain, to keep it bearable.
I have sex because I can't bear to be alone.
I am aggressive because I feel unsafe, even when there is no need to, and with this aggression I defend myself.

The child can be taught to see all his behaviour, terrible as it may be, as an attempt to achieve goals that were important in the past. These goals may not be relevant anymore in the present, but if that part of the child still thinks it is unsafe, these goals may still be actively pursued in the present. If the child starts to understand why those parts of him do those terrible things, this behaviour becomes less frightening: there is a reason for it, and this makes it predictable.

In this way the child's phobia for his own inner world is neutralized. Children are usually most frightened of the aggressive parts. Sometimes the child may hear voices giving him aggressive orders. When the child starts to understand that anger is useful and not bad, he will be better able to accept his own anger. This can be explained as I did with Sandra.

Sandra (7)

Of course it is not nice when angry Sandra breaks things and calls your foster mother names. But I think she doesn't do that to upset you. The angry Sandra in you tries to protect you. Very bad things happened when she was little. You couldn't be angry then, that was very dangerous when you were so small. Angry Sandra has stored up all that anger from long ago for you. That is how she took care of you and protected you when you were so small. She was a hero. Angry Sandra has kept all those bad things that happened to you, so you don't have to think about them all the time.

But now angry Sandra does not have to take care of you anymore, your foster parents do that now. But angry Sandra does not know this. She thinks everybody is there to hurt you. We should tell her, so you can also use her anger without getting into trouble because of it. Angry Sandra is very strong, and that can come in handy. Anger can also help you to stand up for yourself and let others know you don't like something. Angry Sandra just has to learn that you are safe now and that your foster parents take care of you.

When the child learns to control his anger, the need to structurally dissociate the anger disappears. The same goes for the other parts. The child learns to make better use of the different parts of his personality and to use his feelings adaptively. The internal cooperation improves and the internal conflicts diminish.

14.1.11 Cognitive Shift: working with biological parents

Working with the biological parents to create more safety and provide the child with acknowledgement for his innocence is often imperative to access the deeper dissociated negative ideas about themselves including the perpetrator parts.

14.1.12 The Nutshell: gradually exposing the child

If a child is gradually subjected to traumatic memories he will be more in control. The Nutshell Check is an initial step. But it may be necessary to go even slower. A summary of experiences can be made if a child has had a lot of similar experiences – for example, years of sexual abuse. It may then be hard for a child to choose the worst experience. Scanning the various videos or images in his head is in itself too overwhelming. The child can then make a summary of the most important elements in all those memories, and incorporate these in, as it were, a compilation video. A video can be cut into sections, and the child can deal with one section of the video in each session. A plan can be made to help the child to stay in the present. If necessary, the child can bring an object that helps him with this (such as a stuffed animal).

14.1.13 Trauma processing with EMDR therapy for children with dissociative disorders

In their articles, van der Hart et al. (2013, 2014) outline how EMDR therapy can be integrated into the treatment of dissociative disorders in adults. Even though EMDR therapy with dissociative children differs from adults, these articles can be useful to understand the structure of treatment. Two book chapters describe the use of EMDR therapy with children and adolescents with a dissociative disorder (Hauber, 2017; Struik, 2017a). Keep in mind that this description alone is not sufficient to attempt to apply these techniques. It is essential that the therapist is trained in the assessment and treatment of structural dissociation. In children with a dissociative disorder trauma processing very often takes place in layers, especially when the structural dissociation is more elaborate. They go through several cycles of stabilization, trauma processing and integration, and back to stabilization.

14.1.13.1 Involve all parts during processing

Depending on the degree of separation between the various parts, it may be necessary to actively involve the various parts of the personality in treatment. As the child grows older, the phobia for the different parts of the personality increases, and more parts of the personality may develop, which are more clearly differentiated. In adolescents, structural dissociation is generally further advanced and the phobia for traumatic memories and parts is strong. The following examples illustrate how to involve all the parts of the child in the process.

All the Ellies are looking at the picture now – Ellie who is seven, and scared Ellie from when you were two and couldn't talk yet, and angry Ellie. What is it like looking at the picture now? Does it feel better? And how bad is it for scared Ellie? Where inside you is scared Ellie? In your tummy? Okay, just try to concentrate on how scared Ellie feels in your tummy. And how bad is it now? Not bad anymore? Is scared Ellie still there? Is she really quite gone or is there still a bit of a scared feeling left in your tummy? Can you tell that scared Ellie inside you that she doesn't have to be scared anymore? That you aren't two anymore but seven? That you have grown very strong and that it can't ever happen anymore. That you are safe now.

When you were small you were all alone and there was nobody who could comfort you. Little Ellie must have felt terribly alone. And now? Are you still all alone? Do you feel that mother is comforting you now? There wasn't any comfort then, and now there is. Isn't that nice? We've worked on all the pictures now, you said. Has angry Ellie got any more pictures? Okay, then angry Ellie can draw those pictures. Wow, that Ellie can really get angry! Isn't it great that you've got such a strong Ellie inside? She can protect you really well. If you look at the picture now, and scared Ellie and angry Ellie also look, all of you look at the picture together, how bad is it now? Not bad anymore? Okay, now imagine that scared Ellie gets older and older, from two to seven. Can you see that in your mind? Scared Ellie doesn't have to be afraid any more, she is seven years old now. You aren't two anymore, you're seven. Now imagine angry Ellie getting older and older, from two to seven. Just concentrate on that.

And angry Ellie also becomes you. Then you are one Ellie, who can get really angry sometimes and sometimes scared, but doesn't have to be afraid of daddy any more. That is all over now and it is safe. Just concentrate on that.

14.1.14 Integration and dissociative disorders

For children with a dissociative disorder, integration means accepting all the parts of themselves. Trauma processing is complete when a child with a dissociative disorder realizes that he *himself* has had all these experiences (personification) and that they are experiences from the *past* (presentification) (Van der Hart et al., 2006). The child's explanation was initially: 'This is so bad, it can't have happened to me so it must have happened to someone else.' In this way the child has come to experience a part of himself as a different person. After processing the memories and integration, all the parts of the personality realize that they exist in the present and their traumatic experiences happened in the past. They are just memories. If, after trauma processing, spontaneous integration of parts of the personality has not taken place, it will be necessary to help the child with this. The following exercise can be used.

Imagine that you are a river, a big, wide, flowing river. And all your parts are small rivers, flowing down from the mountains. Imagine that all those small rivers flow out into the big river. All the water comes together in one big stream that continues to flow on. All the parts of you come together and become one part; one you, in which all the parts are united. Nothing is lost – the anger, the sadness, the distress, those parts that have now become helpers – they all come together and you become one. Because the big river has taken up all the small rivers it is very strong and it just flows on and on.

A different metaphor can be used, such as beams of light, or a rainbow.

When children integrate, their physical appearance can change. They seem more relaxed and more flexible. They are more able to use fantasy and play, they start exploring and experimenting, and school results can improve significantly. Their feelings become more visible to others and caretakers often say they feel more connected to the child and there is more intimacy. They are more able to tolerate ambivalence, internal conflicts and contradictory thoughts and feelings. The black-and-white thinking which is typical for traumatized children is the opposite of integrated thinking. This can initially complicate life as 'ambivalence is a price of increasing integration' (Van der Hart et al., 2006, p. 346).

14.2 Specific aspects in the treatment of conversion

Traumatic memories are seldom accessible when children use somatic dissociation (conversion) as a psychological defence. They suffer from amnesia, or from conversion symptoms as soon as the child even thinks of the traumatic event. The child does not appear to be stressed, but in reality the stress level of the brain is outside its Window of Tolerance. These children first need to be stabilized. Children with somatic dissociation first need to improve their active defence reactions such as fight, flight or hide (from the hyperarousal state). When the active reactions offer sufficient stress reduction, conversion as a last resort is no longer necessary. They need to become more aware of the stress in their bodies so they actually feel the anger, anxiety or sadness and use their active defence reactions to protect themselves.

Since the amnestic barrier is lowering, this may lead to an increase in flashbacks, nightmares and hypervigilance, even when the child did not have these before. Once the first step has been taken and there are fewer conversion symptoms, the child can learn to gain more control of his stress regulation and stay inside his Window of Tolerance. It may seem as if the problems are initially getting worse. Children often do not like this, because avoidance and not feeling anything, their survival strategy, feels more comfortable than actually experiencing stress. Conversion has become an effective way of avoiding for these children, and as soon as they sense that their stress level is rising, they will prefer to keep avoiding. For the parents too, it is important to predict this interim phase and to label it as a positive effect: it is actually a good thing that their child is more often irritated and angry. It is often necessary to pay attention repeatedly to the child's motivation. Another thing to keep in mind is that the longer the conversion lasts, the more difficult it is to change.

Conversion will disappear completely after trauma processing has been completed successfully. However, because the brain has become used to conversion as a solution for extreme stress, chances are conversion will return if a new stressful situation arises. In the integration phase, the child will have to practise a lot in order to learn new techniques for stress regulation and to deal with his emotions in a different way. The brain has to let go of the old ingrained habit – conversion. With these children more work needs to be done on emotion regulation.

14.3 People with an intellectual disability

The Sleeping Dogs method is used for children and adults with an intellectual disability. The concrete simple interventions combined with the systemic approach, suits this group. Since it is not enough to simply use the developmental age instead of the calendar age, this chapter describes the specific aspects of working with this group. Barbara van Blanken, Susan van der Woude and Joss Schrijver, psychologists working with children and adults with an intellectual disability, co-authored a chapter on the Sleeping Dogs method for children and adults with an intellectual disability in the Netherlands (Struik, 2016). The following paragraphs are based on this chapter.

14.3.1 Intellectual disability

In this chapter the term 'people with an intellectual disability' is used to indicate 'children and adults with an intellectual disability'. Children and adults with an intellectual disability can present very diversely. They not only have cognitive problems, but also have difficulties in adaptive functioning and they need permanent support. It is often assumed that the impairment of people with an intellectual disability function is similar to the way young children function. However there are significant differences. People with an intellectual disability can have a disharmonic profile of functioning. Contrary to young children, they are surrounded by peers who function at a higher level. Because they try and hide their impairment and it is not recognized, they are frequently overrated. Many experiences of failing can lead to a negative self-image and behavioural difficulties. They want to be accepted and depend on external support, which makes them an easy prey for abuse. They can grow up in multi-problem families without the social support to protect them from traumatization. So in a way, trauma treatment for people with an intellectual disability can be compared to the treatment of a younger child, but only when one puts in mind that this child grew up amongst smarter and older peers, can feel incompetent, is frequently overrated and has a higher risk to be abused.

14.3.2 Trauma symptoms

According to the DSM-5 an intellectual disability involves impairments of general mental abilities that impact adaptive functioning in three domains or areas which determine how well an individual copes with everyday tasks:

- The conceptual domain includes skills in language, reading, writing, maths, reasoning, knowledge, and memory.
- The social domain refers to empathy, social judgement, interpersonal communication skills, the ability to make and retain friendships, and similar capacities.
- The practical domain centres on self-management in areas such as personal care, job responsibilities, money management, recreation, and organizing school and work tasks (American Psychiatric Association, 2013).

The consequences of traumatization as described in this book are the same for this target group, with some specific aspects. The lack of research and assessment tools makes it difficult to recognize traumatization. Trauma symptoms are more often expressed in aggressive or sexualized behaviour, self-harm, dissociation, physical symptoms, withdrawal from and avoiding emotional or any kind of contact with others. Medical trauma is more prevalent (Mevissen, 2016; Mevissen & Didden, 2017).

14.3.3 Trauma-focused treatment

Even though they are more at risk of being traumatized, very few people with an intellectual disability receive trauma-focused treatment. Clinicians struggle to adjust treatment to their abilities and can be scared to make things worse, they underestimate or minimize the impact of traumatizing circumstances and are unaware of the huge positive changes that are possible.

One of the necessary adaptations when providing trauma-focused treatment is to collaborate with the caregivers. The caregiver preferably joins in the sessions for several reasons. People with an intellectual disability struggle to generalize and caregivers can assist them to use skills they have learned in daily life. Their self-report is often unreliable and caregivers can inform the clinician about the effect of interventions. The interventions can be made more concrete by drawing what has been explained, constructing things or acting them out. They need to be repeated over and over. Video recordings can be helpful so the caregivers can repeat the interventions at home.

14.3.3.1 Analysis of barriers for awake dogs

People with an intellectual disability may speak about their traumatic memories, and therefore have awake dogs. However because they do not always oversee the consequences of discussing their memories, they get stuck during processing more easily. Their strong feelings overwhelm them, they feeling guilty and ashamed or they become scared of the consequences. It is therefore advised to analyse possible barriers even when the child or adult talks about the traumatic memories, just to be on the safe side.

14.3.3.2 Psychoeducation

The psychoeducation interventions need to be adapted. They are very important to increase the child or adult's competence and autonomy and improve their negative self-image. Taking the time to explain things so they get an understanding of themselves is worthwhile. Involving the caregivers in this psychoeducation can increase their trauma-sensitive approach.

14.3.3.3 Safety

People with an intellectual disability are easy prey for (sexual) abuse or bullying. Threatening them can be very effective. Their network is limited which can make it harder to disclose. They can think things are normal and therefore not say anything. Besides safety in regards to past abuse, it can also be necessary to work on safety in daily life. When they continue to be dysregulated or abused by contacts via social media and the Internet, the use of those may need to be restricted. The attachment figure's support is more important and needs to be made concrete. He can take the child to therapy, phone or send a text or video message or a postcard. He can lend the child his favourite T-shirt to wear to the sessions. Even adults need this support from family members or their network. When adults get older their family may have died or they may not have a network anymore. Then friends, professional caregivers or even an animal may need to take this role. It is difficult for them to know what others think and permission from their parents needs to be made explicit.

14.3.3.4 Daily life

People with an intellectual disability can experience many problems in daily life. Their behavioural symptoms can be difficult to manage. The course of their healing process is more unpredictable. Their family, caregivers, school and work need to be able to deal with a temporary worsening of symptoms. This requires extensive preparation and psychoeducation.

The concrete interventions described in Chapter 7 can be very helpful.

14.3.3.5 Attachment

Talking about traumatic memories can disrupt people in the network, especially when they also are traumatized or have an intellectual disability. Extra psychoeducation and support may be needed for them to keep a calm brain. Support workers from family members are involved in the treatment so everyone is on the same page. This can be a huge, but necessary, investment. Making a life-story book can be helpful for people in out of home care.

14.3.3.6 Emotion regulation

Fear of strong emotions or dissociation can form a barrier with people with an intellectual disability. It can be hard to predict what they are going to feel and how they will react. This may require preparation. Experience-oriented therapies can support emotion regulation.

14.3.3.7 Cognitive shift

Since it is more difficult to understand cause–consequence and their self-image largely depends on what others think of them, extra work can be needed to overcome guilt and shame. They need to understand and tolerate their mixed feelings about the abuse (It was painful to be hurt, but it was nice to get attention) or the abuser (I love mum but I do not like what she did). Guilt and shame can be very persistent. Making a Trauma Healing Story can be very helpful.

14.3.3.8 Motivation Check

Similar to younger children, motivation for people with an intellectual disability is more externally driven. The caregiver's support is imperative.

14.3.3.9 Nutshell Check

Similar to younger children, people with an intellectual disability can struggle to have an overview of their memories. The clinician needs to have additional information of the traumatic experiences from the child's network or files, prior to doing this check.

14.3.3.10 Trauma processing

There is some evidence that EMDR therapy may be an effective treatment for people with an intellectual disability (Mevissen, Didden, Korzilius, & de Jongh, 2017), but this is not enough to make it evidence based. However, why would EMDR therapy not work? It is much less verbal than TF-CBT, and it is evidence based for children from eight years old. An adapted child protocol for EMDR therapy or the Story Telling Protocol (Lovett, 1999) for infants can be used for people with an intellectual disability according to their developmental age.

14.3.3.11 Integration

In the integration phase extensive work can be done on emotion regulation and social skills to prevent future traumatization. Repairing relationships and forgiveness, setting boundaries, having safe contact or no contact with family can contribute to that. The problem areas, which are consequences of the intellectual disability, can be addressed such as daily routine, education, work, free time, friendships, use of social media, relationships, sexuality, physical health and self-care.

Twenty-year-old Daisy (IQ 70) was physically and sexually abused and prostituted by her father between the ages of six and nine, when Daisy's mother was at work or asleep. He told her she was a whore and devil and, by sexually abusing her, he would get rid of the devil. When Daisy was nine, her mother took her and her siblings to a shelter. Her mother had an intellectual disability and was sexually abused herself. When Daisy was sixteen, she was hospitalized for a few months because of severe self-harm, hearing voices and extreme fear of men. She was undressed and restrained several times during this period, which traumatized her. She was diagnosed with schizophrenia and borderline personality disorder.

When Daisy was 20 she was admitted to a psychiatric unit because of severe self-harm and suicidal actions. She continued to cut and tried to strangle herself and disclosed that the voices in her head made her do that. She was afraid to be hit or punished. After several months she went home and started treatment. Daisy wanted to get rid of the people in her head and wanted her nightmares to stop. She wanted to no longer hate herself. She wanted not to be afraid of men anymore and learn to tolerate touch.

Daisy lived with her husband. She visited a care facility for people with an intellectual disability during working hours and a support worker visited her weekly. Daisy became increasingly triggered by seeing dark men, touch, brushing teeth, eating meat, yelling and loud noises. She had flashbacks of the restraining during hospitalization and wanted to process her memories. After starting with trauma processing, she became so suicidal and self-harmed so severely that she was admitted again for three weeks. Daisy had not been stable enough, even though she presented with awake dogs.

Daisy went home and started with Sleeping Dogs treatment. Her support worker joined her in all the sessions. A dissociative disorder was diagnosed and Daisy had several parts of the personality: a young frightened girl and two angry parts with men's voices. The Sleeping Dogs analysis showed several barriers that needed to be worked on.

Psychoeducation was given to Daisy, her mother and husband in the presence of their support workers. These support workers repeated this psychoeducation at home. Periodically Daisy's husband and her mother came to the sessions to repeat psychoeducation and increase their support for Daisy. Daisy increased control over her dissociation with exercises from the Daily Life chapter. Her husband and mother helped her with this. Having sex with her husband continued to dysregulate her. Her support-worker discussed with Daisy and her husband, who also had an intellectual disability, and his support worker that it would be better to stop having sex for a while. He understood, but also struggled. Via the Internet Daisy contacted other victims of sexual abuse and their stories dysregulated her. She could not stop doing that and decided to hand in her phone.

Daisy continued to be afraid and hate and blame herself, despite numerous conversations. She started with experience-oriented therapy in addition to the Sleeping Dogs sessions. She learned to tolerate and express normal anger, which reduced the need to dissociate anger. Her assertiveness was threatening to her husband and mother and they needed several sessions to understand that was progress. She became less afraid and started to understand that she was not responsible. Her mother and husband acknowledged that she was innocent as well. Daisy's mother started to blame herself, which then dysregulated Daisy again. Psychoeducation got them back on track, but many months went by before Daisy was ready for trauma processing.

After fifteen months of stabilization she passed the Nutshell Check. She processed her memories in fifteen EMDR therapy sessions with her support worker present. She changed from a shy, anxious person into a strong young woman. In the integration phase she learned to live 'without the noise in her head' as she called it. The voices had been with her for so long that it felt strange without them. She stopped using medication for her anxiety. She learned how to make friends and wanted to work with animals. She learned gradually to have sex with her husband in a pleasant way. Her mother and husband had to get used to the new assertive Daisy. Her mother warned her numerous times that she was going to have a fall back in winter, which had happened for the past ten years. Daisy reassured her mother every time that was not going to happen, and when spring came, she could proudly say she had healed.

14.4 Cultural adaptations

The Sleeping Dogs method is based on a holistic approach and with adaptations it can be used with children and families from all cultures and can incorporate religious beliefs.

14.4.1 Find out the families' views

The concept of trauma differs greatly amongst cultures. The first step is to find out how the child's family and network views trauma and how they believe the consequences of trauma can be dealt with. The Sleeping Dogs method is based on the view that children and their families are provided with knowledge through psychoeducation. This knowledge makes the child competent to make decisions on whether the child wants to do trauma treatment. This focus on autonomy may not fit with the expectations in certain cultures, where the medical model is more common. They may expect the professional to advise and determine what to do. Because the Sleeping Dogs method is based on providing knowledge to the child and family so they can determine what is best, the method allows very well for cultural adaptations to fit the child and family's views and beliefs. The simple language and concrete interventions are easy to use with children and families who cannot communicate with the professional in their own language. These paragraphs describe some of the possible adaptations to make this method more culturally appropriate. This however is work in progress and any further suggestions, ideas or feedback are welcomed.

14.4.2 Psychoeducation and motivation

Psychoeducation and motivation interventions need to be adjusted to fit with the family's belief system and ways of thinking. Motivation may need to be increased more by external factors than internal.

14.4.3 Safety

Hitting children to discipline them is accepted in some cultures and not accepted or allowed in others. Parents can struggle with this after immigration. When physical abuse is addressed, the parent claims this to be a way of disciplining. The parent can be made aware of the laws of the country they reside in and it is obvious that those laws need to be obeyed. That means that those parents need to learn new ways of disciplining their children, which can be a struggle. Some parents also claim that because the hitting is culturally accepted, their child is not traumatized. That could be true.

It is not so much the event itself, but the child's *experience* of the event that differentiates between this event becoming a normal or a traumatic memory. A child can have a memory of being beaten with a belt, because he had been naughty. All his friends laughed at him, because he could not sit for a week. This has become a normal memory when the child tells this funny story and says it taught him a wise lesson: not to steal any more candy from the shops. This same event can become a traumatic memory, when the child cannot recall the event without feeling terrified, bad and ashamed. The child remembers his father's uncontrollable rage and he was scared he was going to die. He felt hurt, alone and rejected, and the hitting could not be discussed openly. His brother or friends were never beaten, therefore he must be a bad child and he hates himself.

When it is culturally appropriate to hit children, the child is punished for his behaviour not for his being. When hitting is viewed as an accepted way of disciplining, this can be a protective factor. Because it is a predictable consequence of behaviour, the child is less likely to hate himself. However, this is mostly not the case when child protection services are involved. Hitting turns into excessive beatings where the parent loses control over himself because of the parent's own stress, traumatization or mental health issues. Hitting becomes very frequent and is not so much a predictable outcome of the child's naughty behaviour, but a result of the parent's emotional state. This is neither accepted nor appropriate in any culture. It is child abuse and it needs to stop because it is traumatizing.

14.4.4 Attachment

The theory and interventions on attachment stem from a western viewpoint where the child has one mother and father. Children growing up in other cultures may have a large extended family network with family members who are also regarded as fathers and mothers. This significantly increases the options to find an attachment figure as the child has many more important relationships. The interventions with only the parents then need to be adjusted to involve other family members with parental roles. This support network also offers more options to support the attachment figure when keeping a calm brain.

Children can also feel attached to their country or the land they were born in. Being on their land can provide them with a safe and secure feeling. Participating in cultural, spiritual or religious activities or rituals, and listening to stories can also increase activation of their attachment system. Interventions to overcome barrier 3c need to be adjusted. For example, in a residential facility where many children lived far away, all children received a necklace with a small tube with earth from the land where they were born. The staff invited elders from their cultural group to teach the children songs and dances.

14.4.5 Cognitive shift

The theory and interventions on working on the child's cognitions also stem from a western individual viewpoint. In some cultures the individualistic viewpoint is not so common and the child's core beliefs are not individually determined. The person's self-image continues to depend more on what others think about him or how he is treated, instead of internalizing these views. The ideas about shifting from a negative to a positive cognition may then seem strange or difficult to understand. It can be necessary to include family members as standard in the preparation of the cognitive shift or make a Trauma Healing Story.

14.4.6 The Nutshell and trauma processing

Making an overview of memories in a structured and concrete way may seem strange in some cultures. Life cannot be reduced to files or folders in a drawer.

The overview may consist of a story or a storyboard. Western methods for trauma processing can be used when the traditional ways of healing are not sufficient. EMDR therapy can easily be combined with traditional ways to process trauma such as story telling, painting, singing, dancing, making music to create the bi-lateral stimulation that is required during processing.

Traditional, spiritual or cultural ways of healing can be combined or integrated into the western way of healing to increase the effect of treatment.

Chapter 15

Planning and the treatment process

This chapter describes some practical details of the treatment process in addition to the explanation provided in Chapter 4. Two case examples illustrate the process of Sleeping Dogs treatments.

15.1 Selection

The first selection criterion for this method is that the child needs to have experienced chronic traumatization. The second criterion is that the child cannot participate in regular trauma-focused treatment. Either the child refuses or the caregivers think the child is unable to engage.

15.2 Setting

The Sleeping Dogs method can be used for children living at home, children in foster care or in residential care.

15.3 Planning treatment

The professional leading treatment gathers information and fills in the Case Conceptualization Form with the other professionals to get an overview of the case. When it is unsure whether the child has awake or sleeping dogs, the Motivation and Nutshell Checks can be done. It is a misconception that children who do not spontaneously talk about their memories all have sleeping dogs. When asked, a large number of children actually do want to. It has simply never been suggested to them. When the child has sleeping dogs, the Barriers Form is filled in and an Action Plan is made. This plan consists of concrete actions. A date is set to evaluate which actions have been done and which barriers are still left. After trauma processing, the child's progress on developmental areas is evaluated and new actions are planned. Treatment ends when the goals are reached.

There are a few interventions that are very frequently used in Sleeping Dogs treatments. These are marked bold in the Barriers Action Plan: Inform the child about the parent's emotional permission (if the parent can give that permission), the Safe Deposit Box, finding a princess, the Motivation and Nutshell Checks.

15.4 The Development and Barriers Tool

Children with chronic traumatization suffer from developmental trauma. They struggle not only with traumatic memories, but also with problems on all areas of development. In their reports, child protection and youth workers often need to describe the child's current functioning and make plans to improve the child's health and wellbeing. The five items (safety, daily life, attachment, emotion regulation and cognitive shift) from the Sleeping Dogs method can also be used to assess the child's general development and circumstances with the Development and Barriers Tool (see Appendix 3). This new tool is inspired by a tool that was developed in collaboration with Københavns Kommune in Denmark.

Københavns Kommune, an organization for child protection and youth services in Denmark, has started a trauma project to provide both trauma treatment to children and guide case management to improve their health and wellbeing. The collaboration between clinicians providing treatment and child protection and youth workers forms the basis of this project. The Sleeping Dogs method provides shared language which makes collaboration easier. The Sleeping Dogs method's tools have been adapted to the Københavns Kommune system and the project goals, and translated in Danish into the Analyse- og Arbejdsværktøjet. With this tool, professionals assess the child's traumatization, his development and circumstances, and his barriers, if the child has sleeping dogs. The child participates in trauma processing, if needed preceded by Sleeping Dogs treatment. Parallel or consecutive interventions are planned to improve the child's health and wellbeing. The collaboration with child protection services makes it easier to overcome barriers to treatment, and child protection services have input from clinicians, which gives them clear guidelines for decision-making and planning. The results of the Københavns Kommune trauma project will be published in 2022.

15.4.1 The use of the Development and Barriers Tool

The Development and Barriers Tool consists of two sets of questions. The green questions focus on the child's development and circumstances and the red questions focus on barriers to trauma processing. Overcoming the child's barriers to trauma processing has priority. The green areas that are identified as insufficient (score 1 or 2), are preferably worked on in the integration phase. The child and family need to be able to focus and not have too many meetings and sessions at the same time. However some interventions can be done in parallel, such as finding family that the child has lost contact with and reconnecting them, or improving daily life, finding a new school or working on education, improving the parent's self-regulation.

15.5 Case examples

The following case examples (source: Struik, 2018) illustrate the use of the Sleeping Dogs method for two children. In the first example, Lea, a three-year-old girl, it becomes clear how the Sleeping Dogs method can be used to collaborate with child protection services and how their decisions can have a huge positive impact. The second example, Fiona, a six-year-old girl, illustrates how children can blame themselves and how working with the abuser-parents including the absent abuser-parent, enables children to relieve that self-blame.

15.5.1 Case example Lea

Upon referral, Lea (three years and four months) was hyperaroused and had two or three tantrums a day in which she swore, kicked and screamed at the residential staff. She stayed at a residential facility in a group of six children with rotating staff. Lea expressed being sad, isolated herself from other children and cried several times daily, asking why she could not go home. Two or three times a night Lea woke up screaming and needed up to half an hour to fall back asleep with the help of staff. When mentioning grandmother or mother Lea became terrified, started screaming and kicking and she refused to discuss or visit them.

Lea's parents were methamphetamine users, and her father dealt drugs from home. Lea's twin brother had died at birth. Lea's parents were incarcerated when she was nine months old and she then lived with her paternal grandmother. Child protection services were notified several times by neighbours, as they heard the grandmother yelling and hitting and Lea crying. After an investigation, Lea was found to have unexplained scars and broken bones and child protection services suspected Lea was neglected and possibly physically and sexually abused in her parents' and grandmothers' care.

Lea (one year and nine months) was placed in foster care, with a single mother, who reported Lea struggled with anxiety, sleeping difficulties and defiant behaviour. She was terrified of people with a deep voice and dark, heavy eyebrows. Lea had supervised contact with her grandmother fortnightly, but she would often refuse to visit. The child protection worker dragged her from the car screaming and kicking, asking her foster mother to help her. The foster mother had to leave her for an hour, after which Lea would return exhausted and non-responsive. Lea had told the foster mother that she was scared of her grandmother as she yelled and hurt her and that men had hurt her as well. After thirteen months, the foster mother was exhausted. The child protection worker suddenly decided to remove Lea (three years and two months) and placed her in the residential facility. Her foster mother visited weekly, and Lea kept asking why she could not go home with her. The caseworker had ceased contact with the grandmother, who was pressuring for contact to start again. As too was Lea's mother, who was released from prison.

The referring psychologist requested EMDR therapy for Lea to process the traumatic memories of the verbal, physical and possible sexual abuse while in the grandmother's care, and the possible neglect and abuse by the parents. It was believed her sleeping difficulties and refusal to have contact with her mother and grandmother were a consequence of posttraumatic stress. Child protection services had decided that the foster mother could not be involved in therapy, and Lea could not be reunified with her, or with her biological family. It was expected that trauma processing would normalize her sleeping after which she could transition into another foster family, and supervised contact with the mother and grandmother could be resumed. The referral stated that Lea refused to talk about her mother or grandmother.

15.5.1.1 Analysis

Young children under four, like Lea, have not developed emotion regulation skills yet and they do not have the cognitive ability to oversee the consequences of their actions. Therefore, some of the barriers do not apply for young children. Lea's information suggested that the removal from her foster mother and the contact visits had been additional traumatic events that needed to be addressed in trauma treatment. The analysis revealed several possible barriers around test 1. Even though Lea's physical safety was ensured, Lea may have felt physically unsafe during contact with her grandmother, and abandoned by her foster mother, who did not protect her (1a). It was unclear whether Lea was going to be forced to have contact again. It was also unclear who could be an attachment figure for Lea (1b). Lea was confused about the removal from her foster mother, and she may have feared that she would have to go back to her grandmother or parents (1a and 1c).

Important in the analysis of possible reasons for Lea's refusal was the fact that she was already refusing contact with her grandmother when she was still living with her foster mother. Therefore, some of the identified possible barriers, like the lack of attachment figure and perspective as to where she was going to grow up, may have aggravated her refusal, but could not be the main barriers. At the start of the placement, Lea had told her foster mother about her fear and her traumatic memories and her trauma had been accessible, her 'dogs were awake'. However, from her perspective, contact continued and she had not been protected by her foster mother, eventually leading to her refusal to discuss these memories, her 'dogs were now asleep'. In hindsight, Lea might have participated in EMDR therapy at an earlier stage. Decisions made by child protection services can contribute significantly to a positive outcome, but sadly also unintentionally traumatize children further.

The referring psychologist and clinician were unable to complete the analysis and plan interventions, with the limited information given. If Lea had also been traumatized by the forced visits and the sudden removal from her foster mother, these traumatic memories needed to be included in trauma treatment. Information from a caregiver, who knows the child well, was needed to check the hypotheses, but child protection services had decided the foster mother could not be contacted.

15.5.1.2 Treatment

Decisions by child protection services formed the main barriers for Lea. Therefore treatment started with discussing these with the caseworker. Only with more clarity around the options to contact the foster mother could a focused treatment plan be made. The clinician explained the impact of child protection services' decisions to the caseworker by using the Barriers analysis and requested these decisions be reviewed.

The clinician explained the impact of traumatization by using the Window of Tolerance and explained how Lea possibly had perceived the contact visits with her grandmother. The insight that Lea was not a stubborn, naughty child, but rather a terrified, frightened child had a profound impact on the caseworker. She then guaranteed that Lea was not going to be forced to contact again, if maximum effort was exhibited to reduce her fear, and make voluntary contact possible in the future. The connection between traumatic memories and Lea's symptoms were explained using the Volcano metaphor, which led to the caseworker seeing how EMDR therapy could possibly lead to a reduction in symptoms in Lea, which could make reunification with her foster mother possible. Eventually permission was granted to contact the foster mother to provide further information and discuss prerequisites for reunification.

The foster mother confirmed the hypotheses by stating that Lea had attached to her, and that she felt visits had damaged Lea's trust. She said that they were both traumatized and confused by the sudden removal and Lea blamed herself (5c). She said it was likely that Lea did not know who her main attachment figure was (1b) and that she was worried that she may be returned to her grandmother's care (1a). Lea's behaviour was explained with the Window of Tolerance and the Volcano metaphor and the foster mother expressed the strong desire to reunify with Lea. With this information a new treatment plan was developed with interventions focused on overcoming further barriers. Lea's trauma about the removal was accessible, 'those dogs were awake', the memories of the visits and abuse, were not accessible, 'sleeping dogs'.

The first goal was for Lea to feel safe through understanding that she would not return to her biological family. The caseworker decided to approve increased contact with the foster mother, starting with an overnight stay once a week with assistance from her network. In the foster mother's presence, the caseworker explained to Lea that she was not going to return to her family and she apologized for forcing previous contact. She explained that the hope was to work towards her returning home to her foster mother, and that when she was ready she could visit her family again. At this suggestion Lea started to scream 'no, no, no' and ran off.

Session 1 Sleeping Dogs (Lea and foster mother)

In the first Sleeping Dogs session with Lea and her foster mother, the clinician repeated this explanation and used stuffed animals to illustrate the different houses where she stayed and where her home was. All the bad memories were then stored away with the Safe Deposit Box intervention. Lea put her bad feelings and memories in the pouch of a kangaroo stuffed animal. The residential staff were instructed to use the intervention daily.

Session 2 EMDR (Lea and foster mother)

Because the removal from her foster mother seemed to be an accessible memory, 'an awake dog', Lea was asked if she wanted to get rid of her bad memories about leaving her foster mother (Motivation Check). Due to Lea's age, the Nutshell Check was skipped. Lea agreed and that memory was processed in a subsequent EMDR therapy session with Lea and her foster mother, by using the foster mother's narrative. Lea processed fear and anger. The foster mother apologized in tears for not being there for her. Lea hugged her, said she loved her and was affectionate towards the foster mother at the end of the session. All the bad memories were then stored away with the Safe Deposit Box. The foster mother reported that she felt the trust between them had grown in the weeks after this session.

Home-visit to the grandmother by clinician and caseworker

The clinician visited Lea's grandmother with the caseworker at home to discuss her views on what Lea had experienced, and to get an idea of the circumstances Lea had lived in. Lea's grandmother was a heavy smoker with a raw deep voice and dark, heavy eyebrows. Her house was filled with picture frames of Lea and she expressed missing her so much. She gave the clinician pictures of Lea's father and mother and told some stories about how they played with her when she was young and how much her parents loved her. The caseworker and clinician explained why contact had ceased and that there was a plan to reduce Lea's fear. The grandmother denied the allegation against her, but stated that her son and his partner had neglected and abused Lea. She recorded a one-minute video message for Lea expressing how much she loved her, that she respected her refusal and that she hoped Lea would one day change her mind. She agreed to regularly send postcards for Lea to the caseworker.

To increase Lea's feeling of control, the foster mother showed these postcards to Lea and asked her if she wanted to see them. Lea refused, but it was hypothesized that her saying 'no' would empower her. Her foster mother then repeated that the caseworker had said that she was never going to live with her family anymore and contact was her choice. Gradually Lea gained trust and felt more in control of her life. The foster mother reported that Lea started to disclose again about her grandmother yelling and hitting her and about the bad men that came and hurt her between her legs. She was instructed to use the Safe Deposit Box intervention after each disclosure.

Session 3 Sleeping Dogs and EMDR (Lea and foster mother)

The clinician then explained to Lea that her bad memories about 'the thing she did not want to talk about' caused her to be afraid and not sleep well. Lea was offered EMDR therapy to overcome these memories and encouraged by her foster mother, she agreed. Lea stated that she had three traumatic memories. In this session she processed two traumatic memories with EMDR therapy. Lea expressed feeling scared and angry, her body tensed and heated up excessively during processing. The session was concluded with the Safe Deposit Box. After this session, the foster mother reported improvement in behaviour and sleep. She decided to extend the overnight stay to two nights and requested to change it to weekly.

Session 4 EMDR (Lea and foster mother)

Four weeks later Lea processed the third memory with EMDR and stated not to have any more bad memories. After two months Lea's behaviour had improved so much that the foster mother had decided, with consent from the caseworker, not to return Lea to the residential facility after a weekend. Lea slept undisturbed, was less frustrated and more able to verbalize her feelings. She was less defiant, more affectionate towards the foster mother and shy with strangers.

Session 5 Sleeping Dogs (Lea and foster mother)

The positive changes were discussed and Lea stated not to have any more bad memories. The clinician informed Lea of her visit to her grandmother and the video message that was made. She gave the recording to her foster mother and instructed the foster mother to store the recording somewhere visible and ask Lea regularly whether she wanted to watch it.

15.5.1.3 Results

The clinician evaluated treatment with the foster mother and caseworker and made a plan on how the foster mother would continue to mention the biological family, how the family could be introduced once Lea decided to allow contact, what difficulties to expect in development and when to return for therapy. The foster mother was referred to a psychoeducation programme and treatment was ended. One-and-a-half years later, Lea (five years and ten months) returned to treatment. She was struggling with being disciplined, and feared her foster mother would send her back to the residential facility. This time, instead of the Story Telling, her own memories of the removal were processed with EMDR. Two years later (seven years and ten months), the foster mother contacted the clinician via email for advice on some peer difficulties at school. Lea was reportedly doing well.

15.5.2 Case example Fiona

Fiona (six years and one month) was described as a tornado, hyperaroused and clumsy. She could hardly concentrate in school and daydreamed often. Fiona stayed at a residential facility in a group of six children with rotating staff. Her caregivers and family were worried about her depressed mood. She missed her mother and asked nearly every day why her mother did not come and visit her.

Fiona was born missing a toe on both feet, which did not influence her mobility. Fiona's parents were heavy drug-users and after a period of domestic violence, they separated when she was two. She stayed with her mother and new partner, where she experienced domestic violence, physical abuse, possible sexual abuse and neglect. Child protection services then placed Fiona (three years and seven months) with her father, who had stopped using drugs. He struggled with her behaviour, and Fiona (four years and three months) was placed with her paternal aunt and uncle and their four children. They loved having Fiona, but also struggled with her 'wild' behaviour and violence. Fiona's mother often appeared intoxicated for the monthly, supervised contact visits and stopped attending after six months. No one was able to contact her after that. Fiona had always been very fond of her mother and loyal towards her. She did not understand why her mother stopped the visits and missed her mother intensely.

Fiona became more defiant and violent and was placed in a residential facility (five years and five months) to learn to control her behaviour so that she could return home. In the residential facility Fiona's violence and defiance decreased, but she remained hyper-vigilant and became increasingly depressed. She idealized her mother and denied the neglect, domestic violence, physical abuse and drug-abuse by her mother. She had fortnightly weekends with her aunt and uncle, who missed her very much and wanted her to return to their family. During the weekend, she visited her father but kept her distance from him in these contacts. Fiona's father was clear that he was unable to take care of Fiona and he was supportive of therapy and wanted her to return to his sister's family as soon as possible. The caseworker was supportive of therapy and reunification with the aunt and uncle.

The referring clinician believed that Fiona's hyper-vigilance would decrease and she would become less depressed if she could process her traumatic memories with EMDR therapy. Since she denied everything, Fiona was provided with the Sleeping Dogs method and EMDR treatment.

15.5.2.1 Analysis

In a meeting with the clinician, the referring clinician, the caseworker, residential staff and a meeting with the aunt, all possible reasons for Fiona to deny her trauma were discussed. The aunt and residential staff, who knew her best, believed that Fiona blamed herself for her mother not visiting. She often wondered if her mother did not love her anymore, or that she had done something to upset her. Maybe her mother had told her not to talk about what happened at home (1e), or she was afraid to upset her mother even more by talking about what her mother had done wrong (3a). Fiona might think that, if she talked about what her mother had done wrong, the caseworker would not allow her contact with her mother (1d), or she might believe she had been naughty and therefore deserved being hit and neglected making it hard to acknowledge her mother's responsibility (5a). According to Fiona's aunt, Fiona blamed her father for leaving her mother, as he made her unhappy. Fiona had also said to her aunt that her father did not like her, and therefore she could not live with him anymore (5b).

15.5.2.2 Treatment

Fiona needed clarity on whom she could rely. Fiona's father struggled with his own emotions and decided to collaborate, but not participate, in the treatment, as he did not want to burden his daughter with his own guilt. Fiona's aunt and uncle became her main attachment figures and they participated in some sessions. In Fiona's presence, they gave permission to the residential staff to support Fiona when they were not able to attend. To address Fiona's denial, she needed information about her history and her mother so she could understand that her mother abandoning her was not her fault. In addition, she needed information from the caseworker about the consequences of her disclosures, for contact with her father and, in the future, with her mother.

Session 1 Sleeping Dogs (Fiona, aunt, residential staff and caseworker)
The clinician explained to Fiona that she was referred for EMDR therapy because everyone worried about her sad feelings and wanted her to feel better, so she could go home to live with her aunt. With the Volcano metaphor, it was explained that bad memories can make you sad or upset, and that processing those memories with EMDR therapy could make her feel happy again (psychoeducation). Fiona sighed: 'I can never be happy again.' The clinician explained that she was aware that Fiona did not want to talk about what happened and that, therefore, the adults were going to make a story for her about her life. The caseworker then explained that whatever Fiona would tell about her past, that would not influence contact with her mother or father (1d). The session concluded with the Safe Deposit Box. The residential staff, aunt and father were asked to discuss the Volcano metaphor with her regularly to encourage her to open up, and the residential staff were asked to practise the Safe Deposit Box daily.

Interventions with father and family
A Trauma Healing Story was made with Fiona's father and caseworker, and they included the mother's views (1e, 5a and 5b). The maternal grandmother was asked to review the story and provide input on the mother's views such as: 'Grandma says that mum tried to stop using drugs because wanted to be a good mum. Grandma thinks that mum thinks about Fiona every day and loves her, but the drugs might make her not able to contact Fiona.'

Session 2 Sleeping Dogs (Fiona, residential staff and caseworker)
The Trauma Healing Story was read to Fiona and she was amazed by all the information and kept saying: 'Really? Really?' She was unaware of her

parents' drug use and was surprised and proud that her father had stopped using drugs for her. Fiona consented to recording the session, so Fiona's father could be part of it and discuss it with his daughter. She was told that he chose not to attend the session, as he was afraid he would cry because he loved her so much. Fiona said into the camera: 'Does he really love me? I love you too dad! Very much!' With Fiona's consent, the recording and story were stored by the caseworker to show to the mother and ask for her views, when she would surface.

Sessions 3–5 Sleeping Dogs (Fiona and residential staff)
In the next two sessions the story was read again and Fiona's questions were answered. She mainly wondered about the possible reasons why her mother did not visit her, but became more and more sure that it had nothing to do with her. She even started to criticize her mother's continued drug use, comparing it to her father who'd stopped. Fiona became less depressed and more open about her traumatic memories and consented to begin EMDR therapy (Motivation Check).

Sessions 6 and 7 EMDR (Fiona)
Fiona made an overview of her traumatic memories without becoming too over-whelmed and passed the Nutshell Check. She processed the first three memories in the first, and the last two memories in the second, session. She expressed anger towards her mother and father and felt relieved, as her life was good now.

Session 8 Sleeping Dogs (Fiona and residential staff)
Fiona reported not having any more memories and felt happy now and calm. She still hoped her mother would contact her, but she did not think about it anymore every day.

15.5.2.3 Results

Fiona's aunt reported that the weekend visits went very well and she was much easier to manage. The contact with her father had improved, and she enjoyed visiting him and missed him more. The caseworker and aunt decided to increase contact to weekly visits and she was reunified after six weeks. Fiona's concentration had improved slightly, but was still poor and she was still daydreaming, and was therefore referred for an assessment for ADHD. Treatment was ended. Nine months later the caseworker informed the clinician that Fiona was doing well. She had been diagnosed with ADHD, and medication had improved her functioning both in school and at home. Her mother had contacted the caseworker and watched the recording and had told Fiona that everything in the Trauma Healing Story was true. She explained that she had gone to prison for two years for drug-related crimes, after which she had sought treatment and was no longer using. She said that she was sorry for what she did and was very proud of her daughter.

Figure 15.1

15.6 Swimming against the current

Working with this method and trying to wake up sleeping dogs, means difficulties, strong emotions, crises, conflict, resistance from all areas. It can feel like swimming against a strong current. Nobody likes to talk about traumatic memories and tends to rather suppress or ignore the pain and suffering connected to them. Caregivers can be scared of the child's pain or dysregulation. Professionals might be afraid they are not able or skilled enough to handle the child's needs, especially when working in more remote and isolated areas. Schools can be afraid they cannot manage the child's behaviour. Biological parents, with their own sleeping dogs, can wrongfully be afraid they will have to go through their own trauma and pain or want to minimize their child's pain out of guilt. Foster parents often have only just managed and worked hard to stabilize the child. They fear not being able to cope with a deterioration in behaviour. Child protection services can be afraid that involving the biological parents might lead to more contact with the child or new court cases. Unresolved lingering conflicts between parents, child protection services, foster caregivers or residential facilities often lead to the child being stuck. These conflicts need to be resolved and decisions need to be made. This is difficult, which is why decisions are postponed.

Even when the adults are aware of the need and benefits to wake up sleeping dogs and agree to start this treatment, their difficulty with doing this often lingers. They cancel meetings, postpone answering questions, need extra explanations, express their opinions etc. Accepting this as part of working with this method and happily investing most of the time in swimming against the current and keeping everyone on track, is the biggest challenge of all. The more players that are involved in the child's life, usually in out of home care, the harder this becomes. Waking up sleeping dogs is a choice for short-term struggle and conflict, but long-term healing and recovery.

15.7 Managing the treatment

One person manages the treatment plan, alone or with other professionals. In between evaluations, the professional leading the treatment regularly (every two or three weeks) informs other professionals about the progress on the actions, or asks for an update. Professionals working with the Sleeping Dogs treatment need to resist the natural tendency to avoid and swim against the current. They need to be encouraged to keep swimming by actively leading treatment and reminding professionals about their actions. Professionals working with the child tend to stabilize for an unnecessarily long time because their close collaboration with the child makes them more sensitive to the child's anxiety and avoidance. It may be hard to stay focused during treatment, precisely because the internal chaos of these children – and often of their families – also creates external chaos. Problems and goals keep dissolving and shifting. First sleeping is the problem, then aggression, then eating. Now the parents want a divorce, then they get back together again. The child is expelled from school, the parents insist on medication. Other professionals, such as child protection workers or foster care workers lose track. This is frightening to the children and their families. A long-term plan with concrete goals, predictions of possible bottlenecks and criteria for evaluation will help all the people involved to get on track again.

15.8 Timing and order

The Sleeping Dogs interventions are grouped around five items in a fixed sequence. In principle, the interventions from the first item are worked on first, after which interventions from the next item are worked on. However some interventions can be done in parallel or can be combined.

15.9 Duration

The duration of treatment can vary considerably, depending on the circumstances, the symptoms and the child's age. Treatment for young children is usually short. Young children (up to six years old) have formed only a few networks in their memory and their cognitions are not yet solidly fixed. They also more easily give in to suggestions. In addition, young children are often so dysregulated already that it can hardly get worse. Re-traumatization takes place on an almost daily basis. They are hyperaroused, have flashbacks, sleeping problems and nightmares. Young children however often return for further treatment. Duration usually increases the older the child is. Considerable time can be used to work on preconditions, such as decisions by child protection services, finding an attachment figure or the parents having to provide safety.

Thirteen-year-old Peter was sexually abused repeatedly by his older brother who was on drugs. His brother denied this. When Peter was referred for trauma processing, he was living in a residential facility. His guardian had to decide whether he could go home. Peter was improving, but he still had fits of rage as a result of the abuse. The fits were so violent that his mother couldn't handle him, and so he could not go home. His legal guardian thought trauma processing could cure these symptoms and then he would be able to go home. But his brother and his mother were living at home. His mother still didn't know which of her two sons she should believe. The situation at home was unsafe for Peter because his brother lived there. Peter refused to talk about what had happened.

The analysis showed that he would probably not be able to make the cognitive shift during trauma processing because his brother did not take responsibility (5c) and his mother did not acknowledge his traumatization. He would get angry with his brother and risk rejection by his mother (5a). And what was his princess? To be allowed to go home to his unsafe brother (1a)? Not a very attractive princess. This deadlock situation was discussed with his mother. She decided to guarantee Peter's safety and take his story seriously. She decided to let her eldest son move out. Peter was only to have contact with his brother when his mother was present (1a). This took six months to arrange, and Peter received medication in this period to help control his anger. This was not a barrier, but a developmental area that needed to be addressed parallel to working on the barriers. When his brother had actually left the home, Peter was able to start trauma processing. In the first session he indicated that he was afraid of becoming angry (4b). After a stop sign was agreed, Peter explained what it would look like when he would get angry and what would help him (take a break and leave him alone). He started to become confident that he could do it. He passed the Motivation and Nutshell Checks. After two EMDR therapy sessions he had finished trauma processing, without getting angry.

Ten-year-old Bastian took one-and-a-half years before he was able to start trauma processing. His mother established safety first (1a). She arranged for contact with his abusive father to be stopped (1c). Then she started treatment herself, to be able to better regulate her emotions and be there for him (3a). Because she herself might not be able to tolerate hearing about what had happened, a friend was enrolled as a support figure (3b). Bastian could talk to this friend when he needed to. Bastian himself was not involved during the stabilization phase. When his mother was ready, he was able to start trauma processing immediately, and the EMDR therapy itself took only three sessions.

Children may be ready for trauma processing much faster than was thought.

Six-year-old Sandy lived with her grandmother and grandfather. She had gone through traumatic experiences with her psychotic mother. During the screening by telephone, her grandmother said that Sandy couldn't handle conflicts and correction – she would freeze. She didn't play freely like other children and was over-adapted. She had nightmares every night and kept her grandparents awake. They were at their wits' end. During the first session, the grandparents showed themselves to be adequate attachment figures. When asked about Sandy's future, it turned out that they had already decided that Sandy would stay with them and would not return to her mother. Sandy heard this crucial piece of information for the first time (1a, 1b, 1c OK). Grandmother and grandfather told Sandy that her mother had agreed on her treatment and was very sorry for what she had done (1d and 5a OK). Halfway through the session I decided to do the Nutshell Check right away. Why wait when everybody was suffering because of Sandy's symptoms? Sandy passed. Grandmother and grandfather were seated in the waiting room while Sandy did an EMDR session; half an hour later she was finished. The following night she slept like a baby.

15.10 Child's relationship with the professional

15.10.1 (Counter) transference processes

Some elements can intensify (counter) transference processes, for example therapists working one on one with a child, engaging in more long-term contact. The stronger the child's structural dissociation, the stronger usually the (counter) transference processes. For professionals with caregiving tasks, such as residential staff, the (counter) transference processes can become more intense, especially when the child does not have an attachment figure responsible for his wellbeing, and the child lives there for a long period of time. On the other hand, residential staff work as a team and the child therefore has several different caregivers, which again weakens the transference and counter transference. For residential staff the principles are the same but because of their caring tasks it will not always be possible for them to act in the same way. The professional can experience counter transference, such as feeling anger or shame, distancing himself from the child, starting to dread contact, viewing the child as manipulative, becoming passively or actively aggressive. Or professionals can start to care too much and feel too responsible or wanting to adopt the child. These feelings are natural and normal and do not mean that the professional is overinvolved and unfit for the job. When these feelings occur, it is important to notice them, discuss with a colleague what these feelings indicate about the child's situation (often that the attachment figure is not good enough). Then a plan needs to be made to address the child's situation pro-actively, because if the professional continues to react on the basis of this counter transference, the old experiences of the child will be re-enacted, which will make it impossible for the child to learn new ways of handling these emotions.

15.10.2 The professional's attitude

The professional's attitude is very important in the treatment of these children. The confidence of the professional compensates for the children's insecurity; the professional has treated many more of these children, nothing surprises him anymore and he knows exactly what he is doing. The professional listens to the most horrific stories without showing incredulity or disgust. His calm brain organizes their chaotic brains and regulates the stress for them. For a professional it is very important to properly establish the boundaries of treatment and the relationship with the child. Adolescents especially tend to test these boundaries; they may call up or show up in between sessions, or want to visit more often. Setting limits for these children will provide safety for them.

Traumatized children are suspicious because, in their experience, adults do not always take care of them, and may hurt them just like that. They will be extra careful when a care professional says: 'Trust me, I will help you. I know what is good for you.' They only trust in themselves. Their brain will calm when they know what they have to gain and when they can decide for themselves if they want to do it. This provides predictability and a sense of control and that makes the professional safe. Even four or five year olds can decide whether they want to do an exercise or not. Sometimes a reward offered by their parents (a sweet for instance) may persuade them. The same goes for these children's parents, who are often traumatized themselves. The professional can think along with them and share ideas with the family, offer them things and discuss the consequences of certain choices. But the professional does not give them advice, especially not about what the family should do. The professional should not act like an expert or a doctor who is going to make them better, for this would put them in a dependent position. A traumatized child is addressed as a strong and competent survivor and not as pitiful or helpless. So: 'How clever of you to survive all that, how did you manage that?' Rather than: 'How terrible, I feel sorry for you!'

15.10.3 The professional's self-care

It is important to carefully establish who is responsible for what and to only set goals, which can be achieved by oneself. For instance: 'establishing whether these parents are willing or able to acknowledge their child. If they are not, discussing with the guardian how the requirements for treatment may be achieved and putting the treatment plan on hold until this is taken care of.' Or: 'If the guardian places the child outside the family, I can start with: … If the child remains at home, I can do the following: …'. Apart from this, it is important to make sure to have regular supervision and support. Despite all these difficult issues, working with these children and their families can also be tremendously rewarding and their resilience and strength encourages me to continue this difficult but fantastic work. I hope this book will be a contribution to the reader's work and will help others to help more children and families.

And the prince and the princess? They lived happily ever after …

Figure 15.2

Appendix I

Sleeping Dogs® Case Conceptualization Form

|———|———————————————————————————————|

Note the traumas and other important events for the child such as separation or going to foster placement on this timeline (conception–birth–now).

Child's Symptoms *Which trauma-related symptoms does the child display, that are expected to reduce after trauma processing?*

	Age: IQ if determined: Diagnosis if determined: Child Protection Order if applicable: Motivation for trauma treatment: Yes/Not sure/No

Traumas *Note the traumas from the timeline in keywords (for example DV/SA/ Neglect) and circle whether these are awake (AD), sleeping (SD) or preverbal dogs (PD). Fill in the Barriers Form for the sleeping dogs.*

....	AD/SD/PD
....	AD/SD/PD
....	AD/SD/PD
....	AD/SD/PD
....	AD/SD/PD
....	AD/SD/PD

Network *Note here complicating factors with the biological mother and father, if applicable with others (foster parents/grandparents), such as parents' diagnoses, IQ, drug/alcohol use, imprisonment. Note here the contact arrangements in frequency, supervised or unsupervised. Describe the relationship briefly such as the child is overly loyal, close, normal attached or distant.*

Biological mother	Biological father
Contact arrangements with mother	Contact arrangements with father

Others/family
Contact arrangements

Questions/unclear?	How can I get this information?

Appendix 2

Sleeping Dogs® Barriers Form

Name child: DOB: Date:

Who is/are the child's main attachment figure(s)? ....

Who is/are support person(s)? ....

Which parent gives the child permission to talk about memories? ....

Sleeping dogs	Child's negative cognition	Shift to positive cognition

Fill in for which sleeping dogs the barriers are analysed, which dysfunctional cognition the child may have and which shift the child needs to make.

Instructions

The questions in the Barriers Form focus only on whether or not this item from the child's perspective potentially forms a barrier and does not reflect the child's daily life functioning. The goal of this form is to find out what could be the main reasons for the child not wanting or being able to talk about his/her traumatic memories. The questions are numbered 1a, 1b, 1c etc. The questions are answered from the child's perspective, what would he/she think or feel. Tick the box as yes or no. Focus only on the main barriers, so do not tick nearly all. Interventions are planned in the stabilization phase on the Barriers Action Plan. These interventions have priority.

Motivation and Nutshell Checks

Ⓨ Ⓝ The child has passed Motivation Check. If yes, discuss whether to fill in this form.

Ⓨ Ⓝ The child has passed Nutshell Check. If yes, discuss whether to fill in this form.

		Barrier I Safety
Ia	Ⓨ Ⓝ	Is not being or feeling safe because the abuse could happen again a barrier?
Ib	Ⓨ Ⓝ	Is not having an attachment figure or is not being sure who is an attachment figure a barrier?
Ic	Ⓨ Ⓝ	Is not having regular contact with that attachment figure, or not being sure that contact is guaranteed to continue, a barrier?
Id	Ⓨ Ⓝ	Is being afraid that disclosures will have legal consequences and/or that contact arrangements will be changed, and/or that the child will be removed or not reunified a barrier?
Ie	Ⓨ Ⓝ	Is not having permission from the biological parents to talk about the memories and being afraid of being punished a barrier?

		Barrier 2 Daily Life
2a	Ⓨ Ⓝ	Is having too many problems at home, and/or the child being afraid to be removed from home, a barrier?
2b	Ⓨ Ⓝ	Is having too many problems at school, and/or the child being afraid of getting expelled from school, a barrier?
2c	Ⓨ Ⓝ	Is the child or caregivers being afraid the child does not have enough distraction because the child does not have a daily routine a barrier?
2d	Ⓨ Ⓝ	Is the child or caregivers being afraid of not being able to handle an increase in flashbacks and/or sleeping problems a barrier?
2e	Ⓨ Ⓝ	Is the child or caregivers being afraid drugs and alcohol abuse will increase and/or lead to serious problems a barrier?

		Barrier 3 Attachment
3a	Ⓨ Ⓝ	Is the child being afraid of upsetting the attachment figure who would not keep a calm brain when the child would process the traumatic memories a barrier?

Question 3b is only relevant when 3a forms a barrier

3b	Ⓨ Ⓝ	Is not having a support person with a calm brain in daily life who can compensate for the attachment figure with his permission a barrier?
3c	Ⓨ Ⓝ	Is being afraid that the child cannot stay in contact with the therapist during trauma processing a barrier?

		Barrier 4 Emotion Regulation
4a	Ⓨ Ⓝ	Is the child not being able to feel and tolerate bodily sensations during trauma processing a barrier?
4b	Ⓨ Ⓝ	Is the child not being able to feel and regulate the feelings during trauma processing a barrier?

		Barrier 5 Cognitive Shift
5a	Ⓨ Ⓝ	Is the child fearing that the mother blames him/her for the abuse or neglect and will reject him/her when the child would believe he/she was innocent, and the child does not want to risk this a barrier?
5b	Ⓨ Ⓝ	Is the child fearing that his/her father blames him/her for the abuse or neglect and will reject him/her when the child would believe he/she was innocent, and the child does not want to risk this a barrier?

If applicable otherwise skip:

5c	Ⓨ Ⓝ	Is the child fearing that .... (other person) blames him/her for the abuse or neglect and will reject him/her when the child would believe he/she was innocent, and the child does not want to risk this a barrier?

Question 5d is only relevant when 5a and 5b both form barriers

5d	Ⓨ Ⓝ	Is the child not having an alternative attachment figure acknowledging the child's innocence and the child not wanting to risk ending up alone a barrier?

Appendix 3

Sleeping Dogs® Development and Barriers Form

Name child: DOB: Date:

Who is/are the child's main attachment figure(s)? ....

Who is/are support person(s)? ....

Which parent gives the child permission to talk about memories? ....

Sleeping dogs	Child's negative cognition	Shift to positive cognition

Fill in for which sleeping dogs the barriers are analysed, which dysfunctional cognition the child may have and which shift the child needs to make.

Instructions

The form has two goals:

Green (light shading) – These are questions to assess which developmental areas and circumstances need improvement for the child to grow up as safe and healthy as possible in his circumstances. The questions are numbered 1aa, 1bb, 1cc etc. The questions are scored from the professional's perspective:

1 = no, this area needs a lot of improvement for the child to grow up safe and healthy

2=to some degree, this area may need improvement for the child to grow up safe and healthy

3=yes, this area is good enough and does not need improvement for the child to grow up safe and healthy.

Plan interventions on the Integration Action Plan, for all scores '1' and discuss for scores '2', whether interventions are needed.

Red (dark shading) – These are questions to find out what could be main reasons for the child not wanting or being able to talk about his/her traumatic memories. The questions are numbered 1a, 1b, 1c etc. The questions are answered from the child's perspective, what would he/she think or feel. Tick the box as yes or no. Focus only on the main barriers, so do not tick nearly all. Interventions are planned in the stabilization phase on the Barriers Action Plan. These interventions have priority.

Motivation and Nutshell Checks

(Y)(N) The child has passed Motivation Check. If yes, discuss whether to fill in this form.

(Y)(N) The child has passed Nutshell Check. If yes, discuss whether to fill in this form.

		Development and Barrier I Safety	
I aa		The child is safe enough	①②③
I a	(Y)(N)	Is not being or feeling safe because the abuse could happen again a barrier?	
I bb		The child has enough attachment figures	①②③
I b	(Y)(N)	Is not having an attachment figure or is not being sure who is an attachment figure a barrier?	
I cc		Contact arrangements with attachment figures are clear and sufficient	①②③
I c	(Y)(N)	Is not having regular contact with that attachment figure, or not being sure that contact is guaranteed to continue, a barrier?	
I d	(Y)(N)	Is being afraid that disclosures will have legal consequences and/or that contact arrangements will be changed, and/or that the child will be removed or not reunified a barrier?	
I ee		The child can talk freely about his thoughts and feelings	①②③
I e	(Y)(N)	Is not having permission from the biological parents to talk about the memories and being afraid of being punished a barrier?	

		Development and Barrier 2 Daily Life	
2aa		The child has no problems at home or they are under control	①②③
2a	ⓎⓃ	Is having too many problems at home, and/or the child being afraid to be removed from home, a barrier?	
2bb		The child has no problems at school or they are under control	①②③
2b	ⓎⓃ	Is having too many problems at school, and/or the child being afraid of getting expelled from school, a barrier?	
2cc		The child has sufficient daily routine	①②③
2c	ⓎⓃ	Is the child or caregivers being afraid the child does not have enough distraction because the child does not have a daily routine a barrier?	
2dd		The child sleeps well and sufficiently	①②③
2d	ⓎⓃ	Is the child or caregivers being afraid of not being able to handle an increase in flashbacks and/or sleeping problems a barrier?	
2ee		The child does not use alcohol and drugs or this is not a problem	①②③
2e	ⓎⓃ	Is the child or caregivers being afraid drugs and alcohol abuse will increase and/or lead to serious problems a barrier?	

		Development and Barrier 3 Attachment	
3aa		The attachment figure has a calm enough brain in daily life	①②③
3a	ⓎⓃ	Is the child being afraid of upsetting the attachment figure who would not keep a calm brain when the child would process the traumatic memories a barrier?	
Question 3b is only relevant when 3a forms a barrier			
3bb		The child has enough support persons with a calm brain in daily life	①②③
3b	ⓎⓃ	Is not having a support person with a calm brain in daily life who can compensate for the attachment figure with his permission a barrier?	
3cc		The child's attachment system is sufficiently activated in daily life	①②③
3c	ⓎⓃ	Is being afraid that the child cannot stay in contact with the therapist during trauma processing a barrier?	

		Development and Barrier 4 Emotion Regulation	
4aa		The child can feel and tolerate bodily sensations sufficiently	①②③
4a	Ⓨ Ⓝ	Is the child not being able to feel and tolerate bodily sensations during trauma processing a barrier?	
4bb		The child can feel and tolerate and express feelings sufficiently	①②③
4b	Ⓨ Ⓝ	Is the child not being able to feel and regulate the feelings during trauma processing a barrier?	

		Development and Barrier 5 Cognitive Shift	
5aa		The child does not have sufficient acknowledgement of his/her innocence	①②③
5a	Ⓨ Ⓝ	Is the child fearing that the mother blames him/her for the abuse or neglect and will reject him/her when the child would believe he/she was innocent, and the child does not want to risk this a barrier?	
5b	Ⓨ Ⓝ	Is the child fearing that his/her father blames him/her for the abuse or neglect and will reject him/her when the child would believe he/she was innocent, and the child does not want to risk this a barrier?	
If applicable otherwise skip:			
5c	Ⓨ Ⓝ	Is the child fearing that .... (other person) blames him/her for the abuse or neglect and will reject him/her when the child would believe he/she was innocent, and the child does not want to risk this a barrier?	
Question 5d is only relevant when 5a and 5b both form barriers			
5d	Ⓨ Ⓝ	Is the child not having an alternative attachment figure acknowledging the child's innocence and the child not wanting to risk ending up alone a barrier?	

Appendix 4

Sleeping Dogs® Barriers Action Plan

Name child: Date:

DOB: Evaluation dates:

Current owner of the plan:

	Circle Barriers	Example interventions	Describe actions with barrier numbers	Who will do this?	With whom?	OK
1a	Safety	Safety Plan (SP) Inform child of SP				
1b	Attachment figure (AF)	Discuss with network who is AF Find new AF Inform child of AF				
1c	AF stays in child's life	Clarify with AF/child protection worker (CPW)/organization/police Establish or intensify contact with AF Inform child of contact				
1d	Consequence Disclosure	Clarify legal consequences Clarify consequences contact arrangements Inform AF and/or child				
1e	Emotional permission	Ask mother Ask father **Inform child**				

2a	Home	Caregiver support and				
2b	School	Compensation plan				
2c	Daily routine	Within Window of Tolerance Prevent trigger plan				
2d	Flashback and sleep	**Safe Deposit Box** Safe Place Here and Now				
2e	Drugs Alcohol	Relaxation School support and compensation plan Distraction plan Sleep plan Drug/alcohol plan				
3a	Calm brain	Compensation plan AF Self-regulation AF AF informs child				
3b	Other calm brain	Assess other calm brain Discuss with AF AF gives child permission for other				
3c	Attachment system	Increase contact AF/ biological parents Life story work Attachment exercises/therapy				
4a	Bodily sensations	Sensory exercises/ therapy Relaxation				
4b	Feelings	Psychoeducation Management plan Self-harm/suicide plan Intensive work/ therapy				
5a	Mum not acknowledge	Discuss with mum/ dad/other				
5b	Dad not acknowledge	Find other to acknowledge Inform child in				
5c	Other not acknowledge	session/letter/video message or note Trauma Healing Story				
5d	No other to acknowledge					

Circle Barriers	Example interventions	Describe actions with barrier numbers	Who will do this?	With whom?	OK
Motivation	**Find princess** Filing Cabinets Window of Tolerance Volcano Heater Princess story Matryoshka **Motivation Check**				
Nutshell	**Nutshell Check** Remote control				
Trauma processing	Process awake dogs				

Instructions

Fill in the child's name, DOB, date and current owner of the plan. Circle the identified barriers. The numbers correspond to the barriers. Examples of interventions are listed. The **bold interventions** are frequently used. Describe concrete actions with the numbers of the barriers that are addressed by the action (e.g. 1b and 1c, 3a and 5b) or only one (e.g. 1e). Fill in who is going to do this action (e.g. foster care worker Sonja) and with whom this action is going to be done (child protection worker Tina, biological mother and child). Several interventions can be combined into one action. Note an evaluation date.

When evaluating this Action Plan, tick 'OK' for the completed actions. Describe new or altered actions. Note a new evaluation date. Continue until all barriers are removed. Then describe actions for Motivation, Nutshell and trauma processing. Note an evaluation date.

After trauma processing evaluate the child's symptoms. Set goals and describe actions for the integration phase. Note an evaluation date and evaluate until goals are reached.

Sleeping Dogs® Integration Action Plan

	Circle areas	Tick interventions	Describe actions with area numbers	Who will do this?	With whom?	OK
1	Safety	Safety Plan Find new AF Inform child of AF Execute consequences AF/CPW/organization/ police Inform child Ask mother Ask father Inform child				
2	Daily Life	Carer support and home improvement plan School support and improvement plan Safe Place Relaxation Sleep plan Drug/alcohol plan Difficult circumstances				
3	Attachment	Improvement plan Therapy parent Assess other calm brain AF gives child permission for other Start contact with parent Increase contact parent/AF/siblings Reunification plan Life story/video Visit former houses Attachment exercises/ therapy				
4	Emotion Regulation	Sensory therapy Relaxation Intensive work/therapy				
5	Cognitive Shift	Assess child's wish Family therapy Trauma Healing Story Forgiveness plan				

Appendix 5

Manual of the Sleeping Dogs® Barriers Form

Name child: DOB: Date:

Who is/are the child's main attachment figure(s)? ....

Who is/are support person(s)? ....

Which parent gives the child permission to talk about memories? ....

Sleeping dogs	Child's negative cognition	Shift to positive cognition

Fill in for which sleeping dogs the barriers are analysed, which dysfunctional cognition the child may have and which shift the child needs to make.

Instructions

The questions in the Barriers Form focus only on whether or not this item from the child's perspective potentially forms a barrier and does not reflect the child's daily life functioning. The goal of this form is to find out what could be the main reasons for the child not wanting or being able to talk about his/her traumatic memories. The questions are numbered 1a, 1b, 1c etc. The questions are answered from the child's perspective, what would he/she think or feel. Tick the box as yes or no. Focus only on the main barriers, so do not tick nearly all. Interventions are planned in the stabilization phase on the Barriers Action Plan. These interventions have priority.

Motivation and Nutshell Checks

(Y)(N)   The child has passed Motivation Check. If yes, discuss whether to fill in this form.

(Y)(N)   The child has passed Nutshell Check. If yes, discuss whether to fill in this form.

Barrier 1 Safety

1a   Is not being or feeling safe because the abuse could happen again a barrier?

Ongoing abuse, being or feeling threatened can form a barrier when the child is afraid that the abuse *from the past* will continue to happen in the future. The adults may know the child is safe, but the child has not been explicitly informed about the safety measures that are in place. If this forms a barrier, not all abuse needs to be stopped in order to overcome this barrier. For example, it may be possible to process memories of domestic violence in the past, even when emotional neglect is ongoing, or to process the memories of dad hitting mum without being able to address 'mum not protecting the child'. The child can be currently unsafe because of problem behaviour or fighting in school, or bullying, but those only form a barrier when the child is constantly terrified and outside his/her Window of Tolerance.

1b   Is not having an attachment figure or not being sure who is an attachment figure a barrier?

This can form a barrier, when a child does not want to talk about his/her memories mainly because he/she does not have anyone who thinks of him/her and supports him/her. Why would he/she do it, for whom? In the Sleeping Dogs method, an attachment figure is defined as someone who loves the child and who wants to stay in the child's life. The attachment figure would want to be informed when the child for example would get severely injured, moves elsewhere or when a placement ends. When the child would get married, the attachment figure wants to come to the wedding and sit in the front row. When children are born, the attachment figure will want to know. The child does not have to live with the attachment figure or have intensive contact. Most children have one or both of their parents as an attachment figure.

The primary focus here is the quantity 'is there an attachment figure?' The quality of the relationship does not have to be good and the child does not have to be attached to that person, as this is addressed in barrier 3. The attachment figure can even be a father in prison, a grandmother who visits every two years or mother with a borderline personality disorder who lives in a psychiatric hospital and has, once every two months, two hours supervised contact with her daughter. She loves her and wants the best for her. Sometimes she is too unwell and the visits are cancelled, but the daughter knows mum still thinks of her and approves of her talking to the residential staff.

Children in residential care with staff on a rotating roster without any contact with family, mother died and father in prison, can have this barrier. They do not have anyone to do this difficult therapy for. More often than one would think, lack of an attachment figure is a reason for depression in children (manifesting itself as problem behaviour). For those children an attachment figure needs to be found in order to wake up sleeping dogs.

1c   Is not having regular contact with that attachment figure, or not being sure that contact is guaranteed to continue, a barrier?

This forms a barrier when the child's main reason not to start talking about his/her painful memories is that he/she cannot rely on the attachment figure to continue to be there for him/her. The child needs to be certain that the attachment figure will stay in his/her life and cares about his/her well-being. Contact does not have to be regular or intensive, as long as the child has another temporary support person to talk to and the attachment figure has approved that. Some parents can be unpredictable and say they never want to see the child anymore during fights, even though they do not mean it. If the child knows that, that is good enough. Contact is not guaranteed when the parent is capable of refusing contact with the child for months until for example the child apologizes. When the parent would then not come to the hospital to see his/her injured child, because he/she is angry, this attachment figure is not good enough and the child needs another attachment figure in addition. This can form a barrier for children in foster care who may not know whether their foster parents want to have a life-long relationship with them, or are only daily caregivers until the placement breaks down or the child becomes eighteen. They need to be informed about that. The child may live with grandparents who are very old or sick and he/she cannot be sure he/she will not end up alone. They need another attachment figure to wake up the sleeping dogs.

1d   Is being afraid that disclosures will have legal consequences and/or that contact arrangements will be changed, and/or that the child will be removed or not reunified a barrier?

This forms a barrier when the child is worried that talking about his/her memories will have consequences for people outside the family. The child can be afraid the police will be informed, and his/her parents or he/she him/herself will be convicted. Children can refuse to talk because they fear the legal guardian will reduce contact arrangements, not reunify the child or make contact supervised. Children can also fear the opposite, that the legal guardian will intensify contact, make contact unsupervised or reunify him/her with his/her parents because his/her problems are solved. Besides traumatic memories of incidents that were already disclosed or are known, the child may also have secrets or think he/she has secrets, which would be *new* disclosures. Reassurance needs to come from people outside the family. The possible consequences need to be clarified to the child, so the child can decide what to do based on this information.

1e   Is not having permission from the biological parents to talk about the memories and being afraid of being punished a barrier?

This forms a barrier when the child is worried that talking about his/her memories will damage the relationship with one of his/her parents or both. H/she is afraid of his/her parent's reaction. The parent may have threatened him/her or the child is not sure if his/her parent approves of him/her talking. Many children do not know what their parents think and they need to be explicitly told by their parents. To overcome this barrier, the child needs reassurance from his/her parent. Parents can also fear consequences from outside the family, which can be the reason for them to tell the child not to talk. Reassurance from outside for the parents can also help to overcome this barrier.

When the child fears abuse as a repercussion, barrier 1a is analysed, as reassurance from the parent is not enough to overcome that barrier. The child needs a Safety Plan. When the child does not really care about what his parents think, this does not have to form a barrier. Or when the child has one parent who gives him permission and he lives with this parent, and does not really care about the other parent not approving.

Barrier 2 Daily Life
Processing traumatic memories requires the child to be calm enough to focus on doing this. It can temporarily increase the child's symptoms. What could be the main reason why the child wants to avoid this?

2a   Is having too many problems at home, and/or the child being afraid to be removed from home, a barrier?

With 'home' is meant where the child currently lives. This forms a barrier when the child has too many problems to deal with and he/she refuses because he/she does not have the headspace to also dig up old memories. Or the child does not want to talk about his/her memories because he/she is afraid he/she will get more difficult to handle and his/her (foster) parents or the residential staff will be unable to handle that. The child's placement can be under pressure, staff can be exhausted, and this can even be discussed with the child. The child rather keeps 'a lid on his/her traumas' than risking being removed. Or the child absconds so much that the caregivers, attachment figure or others cannot talk to the child to motivate him/her, provide psychoeducation or eventually make sure the child attends therapy sessions.

2b   Is having too many problems at school, and/or the child being afraid of getting expelled from school, a barrier?

This forms a barrier when the child is barely managing at school and refuses to talk because he/she does not have the headspace to also dig up old memories. Or the child does not want to talk about his/her memories because he/she is afraid he/she will get more difficult to handle, and the school will be unable to handle that, or the child needs to pass exams. The child may have been expelled several times and been given a last chance, and this can even be discussed with the child. The child rather keeps 'a lid on his/her traumas' than risking being expelled.

2c Is the child or caregivers being afraid the child does not have enough distraction because the child does not have a daily routine a barrier?

This forms a barrier when the child does not go to school, has no job, lies in bed all day or hangs around with too much time to think. Waking up sleeping dogs can be difficult and the child needs to have some distraction. The child does not have to go to school or have a job, a schedule with activities can be good enough.

2d Is the child or caregivers being afraid of not being able to handle an increase in flashbacks and/or sleeping problems a barrier?

This forms a barrier when the child has so many flashbacks and sleeping problems, that he/she can barely function. Or the child's caregivers are exhausted, and they fear that talking about memories would cause more flashbacks and sleeping problems and they would not be able to handle that. They can fear not being able to take care of the other children, losing their job or failing at work. However, in most cases this does not form a barrier and flashbacks reduce significantly and sleeping problems become less after processing traumatic memories.

2e Is the child or caregivers being afraid drugs and alcohol abuse will increase and/or lead to serious problems a barrier?

Children use alcohol and drugs to numb their feelings, they 'self-medicate'. In most cases bad feelings reduce significantly after processing traumatic memories and the need to use drugs and alcohol also reduces. It becomes much easier to stop afterwards. This only forms a barrier when the child or his/her network fear that the child cannot come to the sessions sober, and when they fear that that talking about memories would increase the child's need to numb bad feelings with alcohol or drugs and this would lead to an overdose, serious injuries or death.

Barrier 3 Attachment
The child needs to feel supported to process trauma. What could be the main reason why the child is not supported enough?

3a Is the child being afraid of upsetting the attachment figure who would not keep a calm brain when the child would process the traumatic memories a barrier?

This forms a barrier when the child fears the attachment figure will become upset *when he/she would talk about his/her memories*. For example when the attachment figure is traumatized, overwhelmed, has experienced the same trauma such as domestic violence or has become upset in the past. By avoiding traumatic memories, the child cares for the attachment figure.

This does not form a barrier if the parent has severe emotion regulation problems in daily life, but is able to stay calm when the child talks about the traumatic memories and the child is aware of that. Barrier 3a assesses whether the quality of the relationship forms a barrier because the child does not have enough emotional support, whereas barrier 1b assesses whether not having an attachment figure forms a barrier, the quantity. Barrier 3a assesses whether the child thinks that the attachment figure can handle 'talking about memories', whereas barrier 2a assesses whether the attachment figure can handle the child's behaviour.

Question 3b is only relevant when 3a forms a barrier.

3b Is not having a support person with a calm brain in daily life who can compensate for the attachment figure with his permission a barrier?

This forms a barrier when the child's attachment figure does not have a calm brain and the child does not have anyone else to talk to, or the attachment figure does not allow the child to talk to this adult, or the child is not sure if he/she can. This does not form a barrier when the child's parent allows the child talk to the other parent, a grandfather or aunt, foster parents or residential staff.

3c Is being afraid that the child cannot stay in contact with the therapist during trauma processing a barrier?

This forms a barrier when the network or child itself fears that the child will dissociate or run away during the trauma-processing sessions. Many children dissociate or avoid in daily life situations and in therapy sessions where their bad behaviour is discussed, but are very capable of staying in contact during a trauma-processing session. Then this does not form a barrier. Symptoms and daily life are like big clouds of suffocating smoke, while the traumatic memories are the fire causing this smoke. Children can find it easier to get to the fire directly, than talking about the smoke session after session.

Barrier 4 Emotion Regulation
During trauma processing the child needs to tolerate the old feelings. Is the child able to do that?

4a Is the child not being able to feel and tolerate bodily sensations during trauma processing a barrier?
When bodily sensations are not tolerated and they need to be dissociated or blocked, this can form a barrier, for example with children with a dissociative disorder or conversion. The child needs to learn to tolerate these first. However, in most cases this is not necessary and children become more aware of their bodily sensations after trauma processing. When barrier 4a is identified, 4b also forms a barrier.

4b Is the child not being able to feel and regulate the feelings during trauma processing a barrier?

When feelings are not tolerated and they need to be dissociated or blocked, this can form a barrier, because trauma processing can overwhelm the child, for example with children with a dissociative disorder or conversion. Children can be afraid they will become violent and harm someone or themselves, or self-harm or be suicidal. If this forms a barrier, the child can make a plan to control this temporarily, so he/she can get through the trauma-processing phase, after which these feelings often reduce. However, in most cases this is not necessary and children become more aware of their feelings and can express them better after trauma processing.

Barrier 5 Cognitive Shift
These questions are only relevant when the abuser is a parent or someone the child will maintain close contact with. Experience shows that with a stuck case, this is very often one of the identified barriers.

5a   Is the child fearing that the mother blames him/her for the abuse or neglect and will reject him/her when the child would believe he/she was innocent, and the child does not want to risk this a barrier?
     This can form a barrier, when the child's mother blames the child and the child finds her opinion important, or when the child thinks his/her mother blames him/her but is not sure. When the mother blames the child, this does not have to be a barrier. The child can have his/her own view and know he/she was not to blame, or have the father, or foster parents acknowledge his/her innocence. With help, most parents can acknowledge that the child was not to blame for the past. That is good enough, even though they continue to blame the child for his/her current behaviour.
5b   Is the child fearing that his/her father blames him/her for the abuse or neglect and will reject him/her when the child would believe he/she was innocent, and the child does not want to risk this a barrier?
     This can form a barrier, when the child's father blames the child and the child finds his opinion important, or when the child thinks his/her father blames him/her but is not sure. When the father blames the child, this does not have to be a barrier. The child can have his/her own view and know he/she was not to blame, or have the mother, or foster parents acknowledge his/her innocence. With help, most parents can acknowledge that the child was not to blame for the past. That is good enough, even though they continue to blame the child for his/her current behaviour.
     If applicable otherwise skip:
5c   Is the child fearing that .... (other person) blames him/her for the abuse or neglect and will reject him/her when the child would believe he/she was innocent, and the child does not want to risk this a barrier?
     This can form a barrier, when for example the child's sibling, stepmother or grandfather blames the child and the child finds their opinion important, or when the child thinks they blame him/her but is not sure. When the

child's sibling, stepmother or grandfather blames the child, this does not have to be a barrier. The child can have his/her own view and know he/she was not to blame, or have the father, or foster parents acknowledge his/her innocence. It also does not have to form a barrier when the child's sibling, stepmother or grandfather is no longer part of his/her life and he/she does not have to have a relationship with them. However, with help, most people can acknowledge that the child was not to blame for the past. That is good enough, even though they continue to blame the child for his/her current behaviour.

Question 5d is only relevant when 5a and 5b both form barriers.

5d Is the child not having an alternative attachment figure acknowledging the child's innocence and the child not wanting to risk ending up alone a barrier?

This can form a barrier when both parents continue to blame the child and threaten to reject the child when the child would claim innocence, and the child does not have someone else to rely on. To maintain the relationship, the child then chooses to continue to take the blame. This does not form a barrier when the child lives with foster parents who do not blame him for the past and who guarantee to maintain the relationship and will be guests at the child's wedding.

Worksheet: Motivation

What bothers you? What are your symptoms?

- _____

  _____

- _____

  _____

- _____

  _____

Why do you want to get rid of these symptoms? How can working on your memories help you? Draw or describe your princess here.

Worksheet: Daily Life 1 – The Safe Deposit Box

Draw the place where you want to store away all your bad pictures.

Worksheet: Daily Life 2 – The Safe Place

Draw your safe place here.

Worksheet: Daily Life 3 – Within My Window

These things take me outside my Window of Tolerance:

- _____
  _____

- _____
  _____

- _____
  _____

- _____
  _____

- _____
  _____

When I am outside my Window of Tolerance, these things help me to calm down (these things soothe me):

- _____
  _____

- _____
  _____

- _____
  _____

- _____
  _____

- _____
  _____

Worksheet: Emotion Regulation 1 – Physical Sensations

These are things I feel in my body:

- _____

  _____

- _____

  _____

- _____

  _____

- _____

  _____

- _____

  _____

- _____

  _____

- _____

  _____

- _____

  _____

Worksheet: Emotion Regulation 2A – Smileys

Day	Date	Event
Monday		
Tuesday		
Wednesday		
Thursday		
Friday		
Saturday		
Sunday		

In your workbook, this worksheet goes on the left and worksheet Emotion Regulation 2B goes on the right.

Every day you write down the date and an event, something that happened that day, and then you colour the face on the right that fits how you felt. You can also colour more than one face.

Worksheet: Emotion Regulation 2B – Smileys

Happy	Angry	Scared	Sad

Worksheet: Emotion Regulation 3 – More Feelings

These are the feelings I know and they look like this:

Feeling   *Face*

_____

_____

_____

_____

_____

_____

Worksheet: Emotion Regulation 4A – Angry

Indicate with a cross where you are on this line.

X ———————————————————————————— X

I can handle this   I cannot handle this

What do you do to help yourself calm down when you are angry?

- _____

  _____

- _____

  _____

- _____

  _____

- _____

  _____

- _____

  _____

- _____

  _____

- _____

  _____

- _____

  _____

Worksheet: Emotion Regulation 4B – Sad

Indicate with a cross where you are on this line.

X ———————————————————————— **X**

I can handle this   I cannot handle this

What do you do to help yourself calm down when you are sad?

- _____

_____

- _____

_____

- _____

_____

- _____

_____

- _____

_____

- _____

_____

- _____

_____

- _____

_____

Worksheet: Emotion Regulation 4C – Afraid

Indicate with a cross where you are on this line.

X ——————————————————————— X

I can handle this   I cannot handle this

What do you do to help yourself calm down when you are afraid?

- _____

- _____

- _____

- _____

- _____

- _____

- _____

Worksheet: Cognitive Shift 1 – Positive and Negative Characteristics

Make a list of your own good and bad qualities:

Positive   *Negative*

_____   _____

_____   _____

_____   _____

_____   _____

_____   _____

_____   _____

_____   _____

Worksheet: Cognitive Shift 2 – Compliments

Compliments to myself: what did I do well today?

Date   *Compliment*

_____   _____

_____   _____

_____   _____

_____   _____

_____   _____

_____   _____

_____   _____

Worksheet: The Nutshell

Give an overview of all the bad pictures in your head:

This worksheet stays with the therapist!

References

Adler-Tapia, R. & Settle, C. (2017). *EMDR and the art of psychotherapy with children: Infants to adolescents* (2nd ed.). New York: Springer Publishing Company.

American Psychiatric Association. (2013). *Diagnostic and statistical manual of mental disorders* (5th ed.). Washington, DC: Author.

Barrett, P., Turner, C. & Webster-Lowry, H. (2001). *Friends for youth group leader's manual*. Bowen Hill: Australian Academic Press.

Baskin, T.W. & Enright, R.D. (2004). Intervention studies on forgiveness: a meta-analysis. *Journal of Counseling and Development, 82*(1), 79–90. doi.org/10.1002/j.1556-6678.2004. tb00288.x.

Blaustein, M.E. & Kinniburgh, K.M. (2010). *Treating traumatic stress in children and adolescents: How to foster resilience through attachment, self-regulation, and competency*. New York: Guilford Press.

Bongaerts, H., Van minnen, A. & De Jongh, A. (2017). Intensive EMDR to treat PTSD patients with severe comorbidity: a case series. *Journal of EMDR Practice and Research, 11*(2), 84–95.

Boon, S., Steele, K. & Van der Hart, O. (2010). *Coping with trauma-related dissociation: Skills training for patients and therapists*. New York: W.W. Norton.

Booth, P.B. & Jernberg, A.M. (2010). *Theraplay: Helping parents and children build better relationships through attachment-based play*. San Francisco: Wiley.

Braun, B.G. (1988). The BASK model of dissociation. *Dissociation, 1*(1), 4–23.

Bretherton, I. & Munholland, K.A. (1999). Internal working models in attachment relationships: a construct revisited. In J. Cassidy & P.R. Shaver (Eds.), *Handbook of attachment: Theory, research, and clinical applications* (pp. 89–111). New York: Guilford Press.

Burke, N.J., Hellman, J.L., Scott, B.G., Weems, C.F. & Carrion, V.G. (2011). The impact of adverse childhood experiences on an urban pediatric population. *Child Abuse and Neglect, 35*(6), 408–413. doi:https://doi.org/10.1016/j.chiabu.2011.02.006.

Child and Adolescent Committee of the European Society on Trauma and Dissociation. (2017). Guidelines for the assessment and treatment of children and adolescents with dissociative symptoms and dissociative disorders. Retrieved from www.estd.org/sites/default/files/files/estd_guidelines_child_and_adolescents_first_update_july_2.pdf.

Children's Rights. (2015). Children's Rights Works. Retrieved from www.childrensrights.org/wp-content/uploads/2016/01/CR-Works-Brochure-12.9.15-spreads-FINAL.pdf.

Cohen, J.A., Bukstein, O., Walter, H., Benson, S.R., Chrisman, A., Farchione, T.R. & Medicus, J. (2010). Practice parameter for the assessment and treatment of children and adolescents with posttraumatic stress disorder. *Journal of the American Academy of Child and Adolescent Psychiatry, 49*(4), 414–430. doi.org/10.1016/j.jaac.2009.12.020.

Cohen, J.A., Mannarino, A.P., Kliethermes, M. & Murray, L.A. (2012). Trauma-focused CBT for youth with complex trauma. *Child Abuse and Neglect, 36*(6), 528–541. doi. org/10.1016/j.chiabu.2012.03.007.

Convention on the Rights of the Child, G.A. res. 44/25, annex, 44 U.N. GAOR Supp. (No. 49) at 167, U.N. Doc. A/44/49 (1989), entered into force 2 September 1990. Stat. (1989).

Cooper, G., Hoffman, K., Powell, B. & Marvin, R. (2007). The circle of security intervention: differential diagnosis and differential treatment. In L.J. Berlin, Y. Ziv, L. Amaya-Jackson & M.T.T. Greenberg (Eds.), *Enhancing early attachments: Theory, research, intervention, and policy. Duke series in Child Development and Public Policy* (pp. 127–151). New York: Guilford Press.

Courtois, C.A. (1999). *Recollections of sexual abuse: Treatment principles and guidelines.* New York: W.W. Norton.

Cozolino, L. (2002). *The neuroscience of psychotherapy: Building and rebuilding the human brain.* New York: W.W. Norton.

D'Andrea, W., Ford, J., Stolbach, B., Spinazzola, J. & Van der Kolk, B.A. (2012). Understanding interpersonal trauma in children: Why we need a developmentally appropriate trauma diagnosis. *American Journal of Orthopsychiatry, 82*(2), 187–200. doi:10.1111/j.1939-0025.2012.01154.x 22506521.

De Jongh, A., Resick, P.A., Zoellner, L.A., van Minnen, A., Lee, C.W., Monson, C.M. & Bicanic, I.A. (2016). Critical analysis of the current treatment guidelines for complex PTSD in adults. *Depress Anxiety, 33*(5), 359–369. doi:10.1002/da.22469.

de Roos, C., Greenwald, R., den Hollander-Gijsman, M., Noorthoorn, E., van Buuren, S. & de Jongh, A. (2011). A randomised comparison of cognitive behavioural therapy (CBT) and eye movement desensitisation and reprocessing (EMDR) in disaster-exposed children. *European Journal of Psychotraumatology, 2.* doi:10.3402/ejpt.v2i0.5694.

de Roos, C., van der Oord, S., Zijlstra, B., Lucassen, S., Perrin, S., Emmelkamp, P. & de Jongh, A. (2017). Comparison of eye movement desensitization and reprocessing therapy, cognitive behavioral writing therapy, and wait-list in pediatric posttraumatic stress disorder following single-incident trauma: a multicenter randomized clinical trial. *Journal of Child Psychology and Psychiatry, 58*(11), 1219–1228. doi:10.1111/jcpp.12768.

Deci, E.L. & Ryan, R.M. (Eds.). (2002). *Handbook of self-determination research.* Rochester, NY: University Rochester Press.

Delfabbro, P.H., Barber, J.G. & Cooper, L. (2002). Children entering out-of-home care in South Australia: baseline analyses for a 3-year longitudinal study. *Children and Youth Services Review, 24*(12), 917–932. doi:10.1016/S0190-7409(02)00252-9.

Diehle, J., Opmeer, B.C., Boer, F., Mannarino, A.P. & Lindauer, R.J. (2015). Trauma-focused cognitive behavioral therapy or eye movement desensitization and reprocessing: what works in children with posttraumatic stress symptoms? A randomized controlled trial. *European Child and Adolescent Psychiatry, 24*(2), 227–236. doi:10.1007/s00787-014-0572-5.

Dorrepaal, E., Thomaes, K. & Draijer, N. (2008). *Vroeger en verder: Stabilisatiecursus na misbruik of mishandeling.* Amsterdam: Pearson Assessment and Information.

Felitti, V.J., Anda, R.F., Nordenberg, D., Williamson, D.F., Spitz, A.M., Edwards, V. & Marks, J.S. (1998). Relationship of childhood abuse and household dysfunction to many of the leading causes of death in adults: the Adverse Childhood Experiences (ACE) Study. *American Journal of Preventive Medicine, 14*(4), 245–258.

Fisher, A., Murray, E. & Bundy, A. (1991). *Sensory integration: Theory and practice.* Philadelphia: F.A. Davis.

Fitzgibbons, R.P. (1986). The cognitive and emotive use of forgiveness in the treatment of anger. *Psychotherapy, 23*(4), 629–633. doi.org/10.1037/h0085667.

Folensbee, R.W. (2007). *The neuroscience of psychological therapies.* Cambridge: Cambridge University Press.

Fonagy, P., Gergely G., Jurist, E.L. & Target, M. (2002). *Affect regulation, mentalization, and the development of the self.* New York: Other Press.

Ford, J.D., Grasso, D., Greene, C., Levine, J., Spinazzola, J. & van der Kolk, B. (2013). Clinical significance of a proposed developmental trauma disorder diagnosis: results of an international survey of clinicians. *Journal of Clinical Psychiatry, 74*(8), 841–849. doi:10.4088/JCP.12m08030 24021504.

Forgash, C. (2009). Workplace or conference room. In M. Luber (Ed.), *Eye movement desensitization and reprocessing (EMDR) scripted protocols: Special populations* (pp. 221–224). New York: Springer Publishing Company.

Fraser, G.A. (1991). The dissociative table technique: a strategy for working with egostates in dissociative disorders and egostate therapy. *Dissociation, 4(1)*, 205–213.

Golding, K. & Hughes, D. (2012). *Creating loving attachments: Parenting with PACE to nurture confidence and security in the troubled child.* London/Philadelphia: Jessica Kingsley.

Gomez, A.M. (2013). *EMDR therapy and adjunct approaches with children: Complex trauma, attachment and, dissociation.* New York: Springer Publishing Company.

Greenwald, R. (2002). Motivation-adaptive skills-trauma resolution (MASTR) therapy for adolescents with conduct problems: an open trial. *Journal of Aggression, Maltreatment and Trauma, 6*(1), 237–261. doi.org/10.1300/J146v06n01_12.

Greenwald, R. (2005). *Child trauma handbook: A guide for helping trauma-exposed children and adolescents.* New York: Haworth Press.

Greeson, J., Briggs, E., Kisiel, C., Layne, C.M., Ake III, G.S., Ko, S.J. & Fairbank, J.A. (2011). Complex trauma and mental health in children and adolescents placed in foster care. *Child Welfare, 90*(6), 92–108.

Gumbleton, J. (1997). *Untreatable families? Working with denial in cases of severe child abuse.* (MSc Dissertation), University of Bristol, Bristol.

Hauber, K. (2017). EMDR bij adolescenten met een dissociatieve stoornis. In R. Beer & C. de Roos (Eds.), *Handboek EMDR bij kinderen en jongeren* (pp. 318–339). Houten: Uitgeverij Lannoo nv.

Hedges, L.E. (1997). Surviving the transference psychosis. In L.E. Hedges, R. Hilton, V.W. Hilton & Caudill, Jr., O.B. (Eds.), *Therapists at risk: Perils of the intimacy of the therapeutic relationship* (pp. 109–145) Northvale, NJ: Jason Aronson.

Herman, J.L. (1992). *Trauma and recovery.* New York: Basic Books.

Herman, J.L. (1993). Sequela of prolonged and repeated trauma: evidence for a complex posttraumatic syndrome (DESNOS). In J.R.T. Davidson & E.B. Foa (Eds.), *Posttraumatic stress disorder: DSM-IV and beyond* (pp. 213–228). Washington, DC: American Psychiatric Press.

Hughes, D.A. & Baylin, J. (2012). *Brain-based parenting: The neuroscience of caregiving for healthy attachment.* New York: Norton & Company.

International Society for the Study of Trauma and Dissociation. (2004). Guidelines for the evaluation and treatment of dissociative symptoms in children and adolescents. *Journal of Trauma and Dissociation, 5*(3), 119–149.

Jonkman, C.S., Schuengel, C., Oosterman, M., Lindeboom, R., Boer, F. & Lindauer, R.J.L. (2017). Effects of multidimensional treatment foster care for preschoolers (MTFC-P) for young foster children with severe behavioral disturbances. *Journal of Child and Family Studies, 26*(5), 1491–1503. doi:10.1007/s10826-017-0661-4.

Jonkman, C.S., Verlinden, E.F., Bolle, E.F., Boer, F. & Lindauer, R.J. (2013). Traumatic stress symptomatology after child maltreatment and single traumatic events: different profiles. *Journal of Traumatic Stress, 26*(2), 225–232. doi: 10.1002/jts.21792.

Kate, M. (2017). *Aspects of childhood maltreatment and dynamics between a caregiver and child that are most likely to lead to dissociation in adulthood twenty years on: Engaging with complex trauma: Lessons, challenges and opportunities*. Paper presented at the ISSTD Australian Regional Conference, Brisbane Convention and Exhibition Centre.

Kliethermes, M. & Wamser, R. (2012). Adolescents with complex trauma. In J.A. Cohen, A.P. Mannarino & E. Deblinger (Eds.), *Trauma-focused CBT for children and adolescents: Treatment Applications* (pp. 175–196). New York: Guilford Press.

Kliewer, W., Murrelle, L., Mejia, R., Torres de, Y. & Angold, A. (2001). Exposure to violence against a family member and internalizing symptoms in Colombian adolescents: the protective effects of family support. *Journal of Consulting and Clinical Psychology, 69*(6), 971–982. doi:10.1037/0022-006X.69.6.971 11777124.

Klonsky, E.D. (2007). The functions of deliberate self-injury: a review of the evidence. *Clinical Psychology Review, 27*(2), 226–239. doi:10.1016/j.cpr.2006.08.002.

Knipe, J. (2018). *EMDR toolbox: Theory and treatment of complex PTSD and dissociation* (2nd ed.). New York: Springer Publishing Co Inc.

Kohut, H. (1977). *The restoration of the self*. New York: International Universities Press.

Lanktree, C.B. & Briere, J. (2013). Integrative treatment of complex trauma. In J.D. Ford & C.A. Courtois (Eds.), *Treating complex traumatic stress disorders in children and adolescents: Scientific foundations and therapeutic models* (pp. 143–161). New York: Guilford Press.

Legaree, T., Turner, J. & Lollis, S. (2007). Forgiveness and therapy: a critial review of conceptualizations, practices, and values found in the literature. *Journal of Marital and Family Therapy, 33*(2), 192–213. doi:10.1111/j.1752-0606.2007.00016.x.

Levine, P. (1997). *Waking the tiger: Healing trauma*. Berkeley, CA: North Atlantic Books.

Liotti, G. (1999). Disorganized attachment as a model for the understanding of dissociative psychopathology. In J. Solomon & C. George (Eds.), *Attachment disorganization* (pp. 25–51). New York: Guilford Press.

Lovett, J. (1999). *Small wonders: Healing childhood trauma with EMDR*. New York: The Free Press.

McCrory, E.J., Gerin, M.I. & Viding, E. (2017). Annual research review: childhood maltreatment, latent vulnerability and the shift to preventative psychiatry – the contribution of functional brain imaging. *Journal of Child Psychology and Psychiatry, 58*(4), 338–357. doi:10.1111/jcpp. 12713.

MacLean, P.D. (1985). Brain evolution relating to family, play, and the separation call. *Archives of General Psychiatry, 42*(4), 405–417.

Mevissen, L. (2016). EMDR bij mensen met een verstandelijke beperking. In H.J. Oppenheim, H. Hornsveld, E. Ten Broeke & A. De Jongh (Eds.), *Praktijkboek EMDR deel II: Toepassingen voor nieuwe patiëntengroepen en stoornissen* (pp. 251–284). Amsterdam: Pearson Assessment and Information.

Mevissen, L. & Didden, R. (2017). Systeemgerichte diagnostiek en behandeling van psychotrauma bij jeugdigen met een licht verstandelijke beperking. *Onderzoek en Praktijk, 15*(1), 6–14.

Mevissen, L., Didden, R., Korzilius, H. & de Jongh, A. (2017). Eye movement desensitisation and reprocessing therapy for posttraumatic stress disorder in a child and an adolescent with mild to borderline intellectual disability: a multiple baseline across subjects study. *Journal of Applied Research in Intellectual Disabilities,* 1–8. doi:10.1111/jar.12335.

Miller, W.R. & Rollnick, S. (1991). *Motivational interviewing: Preparing people to change addictive behavior.* New York: Guilford Press.

Nathanson, D.L. (1994). *Shame and pride: Affect, sex, and the birth of the self.* New York: W.W. Norton & Company.

Nijenhuis, E.R.S. & van der Hart, O. (1999). Forgetting and re-experiencing trauma: from anesthesia to pain. In J. Goodwin & R. Attias (Eds.), *Splintered refections: Images of the body in trauma* (pp. 39–66). New York: Basic Books.

Ogden, P.M.A. & Minton, K. (2000). Sensorimotor psychotherapy: one method for processing traumatic memory. *Traumatology, VI*(3), 149–173. doi.org/10.1177/15347656 0000600302.

Ogden, P., Minton, K. & Pain, C. (2006). *Trauma and the body: A sensorimotor approach to psychotherapy.* New York: W.W. Norton.

Omer, H. (2004). *Nonviolent resistance: A new approach to violent and self-destructive children.* New York/Cambridge: Cambridge University Press.

Parker, S. (2011). *Partnering for Safety Case Consultation Process: A process for consulting on child protection cases using the Partnering for Safety Risk Assessment and Planning Framework.* SP Consultancy Perth, Australia. Retrieved from www.partneringforsafety.com.

Perry, B.D. & Dobson, C.L. (2013). The neurosequential model of therapeutics. In J.D. Ford & C.A. Courtois (Eds.), *Treating complex traumatic stress disorders in children and adolescents: Scientific foundations and therapeutic models* (pp. 249–260). New York: Guilford Press.

Perry, B. & Szalavitz, M. (2007). *The boy who was raised as a dog and other stories from a psychiatrist's notebook: What traumatized children can teach us about life, loss and healing.* New York: Basic Books, Perseus Books Group.

Potter, D., Chevy, C., Amaya-Jackson, L., O'Donnell, K. & Murphy, R. (2009). *Clinical Guidelines Series. Reactive Attachment Disorder (RAD): Appropriate and inappropriate application of the Reactive Attachment Disorder diagnosis on an age continuum from birth through age 18.* Retrieved from www.pbhcare.org/pubdocs/upload/documents/radguidelines2009.pdf/.

Putnam, F.W. (1997). *Dissociation in children and adolescents: A developmental perspective.* New York: Guilford Press.

Putnam, F.W., Helmers, K. & Trickett, P.K. (1993). Development, reliability and validity of a child dissociation scale. *Child Abuse and Neglect, 17*(6), 731–742.

Rodenburg, R., Benjamin, A., de Roos, C., Meijer, A.M. & Stams, G.J. (2009). Efficacy of EMDR in children: a meta-analysis. *Clinical Psychology Review, 29*(7), 599–606. doi:10.1016/j.cpr.2009.06.008.

Ross, C.A. (2007). *Trauma model therapy: A solution to the problem of comorbidity in psychiatry.* Richardson, TX: Manitou Communications.

Rowling, J.K. (1999). *Harry Potter and the prisoner of Azkaban.* London: Bloomsbury Publishing Plc.

Salter, A.C. (1995). *Transforming trauma: A guide to understanding and treating adult survivors of child sexual abuse.* Thousand Oaks, CA: Sage.

Saxe, G.N., Ellis, B.H. & Kaplow, J.B. (2012). *Collaborative treatment of traumatized children and teens: The trauma systems therapy approach.* New York: Guilford Press.

Schlumpf, Y.R., Nijenhuis E.F., Chalavi, S., Weder, E.V., Zimmermann, E., Luechinger, R., Reinders, A.A. & Jancke, L. (2013). Dissociative part-dependent biopsychosocial reactions to backward masked angry and neutral faces: An fMRI study of dissociative identity disorder. *NeuroImage: Clinical, 12*(3), 54–64. doi:10.1016/j.nicl.2013.07.002.

Schore, A. (1994). *Affect regulation and the origin of the self: The neurobiology of emotional development.* Hillsdale, NJ: Erlbaum.

Schore, A. (2001). The effects of early relational trauma on right brain development, affect regulation and infant mental health. *Infant Mental Health Journal, 22*(1–2), 201–269. doi.org/10.1002/1097-0355(200101/04)22:1<201::AID-IMHJ8>3.0.CO;2-9.

Shapiro, F. (2001). *Eye movement desensitization and reprocessing: Basic principles, protocols, and procedures* (2nd ed.). New York: Guildford Press.

Shapiro, F. (2006). *EMDR new notes on adaptive information processing with case formulation principles, forms, scripts and worksheets.* Watsonville, CA: EMDR Institute.

Sherborne, V. (2001). *Developmental movement for children* (2nd ed.). London: Worth Publishing.

Siegel, D. (1999). *The developing mind: Toward a neurobiology of interpersonal experience.* New York: Guilford Press.

Silberg, J.L. (2013). *The child survivor: Healing developmental trauma and dissociation.* New York: Routledge/Taylor & Francis Group.

Spierings, J. (2012). Stabilisatie, een gestructureerd programma voor taxatie en intervisie. In E. Ten Broeke, A. De Jongh & H. Oppenheim (Eds.), *Praktijkboek EMDR* (3rd ed., pp. 131–150). Amsterdam: Pearson Assessment and Information.

Struik, A.L. (2009). Klinische fasebehandeling van vroegkinderlijke traumatisering bij kin-deren en ouders. *Kind en Adolescent Praktijk, I,* 10–19.

Struik, A. (2015). Denise (10) is gaan praten en verwerken. *Kind en Adolescent Praktijk, 14*(1), 4–11. doi:10.1007/s12454-015-0002-y.

Struik, A. (2016). *Slapende honden? Wakker maken! Een behandelmethode voor chronisch getraumatiseerde kinderen* (2nd ed.). Amsterdam: Pearson Assessment and Information B.V.

Struik, A. (2017a). EMDR bij kinderen met een dissociatieve stoornis of dissociatieve symptomen. In R. Beer & C. de Roos (Eds.), *Handboek EMDR bij kinderen en jongeren* (pp. 340–357). Houten: Uitgeverij Lannoo nv.

Struik, A. (2017b). The Trauma Healing Story: healing chronically traumatised children through their families/Whanau. *Australian and New Zealand Journal of Family Therapy, 38*(4), 613–626. doi:10.1002/anzf.1271.

Struik, A. (2017c). Treating chronically traumatised children with the Sleeping Dogs method: don't let sleeping dogs lie! *Children Australia, 42*(2), 93–103. doi:10.1017/cha.2017.13.

Struik, A. (2018). The Sleeping Dogs method to overcome children's resistance to EMDR therapy: a case series. *Journal of EMDR Practice and Research, 12*(4), 224–241. doi:10.1891/1933-3196.12.4.224.

Struik, A., Lindauer, R.J. & Ensink, J.B. (2017). I won't do EMDR! The use of the 'Sleeping Dogs' method to overcome children's resistance to EMDR therapy. *Journal of EMDR Practice and Research, 11*(4), 166–180. doi:10.1891/1933-3196.11.4.166.

Teicher, M.H. & Samson, J.A. (2016). Annual research review: enduring neurobiological effects of childhood abuse and neglect. *Journal of Child Psychology and Psychiatry, 57*(3), 241–266. doi:10.1111/jcpp. 12507.

Timberlake, W. (1994). Behavior systems, associationism, and Pavlovian conditioning. *Psychonimic Bulletin and Review, 1,* 405–420.

Turnell, A. & Edwards, S. (1999). *Signs of safety: A solution and safety oriented approach to child protection casework.* New York: W.W. Norton.

Turnell, A. & Essex, S. (2006). *Working with 'denied' child abuse: The resolutions approach.* Maidenhead, UK: Open University Press.

Van der Hart, O. (Ed.). (1995, 4th edn 2003). *Trauma, dissociatie en hypnose.* Lisse: Swets & Zeitlinger.

Van der Hart, O., Groenendijk, M., Gonzalez, A., Mosquera, D. & Solomon, R. (2013). Dissociation of the Personality and EMDR Therapy in Complex Trauma-Related Disorders: Applications in the Stabilization Phase. *Journal of EMDR Practice and Research, 7*(2), 81–94. doi:10.1891/1933-3196.7.2.81.

Van der Hart, O., Groenendijk, M., Gonzalez, A., Mosquera, D. & Solomon, R. (2014). Dissociation of the personality and EMDR therapy in complex trauma-related disorders: applications in phases 2 and 3 treatment. *Journal of EMDR Practice and Research, 8*(1), 33–48. doi:10.1891/1933-3196.8.1.33.

Van der Hart, O., Nijenhuis, E. & Steele, K. (2006). *The haunted self.* New York: W.W. Norton.

Van der Kolk, B. (2005). Developmental trauma disorder: toward a rational diagnosis for children with complex trauma histories. *Psychiatric Annals, 35*(5), 401–408.

Van der Kolk, B. (2016). Commentary: the devastating effects of ignoring child maltreatment in psychiatry – a commentary on Teicher and Samson 2016. *Journal of Child Psychology and Psychiatry, 57*(3), 267–270. doi:10.1111/jcpp. 12540.

Van der Kolk, B.A., Pynoos, R.S, Cicchettie, D., Cloitre, M., D'Andrea, W., Ford, J.D., Lieberman, A.F. & Teicher, M. (2009). *Proposal to include a developmental trauma disorder diagnosis for children and adolescents in DSM-V.* Retrieved from www.traumacenter.org/about/Conference2011.php.

Van Mil, E. & Struik, A. (2017). Overweight and obesity in children: more than just the kilos. *Pediatric Physical Therapy, 29,* S73–S75. doi:10.1097/pep.0000000000000384.

Van Olst, E.H. (1972). *The orienting refex.* The Hague: Mouton.

Vissia, E.M., Giesen, M.E., Chalavi, S., Nijenhuis, E.R., Draijer, N., Brand, B.L. & Reinders, A.A. (2016). Is it trauma- or fantasy-based? Comparing dissociative identity disorder, post-traumatic stress disorder, simulators, and controls. *Acta Psychiatrica Scandinavica, 134*(2), 111–128. doi:10.1111/acps.12590.

Waters, F.S. (2016). *Healing the fractured child: Diagnosis and treatment of youth with dissociation.* New York: Springer Publishing.

Went, M.A.T. (2014). Ouder-Kind-Trauma-Therapie. *GZ-Psychologie, 2,* 18–24.

Went, M.A.T. (2018). OuderKindTraumaTherapie Hoe werkt dat nou bij baby's? *Tijdschrift voor Kinder- en Jeugdpsychotherapie, 54*(1), 76–93.

Wesselmann, D. (1998). *The whole parent: How to become a terrific parent even if you didn't have one.* New York: Perseus.

Wesselmann, D. (2007). Treating attachment issues through EMDR and a family systems approach. In F. Shapiro, F. Kaslow & L. Maxfield (Eds.), *Handbook of EMDR and family therapy processes* (pp. 113–130). Hoboken, NJ: John Wiley & Sons, Inc.

Wesselmann, D., Schweitzer, C. & Armstrong, S. (2014). *Integrative team treatment for attachment trauma in children: Family therapy and EMDR.* New York: W.W. Norton & Co.

Wieland, S. (2007). Working with the child's external world. *International Society for the Study of Trauma and Dissociation News, 25*(4), 6–7.

Wieland, S. (Ed.). (2015). *Dissociation in traumatized children and adolescents: Theory and clinical interventions* (2nd ed.). Routledge Psychosocial Stress Series. New York: Routledge.

Wilbarger, P. & Wilbarger, J. (1997). *Sensory defensiveness and related social/emotional and neurological problems.* Van Nuys, CA: Wilbarger.

World Health Organization. (2013). *Guidelines for the management of conditions specifically related to stress.* Geneva, Switzerland: WHO.

Zeanah, C.H., Chesher, T. & Boris, N.W. (2016). Practice parameter for the assessment and treatment of children and adolescents with reactive attachment disorder and disinhibited social engagement disorder. *Journal of the American Academy of Child and Adolescent Psychiatry, 55*(11), 990–1003. doi:10.1016/j.jaac.2016.08.004.

Zeanah, C.H. & Gleason, M.M. (2015). Annual research review: attachment disorders in early childhood – clinical presentation, causes, correlates, and treatment. *Journal of Child Psychology and Psychiatry, 56*(3), 207–222. doi:10.1111/jcpp. 12347.

Index